Leadership And Learning, Inc. is delighted to reprint *Entry: The Hiring, Start-up and Supervision of Administrators*. Though published in 1982, the book's entry-plan approach to beginning a new job is as effective today as it was then. It continues to live by word-of-mouth in the States and in countries around the world.

The companion book to *Entry – Leadership And Learning: Personal Change in a Professional Setting* (1979) is also available. In this book of case stories published prior to *Entry*, we describe the personal learning, change, and growth that enables administrators to implement successfully the methodologies advocated in *ENTRY*.

To order *Entry* or *Leadership And Learning:*

- **E-mail: orders@entrybook.com**
- **Fax: 617-630-0663**
- **Address: Leadership and Learning Inc.**
  28 Nobscot Road
  Newton, MA 02459
- **Cost Per Book: $25 + $4.50 shipping and handling**
- **Please make checks payable to:**
  Leadership and Learning Inc.

Barry Jentz has a new manuscript available, entitled: *Talk Sense: Communicating to Lead and Learn*

ENTRY

ENTRY

The Hiring, Start-up, and Supervision of Administrators

Barry Jentz

with

Dan S. Cheever, Jr.
Stephen B. Fisher
Meredith Howe Jones
Paul Kelleher
Joan W. Wofford

McGRAW-HILL BOOK COMPANY

New York   St. Louis   San Francisco
Auckland   Bogotá   Hamburg   Johannesburg   London   Madrid
Mexico   Montreal   New Delhi   Panama   Paris   São Paulo
Singapore   Sydney   Tokyo   Toronto

Thomas H. Quinn and Michael Hennelly were the editors of this book. Christopher Simon was the designer. Paul Malchow supervised the production. It was set in Caledonia by University Graphics, Inc.

Printed and bound by R. R. Donnelley and Sons, Inc.

Library of Congress Cataloging in Publication Data
Main entry under title:
Entry: the hiring, start-up, and supervision of administrators.

   Includes index.
   1. School administrators—United States.
I. Jentz, Barry C.
LB2831.62.E57   371.2'01'0973   81-14294
ISBN 0-07-032528-6   AACR2

1 2 3 4 5 6 7 8 9 DODO 8 9 8 7 6 5 4 3 2

Contents

SECTION THREE: SUPERVISING

EXERCISES ON SUPERVISING

CONCLUSION TO THE BOOK

APPENDICES

Foreword

WILLIAM R. TORBERT

As practicing administrators and students of administration read this book, you will probably feel as though you are consuming a rich meal which requires leisurely digestion. Indeed, the process of digestion will probably bring you back to the book again and again, in order to compare what it says to your own experience and reflections.

Why is this book so rich? It is rich because of its combination of a very general and inherently dramatic topic—entry—with unusually concrete descriptions of practice.

The topic of "entry" is relevant to anyone who ever enters a new work role—which is to say that it is relevant to virtually everyone, and relevant to most of us many times during our work life. Although the particular examples of entry described in this book all relate to administrators in public educational settings, the general dilemmas of entry which become illuminated are certainly relevant to managers in governmental, medical, or business settings as well.

The topic of entry is relevant not only to that prolonged moment when one takes a new position in a new organization, but also to the many less dramatic moments within any given role when one starts a new project. The general approach of *structured collaborative inquiry* which this book illustrates for entry into new administrative positions can also be applied to starting any new project. The failure to exercise the disciplines of structured collaborative inquiry at the outset of new projects frequently condemns them to uncreative, undistinguished, and unproductive outcomes.

If the foregoing paragraphs provide an overview of how general a concern is the topic of entry, they do not yet explain why entry is so gripping—so dramatic, so significant, so emotional—a concern. Entry is a quintessential human situation, when "the hopes and fears of all the years" are again rekindled—when the dreams and visions of both the person entering and the organization inviting are aroused—when all the anxieties of facing the unknown are at their highest pitch—when one re-experiences the ritual of initiation into the mysteries of this particular tribe—when the advent of someone new is believed to hold the potential for new action and new results—when a human being is believed to be capable of making a difference. Hence, the typical "honeymoon" period when the new arrival seems golden. Hence, the typical sense of letdown, betrayal, and failure that follows this "honeymoon" period. And hence, the growing sense of the cyclical nature of human affairs as one ages—promises followed by betrayals followed by promises followed by betrayals . . . each new ideology becoming its opposite in practice, thereby spawning a new ideology which becomes its opposite in practice . . .

Is there a way to break this tragic cycle of human action? Here lies the special promise of this book, for it claims that the answer is "Yes," and it provides carefully drawn, concrete illustrations of practice to document its affirmation.

How radical a promise this is, and how suspicious we should be of its validity, is emphasized by the dynamics just examined: the dynamics of our deep yearning for a trustworthy promise which frequently leads us first to faith and then to disillusionment. Yet here is a book which promises to help us learn the most fundamental human skill of all: how to make promises come true. Should we believe its message?

How radical a promise this book makes, and how suspicious we should be of its validity, is suggested in another, related way by Hegel's famous dictum "The Owl of Minerva spreads its wings only at dusk." The Owl of Minerva—the symbol of wisdom, of learning from experience—awakens only at dusk *after* the action of the day initiated by the dawn's promise. According to Hegel, wisdom comes only in retrospective reflection toward the end of any particular episode of action, any particular career, any particular historical period. Yet here is a book which counsels reflection and inquiry right in the midst of the very outset of action—just during that frenzied time when the individual and the institution know least about one another: at entry. Is this counsel really practical? Should we believe the book's message?

These are questions which each reader must ultimately answer for himself or herself. Even if the book as a whole seems persuasive upon first reading, each reader's ultimate answer can only come after the pain and perseverance and reward of trying the approaches suggested here in his or her own practice.

But I believe there are some good reasons for *not* dismissing out of hand the special promise of this book *before* reading it. Put another way, there are some good reasons for believing that this book is on the right track.

The first of these reasons is that the approach of structured collaborative inquiry, illustrated in different ways throughout this book, is *hard work*. To already-overworked administrators, this feature may not, at first taste, seem a very positive recommendation for this approach. But if you reflect for a moment, you realize that you are sick and tired of faddish management gimmicks that are supposed to solve all your problems in a cookbook fashion. If there were an easy solution to administrative dilemmas, this book would not be about work at all, but about the dilemmas we would all share in fashioning the life of leisure that would be ours! So, I would argue that the hard work involved in structured collaborative inquiry is the first sign of its validity as an approach to the dilemmas of entry.

To me, the second indication that the promise of "structured collaborative inquiry" is a trustworthy promise is its function not just as answer but as continuing, disciplined inquiry. Inquiry is obviously necessary at the moment of entry when so little is known, yet human inquiry is also most difficult when the new member on the scene does not have established relations of trust through which he or she can be sure of receiving valid information; and when, to make matters worse, the new member is expected to bring solutions to the organization's problems, not "just" questions. The fact that this book offers methods of inquiry at this difficult juncture—methods for interweaving traditional notions of firm, confidence-inspiring leadership with the tentativeness and openness of genuine inquiry—methods for exerting firm leadership toward inquiry-based administrative procedures—is a second sign of the validity of its approach.

The third reason why I find this book credible is its acceptance of the fundamental paradox of all leadership and authority—indeed, all human action. This paradox is hinted at in the tension between the words "structured collaborative inquiry." The word *structured* implies a preformulated process, whereas the words *collaboration* and *inquiry* imply processes for creating or discovering forms. Authority is often defined either as "top-down" (enacting a pre-formulated process) or "bottom-up" (collaboratively creating forms). Leaders are often categorized as either authoritarian and unilateral or as participative and collaborative. But any experienced administrator knows upon reflection that these dichotomous characterizations are fictional caricatures. Authority and leadership are more creative and more paradoxical exercises than either the "top-down" or the "bottom-up" metaphors suggest. In fact, authority is created and genuine leadership is exercised just when "top-down" and "bottom-up" influences somehow interact together in a way that produces collective action which responds to profound human yearnings. This book provides concrete illustrations which make the paradox and the magic of geniuine leadership less mysterious.

A final reason why I find the promise of this book initially trustworthy is that the authors have used the very process they recommend in writing the book itself.

At this point, the reader may be wondering how much to trust this foreword! It seems dedicated to "selling" this book in more dramatic (one might even say more grandiose) rhetoric than the authors themselves use. Mentioning two of the concerns I have about the book may provide a helpful antidote to the tone of the foregoing pages.

The concern I felt when first reading this book was that it was too "neat," almost "too good to be true." In showing how one can turn the dilemmas of entry into opportunities and make the chaos and fear of entry into meaning and fulfilling accomplishment, the authors were in danger, I feared, of perpetrating the illusion that it is possible to "plan out" surprise and frustration. There is a dramatic case of failure included here, but it reads like a "before" story. "Before I took the approach advocated in this book, here is the sort of mess I made. Now, everything is fine." The various authors have made revisions which diminish this tone, and certainly the stories provide a realistic sense of how difficult it is to maintain a consistent commitment to this approach. But my concern remains. As a practicing administrator, I am constantly aware of the multiple, fragmenting demands upon my attention which batter and submerge my planned activities. Sometimes, I later believe myself to have been "open" and "wise" to turn my attention to such demands. Other times I call myself "weak." And beyond the only partially manageable tensions among competing duties on the job lie the still more awesome dilemmas of the proper relationships among work, family, friends, and leisure. Even our greatest mathematicians and physicists no longer agree in the abstract on a single "neat" pattern which encompasses reality. How much less likely are we to find "neat" enduring solutions to our everyday dilemmas?

The second concern I felt when first reading this book was its predominant emphasis on one particular tool (called "activity mapping") for structuring collaborative inquiry. This tool for planning time is particularly appropriate for major organizational projects, such as the entry process of a top administrator, which typically occurs over a period of something less than a year. Thus, in one sense, the emphasis on activity planning is perfectly appropriate for a book on entry. My fear was that this exclusive focus might obscure the likelihood that there are other quite different tools of structured collaborative inquiry applicable to differently shaped dilemmas. For example, Jentz and Wofford's earlier book, *Leadership and Learning*, provides a wonderfully intimate look at how conversations within any given administrative meeting or interview can become structured collaborative inquiries. Anyone who, after reading this book, wishes to develop the skills to structure collaborative inquiry will find *Leadership and Learning* a rewarding companion volume.

In conclusion to this brief foreword and in anticipation of the book which follows, welcome to this rich meal. (And don't forget to leave time for the leisurely digestion it requires.)

Preface

A reader need not go beyond the Contents to find that I have authored a book which I did not write. Nice work if you can get it, sing the words of an old song. Already some advance readers have likened the writing of this book to the painting of Tom Sawyer's fence—did I make the task an opportunity too good to refuse? Actually, I attribute this feat to my outstanding leadership—which amounts to getting other people to do for nothing what you get paid to do.

Of course, the knife cuts both ways, for here I am relegated to a role as master of ceremonies, introducing myself and the talent to follow: my colleague and partner in the organizational consulting business, Joan Wofford; Dan Cheever, a school superintendent, Steve Fisher, an assistant superintendent; Paul Kelleher, a high school principal, and Meredith Jones, a junior high school principal—all active administrators and the writers of the case-stories in this book.[1]

With the exception of my partner in Leadership and Learning, Inc., Joan Wofford, I have had an extraordinary consulting relationship with all of the writer/administrators of this book. Both the length and nature of my work with these individuals deserve brief mention because the book follows directly from this consultation. I have consulted with each of these administrators for four years. In marked contrast, most people think of consultation as short-term in nature. Many people see the nature of a consultant's work as solving a discrete problem, providing a workshop, or producing a tangible product, such as a report. This has not been the nature of my work with the people in this book.

My function has been to help these administrators examine, question, and change their practice of leadership. In pursuit of this goal, I generated data about their current practice by asking them such questions as these:

- If you had no opportunity for further discussion of this matter, what would your decision be, now?

[1] Short biographies of each individual appear in Appendix I, p. 221.

(By taking a position, even temporarily, administrators generate new information within themselves about ambivalences, uncertainties, fears and hopes which we then analyze in a search for new understanding.)

- If you had to set a deadline for completing this project, what would it be? Now, what activities involving which people will have to occur in what sequence to meet those deadlines? Why?

(By mapping deadlines and activities in the form of who does what to whom, when, where, and why, administrators reveal their assumptions about decision making, problem solving, and most importantly, assumptions about how change occurs in organizational settings. Once revealed, these assumptions can be questioned, and changed.)

- If you were facing so-and-so right now, what would you say to this person? Role-play the interaction.

(By role-playing, administrators reveal their characteristic patterns of interaction. Leadership happens *with* and *through* interaction with other people; so examining patterns of behavior and abstracting the assumptions implicit in the behavior is a prerequisite to knowing and developing the capacity to change one's own leadership style.)

In this book, a reader will find no description of the consulting relationship within which these questions are asked and the data analyzed, then used to re-design a person's practice of leadership.[2] This omission is necessary to preserve the focus of the book but unfortunate if it implies that I brought together a group of writer/administrators who had only worked with me on the hiring, entry, and supervision of administrators. The text will evidence a similarity of values, ideas, and practice which make sense only in the larger context of our long-term inquiry into the nature of learning and leadership.

In consulting, my first priority with these administrators has been on "examining practice;" my second concern has been teaching new content. Here that content is about hiring, entering, and supervising. My concern with these topics began fifteen years ago when I started a new high school; continued during my consultant training[3] and practice, came to focus in designing and starting up the Leadership and Learning Cooperative in 1973, and became a service I offer in my consulting practice in 1979, after the writer/administrators here had developed, tested, and made the ideas work.

---

[2] In *Leadership and Learning: Personal Change in a Professional Setting*, McGraw-Hill Book Co., New York, 1979 co-authored with my colleague, Joan Wofford, we described the consulting relationship and the learning process which lie behind the frameworks of thought and administrative activities, the processes, methodologies, procedures, and techniques for successful hiring, entry, and supervision which are the focus here.

[3] I am indebted in particular to Dale Lake, who wrote the "Afterword" to this book, for introducing me in 1971 to the interview and feedback methodology which is used by all of the administrators in this book.

To produce this book we used the very ideas and skills which we advocate here as *structured collaborative inquiry*. In 1978 I designed with Dan Cheever a research project for Marla Colarusso, then a graduate student, to collect and feed back data to Dan and me about Dan's entry into a new superintendency. In the fall of 1979, using Marla's research and the results of other administrator's efforts to use an "entry plan," Dan, Steve Fisher, and I forced ourselves to clarify our ideas about entry by writing a series of articles on the topic. After securing a book contract in December, 1979, I wrote an outline for the book and a work plan for finishing it by January of 1981. Then I presented the outline and work plan to the assembled writers and modified both outline and work plan in response to new information and argument.

For six months, each writer worked alone and in combination with me. In late June, I produced a full draft of the book for review and criticism at a meeting of all of the writers. Again, using critical comment from the review session, each writer worked alone or in combination with me, or with my partner, Joan.

In October, with Joan's help, we produced a second full draft of the book. Each writer read and criticized this draft and engaged at least one outside reader in criticizing the draft before we met together again. In advance of this meeting all readers sent us their critical comments in writing on a form developed by Joan for this purpose; the data were organized, fed back, and analyzed to begin our final, joint meeting to revise the text.

Again, individuals revised their own work in response to a timetable which allowed Joan, Kathy Simons (our assistant), and me to finish a third draft of the whole book by the end of the year.

There were a number of major decisions I made along the way which changed the nature of the book and its ownership.

- Originally, I intended to write much more of the book than I did in the end. Not that I did not write, and write, and write! But. My fellow authors practiced the art of giving negative feedback which is advocated in this book. I practiced the art of receiving it and using it. So, my two hundred pages found the circular file, and the standing joke during the writing process—"You're getting written out of your own book!"—became reality.

- Originally, I had not intended to include exercises in this book. While writing the second draft, I became aware of the potential usefulness of exercises designed to help readers adapt for their own use the methodologies described in the cases. Joan Wofford developed the three hiring exercises with the assistance of Paul Kelleher on the exercise entitled, "Hiring of An Assistant." I developed the entry exercises, building on an original draft by Steve Fisher of "Designing an Entry Plan and

Implementing the Plan." Paul Kelleher also helped with the entry exercises. Joan and I jointly developed the supervision exercises, based in part on work which Dan Cheever and I had done together, and Dan's work in producing the supervisory exercise, "Analysis of Patterns of Withholding Information".

- Originally, I did not conceive the book as including a section on hiring. Paul Kelleher's description of how he set up a screening process along with Joan's simultaneous work as a consultant to a superintendent search led me to broaden the book's scope to include the section on hiring and to invite Joan to play a prominent role in editing and writing the whole book.

Though I made major changes along the way, I maintained from the outset a commitment to writing this book as a companion to Joan's and my first book, *Leadership and Learning: Personal Change in a Professional Setting.* Both books focus on how to bring about organizational change. *Leadership and Learning* focusses on the place of personal and interpersonal skills in that effort. In contrast, this book focusses on the place of structure, process, and procedure in creating conditions for organizational change. My bias toward making this book a companion to *Leadership and Learning* is important to highlight here if only to account for the many references in this text to that book.

A related, early directive to the writers of this book accounts for its final shape, as well. I asked the writers not to try to capture the full tone and content of their jobs—the loose ends, unexpected crises, the general messiness of any administrator's day-to-day life—but to abstract from this chaotic background the elements of planning, process and procedure which they made work during hiring, entry, and supervision. The advantage of this approach is a clearly defined picture of what was done, how, when, where, and why. But, as Bill Torbert points out in the Foreword to this book, the disadvantage is that we can appear to be more clear, planned, and organized than in fact we or anyone can be in managing the unexpected, uncontrollable realities of life in administrative positions.

We hope readers find this book useful, enjoyable, and hopeful.

Acknowledgments

For several years I got little response to my question, asked of administrators taking new jobs, "How do you plan to begin?" Dan Cheever was the first person who risked thinking with me about how to get off to a good start in his new superintendency. He was the first person to make the ideas about entry credible by putting them into practice.

Steve Fisher changed jobs one year after Dan. Steve moved from a junior high principalship to an assistant superintendency, and, like Dan, was working with me regularly at the time of his job change. Steve adapted the work on entry begun by Dan to his own setting; then, after making it work for him, extended it systematically to his supervision of a new administrator who reported to him. This supervision work is described here.

Meredith Howe Jones and Paul Kelleher, like Dan and Steve, are long-term clients of mine who became interested in the entry work and translated it into their own practice. Meredith's special contribution has been in describing the most difficult problem which we have all faced in supervision—how to handle "negative information" about another person's performance. Paul Kelleher's contribution to this book, beyond the three case stories he has written, came particularly at the outset when we were uncertain if we could write useful case-stories about technical material on hiring, entering, and supervising which were also fun to read. Paul wrote the first case-story which "worked." It served as a model from which others of us improvised.

Joan Wofford, my colleague and business partner, joined this project late. But, in the end, she made a major contribution to the writing of the book. Her contribution consists of writing a case and the exercises on Hiring, her editing of the sections on Entry and Supervision, and eventually writing the final draft of the framing materials which integrate the parts of this book into a qualitatively better whole than I could have achieved.

After completing the second full draft of the book, we each asked at least one outside reader to review it and comment. We owe a special thank you to Roland Barth, along with Judith Codding, Kevin Dwyer, Donald Kennedy, Julie Leerburger, Maria Levinsen, Judith Schiffer, Bill Torbert, and Ann Wallace for the timeliness and quality of their criticism. In addition we want to thank Larry Gagnon and Bob Mackin for allowing us to use in the Appendices materials they created as part of their entry into new administrative positions.

The book could not have been produced without our long-time assistant, Tina Renard, who typed two, different, full drafts of the book before she moved to a new part of the country. Kathy Simons rescued us by organizing and producing the final draft.

We had the opportunity to write this book because of Tom Quinn, our publisher, who urged Joan Wofford and me to submit other book proposals to him after we had finished our first book, *Leadership and Learning: Personal Change in a Professional Setting.* I am grateful to him for pushing us at the right time and coming through with a contract. His editing of the final draft of *Entry* made it a tighter and more readable book.

ENTRY

Introduction

Setting the Context

During the sixties and seventies, the hierarchies, policies, and practices of many organizations came under attack as rigid, exclusionary, or unfair. In the interests of making organizational life more fulfilling and productive for individuals, considerable effort went into attempts to alter the structures which had traditionally defined organizational relationships and decision making. Like most efforts at righting balances, the new effort to be humane, trusting, and participatory in decision making tended to go too far. The removal of structural constraints frequently failed to produce the expected positive, collaborative working relationships. Instead, organizational life became filled with good intentions and confusion; people were involved but their involvement was exhausting and frequently ineffective.

Nonetheless, by the eighties most administrators had adopted decision-making practices intended to involve a broad range of participants. Well-intentioned administrators tended to invite participation by saying to groups, "What shall we do about this?" and to experience disappointment and confusion in the face of the alternately chaotic or lifeless behavior this type of invitation produced. This question—both actually and meta-phorically—continues to plague organizational life. The larger question of how effectively to involve people receives little vigorous and imaginative attention.

This book asserts a paradox: To create the kind of organizational climate in which people feel they can contribute and produce requires the use of that which is often thrown out in the effort to create such a climate—structure.

This paradox is enormously confusing, often painful when experienced in practice. Most of us who lived through the sixties and seventies reflexively tend to see those who imposed structures as rigid, authoritarian, and unenlightened. Our instincts run toward egalitarian sharing. Yet as administrators, if we are to put our beliefs into practice and facilitate real sharing, we must use structures. That runs the risk of making us appear (and feel) like those we dethroned: rigid, authoritarian, and unenlightened. To design and use structures is counterreflexive.

The difficulty of doing so—and the success—is at the heart of this book. Throughout the cases in this book, readers will see administrators create and use structures which define who will do what in relation to whom, when, where, and why. In doing so, these administrators confront the risk of appearing to seek unilateral control. In reality, however, they are controlling in the interests of collaboration, unilateral in order to create mutual participation in learning and work.

The writers in this book assert the value and effectiveness of using structure to create conditions for mutual work and learning within three particular areas of administrative responsibility: hiring, entry, and supervision of new subordinates. It is at the start of a new job, or when an organization pauses to consider how it wants to fill a position, that there is the best chance to create new structures which restrain, then modify, the usual organizational forces of competition and fragmentation.

Our efforts to humanize organizations in the sixties and seventies taught us that the forces in organizations which tend toward competition and fragmentation are very powerful and will not submit to talk or to our good intentions for creating conditions for mutual work and learning. If a more collaborative kind of interaction is to take place, structures must be created which block or mitigate the organizational forces pushing toward competition and fragmentation. Persons in positions of authority who wish to create structures not for the purpose of control but for the purpose of collaboration have the best chance of doing so at the beginning of a new job.[1] To do so, however,

---

[1]   This distinction between creating structures not for the purpose of control but for the purpose of collaboration came from Bill Torbert. It helped us define the central thrust of this book. To read more about Bill's work in regard to this distinction, see "Educating toward Shared Purpose, Self-Direction, and Quality Work: The Theory and Practice of Liberating Structure," 0022-1546/78/0378-0109, $.50.© 1978 Ohio State University Press, *Journal of Higher Education*, vol. 49, no. 2.

requires an approach to the hiring, entry, and supervision of new administrators, which differs from normal practice.

Content and Purpose

Nearly everyone has an entertaining story to tell about the difficulties of beginning a new job, supervising a new employee, or trying to find and hire the "right" individual. In these stories, the organization, in the form of the persons who hire or supervise, usually say to a new person, "Here is the job; sink or swim." The new person implicitly responds with the message—"I'll prove I can do it." This tacit contract—sometimes modified by orientation programs or by offers of help if needed—constitutes an initiation rite rather than a rational plan for enhancing both the person's and the organization's ability to learn and perform. It costs individuals hours, weeks, and even years of confusion, heartbreak, and mediocre performance. It costs organizations thousands of dollars in wasted human energy and time. It is not collaborative either in intent or practice.

In this book we present a three-part answer to the question, *How can an administrator who believes in collaboration successfully start a new job or help a subordinate begin well?* First, since the success of newly hired administrators depends not only upon her or his own actions but upon the actions of other people in the new setting, we depict ways in which a hiring process can help an organization clarify its needs, renew its commitment to its goals, and thus help the new person succeed. Second, we examine ways the newly chosen administrator can inquire into self and setting through designing and using an entry plan reflective of the values of collaboration. Finally, we show how an established administrator can supervise the entry of a new subordinate to involve rather than isolate the subordinate and thus enhance the probabilities of success.

We expect people to read this book who are in the midst of hiring or supervising a new administrator or entering a new administrative job themselves. Particularly, we believe the book will be useful to people who design, run, or participate in any phase of a hiring process for administrators; to people entering new administrative jobs, whether experienced or new to administration; and people already established in administrative positions who must hire and supervise a new administrator.

The book comprises seven chapters of case-stories in which five writer-administrators present the frameworks of thought and administrative action—the structures, processes, methods, and techniques they used in their attempts to hire and supervise new persons or to enter a new job themselves in a more planned and collaborative manner. The case-stories serve as handbooks in the best sense: they are personalized tours through unknown territory which will give readers a map to revisit the territory (replicating in other settings what is described here) and to explore new but related territory (creating and implementing a plan of their own, appropriate to a unique setting).

Supplementing the case-stories are sets of exercises designed both for practitioners working alone and for instructors in classroom, workshop, and seminar settings. The exercises will help readers translate into their own experience some of the techniques and procedures depicted in the case-stories.

How to Read the Book

Under the sections (1) Hiring, (2) Entering, and (3) Supervising, we present excerpts from each of the case-stories which give the flavor and suggest the content of each story. Each excerpt also implies some of the traps which make for bad beginnings in hiring, entering, or supervising. The complete case-stories show how to escape the traps which result in bad beginnings. We present the excerpts as an invitation for the reader to sample each case-story, discard the idea of reading the book straight through, and turn immediately to a case-story of personal relevance.

Cases on Hiring

We assume that the participatory hiring practices common everywhere today are necessary and desirable, but often undisciplined and ineffective.

A SUPERINTENDENT SEARCH PROCESS

(Chapter 1)

"The last two times we hired an administrator it was a zoo! Please, let's not do *that* again. There's got to be a better way."

That statement in one form or another—and with lots of grim details to back it up—was uttered by school board members, teachers, screening committees, and administrators as the system prepared to choose a new superintendent.

The "zoo" had consisted of five different interview teams, each simultaneously interviewing five different candidates and then circulating candidates from one team to another. To be sure, a maximum number of interested parties had been involved. . . . [But] almost everyone was left frustrated and angry at the process and therefore predisposed to being dissatisfied with the product, namely, the new administrator. . . . Apparently in the interests of creating maximum participation and involvement, the system found it had produced maximum divisiveness.

The author of this case, Joan Wofford, presents step-by-step the methods she used to engage members of the system in a hiring process which produced not divisiveness but trust, inquiry, and commitment to the system as a whole.

HIRING A NEW ASSISTANT

(Chapter 2)

I recall one day, long after my former assistant, Glen, had "established" himself, when I overheard him discussing what I will simply call "educational issues" with a group of students in the hall while I worked at my desk tallying a column of budget figures. In that moment of epiphany, I realized that he was doing the work that I wanted to do, and, more importantly, felt that I should do, while I was doing work that was more properly his. Somehow I had failed to communicate to him what I expected him to do.

In this case Paul Kelleher goes on to describe how this experience led him to redefine the concept of a "job description" when hiring a new assistant, and he shows in detail how he conceived and managed a screening committee to produce a better decision through the use of effective participatory techniques.

Cases on Entering

We assume that many administrators get off to bad starts because they immediately begin to "solve problems" or "make changes" before planning and executing a set of activities which force them to learn more about the system and test their assumptions before trying to change or direct it.

A BAD BEGINNING AS PRINCIPAL

(Chapter 3)

When the superintendent called me in May 1973 and offered me the principalship, I felt as if a dream had come true. . . . I would have my own school. Even more exciting, I would have a new school. . . . I would have the chance to hire almost half the staff. . . . In addition, I would be working with a superintendent whose ideas I liked. The year was 1973, but my new boss espoused a commitment to the liberal ideas of the sixties that I still loved—openness, freedom, spontaneity, individual growth. He wanted to make the new middle school a place to help young adolescents grow and flourish. What could be better!

In less than two years, my dream turned into a nightmare. I discovered that the fifty miles I traveled from my old system to this one might just as well have been fifty thousand miles as measured by the differences in community ideas

about education. On a rainy April night in the spring of 1975, I sat beside my
lawyer while the School Board announced that it would not reappoint me.
What happened?. . .

In this case-story Paul Kelleher reconstructs his attempt to make change fast,
neither systematically inquiring into the norms and values of the new setting, nor questioning his *own* assumptions about what changes to make and
how to make them.

A GOOD BEGINNING AS SUPERINTENDENT

(Chapter 4)

"Now that you've got the job, when are you going to plan how to begin
work?"
Flushed with my success at having been picked for the job, I reacted angrily
to the question. The previous evening I had been appointed superintendent of
a suburban school district, after a grueling three-month selection process
which culminated in a public interview with the School Board before 200
citizens. I hadn't even finished celebrating, and here my consultant was telling
me to get back to work. More important, the question evoked the fears and
self-doubt deep within me. *"Plan* how to begin work?" I had never thought of
starting a new job in quite that way. How do you do it? Could I do it? If not,
would I fail before I began?
. . . The district, although a good one, had suffered serious problems recently
and I was not confident I could succeed. There were several strikes against me:
I was young, I had never been superintendent in a district which included a
high school, I was appointed on a split School Board vote without full support
from the faculty, and my appointment came after a year-long search in which
the School Board had fired its original consultants and started the selection
process over again.

Dan Cheever continues to show in detail how he planned and executed an
entry design which allowed him to avoid both the traps of the system and his
own reflexes and which enabled him to engage others at all levels of the
organization in systematic inquiry into how the system worked, where it was
headed, and how it would get there.

Cases on Supervising

We assume that supervisors often fail to nurture the growth of new supervisors: (1) Because supervisors often do not analyze and change their own
practice of "sink or swim" supervision (Chapter 5); (2) because supervisors
often do not give and receive negative information about performance, their

own and that of the supervisor, in a timely, effective manner (Chapter 6); and (3) because supervisors often do not adequately plan and take an active part in the supervisor's inquiry into the nature of the new organization and the job (Chapter 7).

SUPERVISING A NEW SPECIAL EDUCATION DIRECTOR

(Chapter 5)

This case begins with the author's analysis of his own sink or swim supervisory practice in a previous job:

> My journey into the past was not a pleasant one. I recalled an assistant principal whom I hired in a previous district. The participatory hiring process was a good one, involving faculty members from the various disciplines of the school in developing and asking questions that measured the problem-solving ability of the candidates and their performance in simulated stress situations. Out of that process I hired an energetic assistant principal. Young, bright, and talented, with a series of successful jobs behind him, my assistant was excited by his first administrative position. I was sure I'd enjoy working with him as he took charge of the instructional program in that large junior high school.
>
> He lasted only one painful year. What went wrong?
>
> Without knowing it, I "threw him to the faculty," as several of my own faculty members flippantly pointed out. Almost like students with a substitute teacher, the faculty took my new assistant apart. His failure, though, was less the faculty's fault than my own.

Steve Fisher's case-story illustrates his sink or swim supervision with this assistant principal and shows his attempt to change this approach in supervising a new special education director.

SUPERVISION: THE GIVING AND RECEIVING OF NEGATIVE INFORMATION ABOUT PERFORMANCE

(Chapter 6)

The administrator in this case supervises a new teacher, rather than a new administrator, and demonstrates the skill of giving and receiving negative information about performance. The discipline necessary to give and receive negative information about performance is difficult to achieve because it runs counter to most people's reflexes to protect others from negative judgments. However, protection of another from the "bad news" can also feel like abandonment as the supervisee is left to make sense of what is happening alone.

> By accident I was passing Sally's room a few minutes before our scheduled meeting in my office, and I saw her sitting at her desk, staring down at a

book. Putting my head in the door, I said that I'd see her in a few minutes. She didn't seem to hear me. As I stepped into the room, she looked up, taken aback, and immediately began to speak "of all the days you should have come to my class"; the day was atypical; the kids behaved differently than usual; "I'm so annoyed with them," she complained.

As I took a seat across from Sally, my silent reaction was, "Hey, wait a minute. I have data here from student folders that has nothing to do with what day I observed. Who are you trying to fool?" I wanted to "shoot her down" with the data I had collected, to disconfirm the case I imagined she was trying to build against the validity of anything I was going to say.

Though the administrator in this case supervises a new teacher, not a new administrator, the case is included here for three reasons: (1) its real content is the giving and receiving of negative information about performance in a timely and effective manner; (2) the content is central to effective supervision of administrators (and teachers); and (3) this case is extraordinary in demonstrating a supervisor's capacity to recognize, question, and verbally test her own observations and assumptions about a supervisor's performance in conversation with the new supervisee.

SUPERVISING A NEW ASSISTANT PRINCIPAL

(Chapter 7)

The approach in this case to supervising a new but experienced assistant includes a number of techniques for jointly clarifying roles and responsibilities and inquiring into the system, of which one of the most important is the mapping of norms:

As an entering administrator, Phil should be like an anthropologist. Like the anthropologist who tries to determine the myths, lore, and traditions of a foreign culture, Phil would need to learn the social and political norms of the school, its traditions, its procedures, and the historical context in which all these phenomena reside. Phil's need to learn about the "culture" of the school is even more imperative than the anthropologist's since he must quickly become an actor in the new setting.

He might decide to break the norms that exist by attempting to change the culture of the school in some way, but that decision ought to be conscious and deliberate and made only after careful consideration of the consequences. In these terms, it would be costly for him to initiate some activity and then discover, to his surprise, that he did not accurately predict its consequences. His actions might have violated someone's sensibilities, intruded on someone's turf, or elicited some other painful response to perceived change. However well-intended, if Phil took significant action in ignorance of the norms of the school, he might find surprising consequences. These consequences might also set up a pattern of resistance to his attempts at change that would have lasting impact.

Paul Kelleher's story shows how he helps his new assistant inquire into the norms of the setting, seize the initiative in defining responsibilities, establish legitimate control of his job, and set about making learning a necessary accompaniment of effective practice.

In general the writer-administrators escaped the traps implied in the above excerpts from each of the seven cases by developing practices which forced them to:

— Inquire into and change their own reflexes
— Inquire into how people within the system view it and each other
— Test that information with the people in the system for its validity
— Develop, test, and utilize a plan to help them resist the combined forces of their own reflexes and organizational pressures toward competition and fragmentation
— Inform all persons involved of the plan prior to its use
— Confront the paradox of using structures for the purpose of fostering collaboration rather than seeking unilateral control

How to Use the Exercise Materials

Each of the three sections of this book, Hiring, Entering, and Supervising, will be followed by a set of materials designed to help readers inquire into their own reflexes, inquire into how others in the system see it, test their information, publically develop plans, and practice using structures to foster collaboration.

Each of the sets of materials will be divided into two parts: materials for practitioners, called "self-help exercises," and materials for use by instructors in classrooms, workshops, and seminars. Each set of materials relates intimately to the case-stories which precede it and is designed to be used after the relevant case-stories. A reader who has not read the case-stories might find the exercise materials difficult and confusing. Additionally, the materials assume a reader's willingness to (1) reread parts of the case-stories and (2) use the materials as guidelines from which to improvise rather than as rules to be followed to the letter. For the most part these exercises are a presentation of the case material in an instructional rather than a narrative form which complements rather than replaces the case-stories.

One of the methodologies used throughout these exercises is role playing. While we are aware of many persons' concerns about the effectiveness of role playing and about its high-risk nature, we recommend and make use of the role-playing methodology because of our experience in using it as a way to reveal reflexes—to expose the discrepancies between administrators' intentions and their actual practice. Role playing allows us to reveal to ourselves (and others, of course) the discrepancy between our espoused theories of leadership and the reflexes or assumptions which actually inform our everyday behavior.[2] However, to be effective, role plays can only be used in a setting where collaborative not competitive effort is valued and insisted upon by the person in charge. They must be followed by rigorous exploration and analysis of what the revealed discrepancies tell us about ourselves and by attempts to invent new, more appropriate, forms of behavior.[3]

[2]   See Argyris and Schon, *Theory in Action*, Jossey-Bass, San Francisco, 1974.
[3]   See "A Framework for Looking at Learning," in Jentz and Wofford, *Leadership and Learning: Personal Change in a Professional Setting*, McGraw-Hill, New York, 1979, chap. 2, p. 6.

Section One:

___

HIRING

___

INTRODUCTION TO THE SECTION

Hiring a new administrator usually involves the participation of large numbers of people. Unfortunately, participatory hiring practices often fail. Thousands of hours of time and effort by people from different levels of the organization do not result in improved information about the nature and needs of the organization, better decisions, or renewed commitment to the organization as a whole.

In this section on hiring we show how Joan Wofford, working from outside the system as a consultant to a school board in its search for a new superintendent, and Paul Kelleher, working from his position within the system as high school principal, employ structures to set up participatory hiring practices which result in increasing the quality of information, fostering organizational inquiry, improving decision making, and renewing commitment among members of the system to the system and to helping the new administrator succeed.

Immediately following the cases are three sets of exercises on hiring, two sets for practitioners and a third for instructors to use in classes, workshops, or seminars.

Chapter 1:

A Superintendent Search Process

by JOAN W. WOFFORD

Introduction

"The last two times we hired an administrator it was a zoo! Please, let's not do *that* again. There's got to be a better way."

That statement in one form or another—and with lots of grim details to back it up—was uttered by School Board members, teachers, screening committees, and administrators as the system prepared to choose a new superintendent.

The "zoo" had consisted of five different interview teams, each simultaneously interviewing five different candidates and then circulating candidates from one team to another. To be sure, a maximum number of interested parties had been involved. Teachers formed one team, administrators another, students a third, School Board members a fourth, and parents the last. The outcome had been that each team received differing impressions, that candidates apparently played effectively to their differing audiences, and that when the School Board made its decision, it inevitably angered those constituent teams which had expressed preferences for other candidates. Almost everyone was left frustrated and angry at the process and therefore predisposed to being dissatisfied with the product, namely, the new administrator. The teachers were mad at the School Board for not selecting any of "their" candidates. The School Board was angry at the teachers for acting as if they had a right to dictate selection to the Board. Even the facts of how the final decision had been made were the subject of a variety of conflicting accounts. But about one central fact there was little disagreement: most participants were exhausted and felt somehow abused. Apparently in the interests of creating maximum participation and involvement, the system found it had produced maximum divisiveness.

The system had benefited from this previous experience to the extent of deciding this time to hire a consultant to help with the search process, but the system's learning was limited. As one of three consultants invited to appear before a Board subcommittee with a proposal for how to assist the search, I encountered the following disturbing series of events.

Among the panel of eight persons who interviewed me, it was unclear who was a genuine, voting member of that subcommittee and who was present as an interested Board member but not as an official subcommittee member. Not only were membership issues ambiguous, but it later emerged that decision-making timetables and procedures were also unclear. An initial subcommittee decision made in favor of another consultant was reached unexpectedly at a time when some of the committee did not know a decision was scheduled. Furthermore, the decision was reached informally, and not by a vote, apparently to avoid having to clarify the issue of who could legitimately vote. Ultimately, this "decision" was overturned by a small number of outraged members (including one not formally on the subcommittee) who chose to do additional research and politicking to reverse it.

By these far from promising methods, I was chosen the consultant. And that choice-making process—with all its unclarity, frustration, and reversal of decisions—offered a frightening paradigm of what the entire superintendent search process might well have turned out to be like.

Fortunately, the opposite proved true. Five months later, with a superintendent chosen, there was virtually unanimous agreement that the process the Board had gone through resulted not only in first-class decisions, but in a kind of orderly participation and level of trust in each other that left members struggling to describe their feelings of hope, personal learning, and organizational commitment. The headline in the local paper read, "School Search Brings Unity." The article began by stating that the union board, made up of the full school board of each of the six towns,

> . . . has been a political battleground in the past, but officials said this week differences were put aside in the search that resulted in [the new superintendent].

The article went on to quote Board members at length, the first of whom had originally opposed my selection:

Sometimes you get into a union meeting and they're very political. It's town against town. But because of the search process, all that was eliminated.

Because everyone had to be heard, we made it a point that everyone was heard. It was really not a typical union meeting in that people were not playing politics. You couldn't. People really sensed the importance.

A second Board member was quoted in the paper as saying:

What surprised me was that there were fourteen individuals who listened to and respected each other and helped each other to hone down into a more concise form what they were really looking for.

Everyone really cooperated with each other to make the process work.

And still another was quoted as stating:

It was an extraordinary experience. I think all of us felt that. I felt more a part of a team than at any time since I've been here.

I think that is the result when people focus on listening. We didn't get just a sense of each other's views on the candidates, but the process got us to talk about our goals for the schools and what we want for kids. We had more of a discussion on education than I've ever seen.

We all felt as though we came through an extremely difficult year and we came through it together. We're proud of each other.

The wonder and excitement expressed by these individuals resulted in part from a shift in the Board's dynamics from a kind of participation that was haphazard and mistrustful to a mode of participation that was orderly, calm, and reflective of the best in people. Board members felt good because they not only chose a good superintendent but because they also ended up working well together and seeing each other in a more positive light. This experience appeared to give them hope that they could continue to learn to respect each other more and thus be able to work better together in the future. In short, broad participation, rather than proving divisive as it had in the past, brought people together, enhancing their commitment to the whole system and to helping the new superintendent succeed.

The purpose of this chapter is to delineate the procedures—and the thinking behind the procedures—through which that shift occurred, from a mode of participation based on competition and conflict to a different kind of participation, one based on collaboration and trust.

The System

There were a number of features of the school system itself which necessitated careful attention to how people would participate. These features included the fact that the system consisted of six separate communities, all with a history of some tension and mutual mistrust. Each of these towns had its own three-member school board, half those members sat in rotation on the Regional School Board, and all eighteen members came together in a Union School Board for the purpose of selecting the superintendent, their only legal function. This Board structure meant that, first of all, there was a large number of people to keep informed and to keep focused, a much larger group of central actors than one normally finds in the usual five- or seven-member School Board.

Secondly, given the history of mistrust between the towns, the political situation was always on simmer, waiting to boil up at the first misunderstanding. It was important that the search process emphasize the whole system and common goals rather than dwelling on issues of any single part of the system.

Thirdly, this group of eighteen people did not have a history of working effectively together but did have daily contact with each other in a variety of roles and, in some cases, had a lifelong knowledge of each other and each other's families. Unlike some organizational settings, individuals in the central group had little history of teamwork, but a long history of personal knowledge, even of mistrust. Individuals simultaneously knew too much and too little about each other for effective group work to be easy. This fact required continual efforts to create the conditions for trust.

Serving on the School Board were a group of bright, energetic, feisty people who had chosen to live in this unusual community and who reflected the rich intellectual, experiential, and cultural diversity that characterized this area.

These factors are described not to claim that the situation was unique but rather to state that there were forces at work which were exaggerated in their intensity and which therefore necessitated greater attention to clear and rigorous procedures if genuine collaboration was to occur.

The Stance

Central to helping the Board move to a more collaborative style of participation was a stance toward information. That stance consisted of a rigorous method of managing information designed to produce trust and of a technique for improving the quality of information best captured by the phrase "to get good information, you have to give good information." Both the management and the quality of information were based on a number of developed procedures or "structures." The first of these structures was the search plan itself, and the second, the method of presenting that plan.

The Plan

Having been told I was selected by the subcommittee to handle the superintendent search, I was also told that the entire Board would like to meet me within the week, to hear what I proposed, and convince themselves they indeed wanted to pay me the fee I had requested. This sounded threatening to me, particularly since my preferred work style at the time was to do some interviewing and pulse taking before I committed myself to a design. Instead, I was expected to appear before eighteen strangers with a known history of wrangling, for what easily could turn into a very bad beginning. My colleague said, "Use that first meeting to present your entire plan and get them to modify and accept it at that meeting." I knew instinctively he was right, but I had never done a superintendent search and I did not have a plan.

Two days later, using a time-line planning technique and reading a helpful brochure on superintendent searches issued by the American Association of School Administrators and the National School Boards Association, I had developed the plan. It consisted of five major tasks:

1. Collection of constituent input on expectations for the new superintendent

2. Recruitment (advertising, developing brochures and forms, screening applicants)

3. Development of goals and criteria (reviewing constituent input, developing criteria for candidate selection, agreeing to statement of system goals)

4. Development and management of the semifinalist and finalist interview process

5. Development of a superintendent's contract (to communicate expectations, identify and eliminate areas of misunderstanding, etc.)

By placing the starting date, February 1, at one end of a time line and the hoped-for final date, June 20, at the opposite end, and then marking off the months and weeks in between, I began to work forward from February and backward from June to figure out what had to happen in what order at what times. Clearly, for instance, ads had to appear before candidates could be screened and application forms had to be designed before candidates could apply (assuming we wanted uniform applications). I ended up with a chart depicting the components and the interrelationships across five months (see Chart 1-1).

At my initial interview with the consultant selection subcommittee, I had

Chart 1-1 Superintendent Search Process

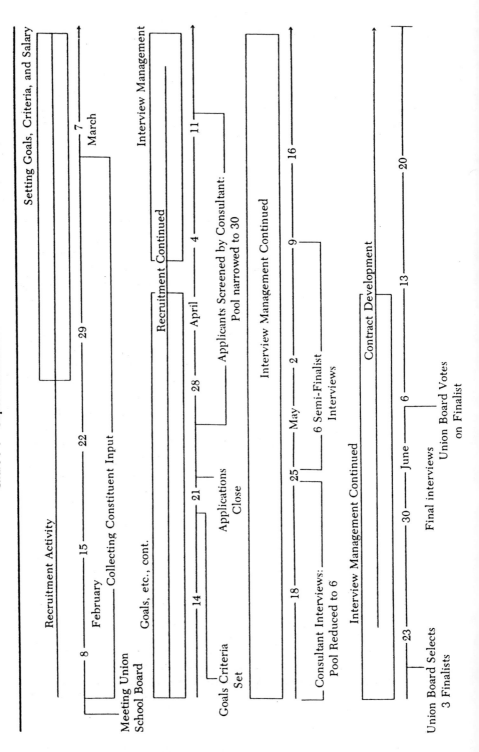

proposed a much less clearly worked out plan of roughly the same obvious components and suggested there be one subcommittee for the whole process which would do all the major work while I served in a staff role. In response to that proposal, the subcommittee had said (1) they wanted the consultant to do more of the work (like initially screening all the applicants) and (2) they felt one subcommittee could not give the required time or sustain the commitment for the entire process, let alone be trusted by the others. Their solution was for the consultant to do most of the work while they all remained somehow involved.

I resisted this solution out of the feeling that the superintendent had to be their choice and that only by making a substantial effort along the way would they develop the faith in their choice—and the commitment to that choice—to make later success likely. Although I did not recognize at the time that what I did was a major contribution,[1] I now see it to be. I simply suggested that for each component there would be a separate subcommittee, and, depending on individuals' interests and energies, people could sign up for as many subcommittees as they wanted.

Given the time line, it was easy to delineate when subcommittees would need to do their major work and when their tasks would be completed. By separately delineating the tasks and timetable for each subcommittee, developing from the time line a master list of significant events, and composing a list of the consultant's functions, I completed the search plan.[2]

The final ingredient was again provided by my colleague. "Get them ahead of time to agree on chairmen for each subcommittee and on a mechanism for resolving subcommittee impasses so that no one subcommittee can mess up the entire design." This was done by asserting, as a part of the plan, that chairmen be chosen and, in the event of a committee impasse, that individual subcommittee chairmen have final authority.

Presentation

With the plan written on large sheets of cardboard, I appeared before the School Board to make the presentation. First I asked the Board members to

---

[1]   The subcommittee structure was significant in:

    (a)   Creating cross-community work teams who developed respect for each other as they effectively accomplished their discrete tasks

    (b)   Requiring the simultaneous self-selection to subcommittees on the basis of interest, not on the political basis of who was serving on what committee

This method of self-selection was later described by a Board member as provoking new and unexpected behavior in that she had not before seen the Board commit itself to a common goal rather than act in a political manner.

[2]   See Appendix II-1, pp. 229–231.

allow me to present the whole plan before we discussed aspects of it. I walked them through the plan in its entirety. One member immediately spotted a weakness: input from the goals committee was needed by the recruitment committee for its brochure, but the goals committee would not yet have received the input it needed. We solved the problem right there.

This structured method of presenting the plan exemplified an important principle about information, namely, its rigorous management in the interests of ensuring that all participants experience the same information. With respect to the plan, specific elements had to be presented at an extremely concrete level and the whole plan presented in its entirety so that all participants could be reasonably sure they were hearing the same information. By insisting they hear the whole plan through, I was rigorously managing information in a way that laid the groundwork for the group's future trust initially in the process and ultimately in each other.

Listing the subcommittees and dates on several more large pieces of paper and placing some magic markers on the table, I asked the Board members to stand up and write down their preferences for subcommittee assignment. Everyone did so. Chairmen were quickly elected, the whole process voted, and the meeting was over. At its completion, six separate people said that they had accomplished more that night than in the past six months.

The plan, then, represented a way to *get* good information from the Board members about what activity they could commit themselves to by *giving* good information, namely, my best picture of what we would do. The presentation represented a way of managing information rigorously so that everyone hopefully shared in the same information. The trust generated by that handling of information was expressed in Board members' committing themselves to the plan and to subcommittees.

Both the plan and its presentation represented the first in a series of structures designed to improve the quality of information used in inquiry and decision making. In subsequent subcommittee meetings, I tried always to make it a practice to present at every meeting a specific written proposal. The concept behind the written proposals was not that they would be accepted totally but rather that they could give the group something to work from on the assumption that a group cannot create something from nothing—it can only create something from something else. So, whether it was selection criteria to be developed or a brochure to be written or interview questions to be decided upon or evaluation criteria to be polished, whatever the task at hand, I attempted to give the relevant group a written statement representing my best attempt to show what a product and process to create it might look like, as an invitation to them to modify and change it (which they always did).

Implicit in the use of the plan and in the structure of the plan's presentation were the following steps:

- Give good information through a carefully designed structure as an invitation to others to give good information
- Receive, collate, and interpret information
- Publicly test the received information by feeding it back as an invitation to others to confirm or disconfirm it
- Publicly reexamine and revise old information in light of new information received and of new interpretations of the old information
- Ask participants, if appropriate, to express their committment by taking action on the information

Fears Associated with Plans

Before going on to depict the structures used during the search process to improve the management and quality of information, I want to comment personally on my decision to present a whole plan to the Board for their review, revision, and acceptance.

The decision to create and present a plan before any work had begun was conscious and frightening. It may sound ridiculous to say that it is frightening to present a plan ahead of time because professionals do just that all the time. Every proposal contains a work plan detailing tasks, deadlines, sequences, and products. As an experienced consultant I had made and presented countless such plans. Yet, frankly, many of them had the quality of fiction because they were developed in the abstract to win a contract and therefore were made in a hypothetical mode, *before* the reality of actually doing the job in the context of real-life constraints made itself felt. Furthermore, they were usually plans detailing what I and my colleagues would do.

This time, having won the contract, I was stating what I expected fourteen other people to do over a period of five months, people who were hiring me and some of whom I was meeting for the first time. Simply put, it was frightening for me to create, present, and in effect impose that plan on them when I did not know them or the situation and when I was presenting myself as facilitator of their participation.

I was presenting myself as collaborative, yet could be viewed as acting unilaterally in walking in, asking them to listen to the whole plan, and asserting what I expected them to do. There is a paradox in this because the unilaterally developed structure is in the interests of collaborative participation rather than competitive participation, yet the act of presenting it can be seen as an act of control which, in turn, produces competition not collaboration. I had come to believe that genuine collaboration requires carefully developed structures, but there was a part of me that feared being seen as arbitrary and controlling if I imposed such structures.

One obvious way to avoid being seen as arbitrary and controlling (and the way I had used in the past) is to present oneself as open to learning as much as possible about the setting *before* presenting a plan and to develop the plan out of the information collected. That helps one appear (and feel) open with respect to both the appearance of control and being right about the issues. Since I had little information to go on, I ran the risk of being perceived as both controlling *and* wrong. That meant being "wrong" in two ways: wrong in my facts and assumptions *about* the system, and wrong *for* that system, which was committed to participation and had chosen me over other consultants because they believed I would enhance their participation in all the steps of the process.

Being wrong is very painful because it carries with it the risk of being exposed as a fraud. Most experienced leaders know the fear that accompanies that possibility—a possibility that lurks inside even though it might have no grounds to exist. In the face of the possibility of being wrong and of being exposed, why choose to offer a plan?

The answer is very simple, though not always compelling—because it works. Because to present one's best image of what ought to happen based on the best information available at the time is to invite others to offer better information available to them by which to alter the plan.

In short, to produce genuine collaboration, one has to risk appearing dictatorial. To avoid dictating structures in the hopes of appearing collaborative is to abandon a group to a competitive and often devisive kind of participation.

A second, related fear associated with offering a tightly structured plan is that even if it is not perceived as an effort to control, it will be felt as eliminating choice, boxing people in, and limiting their mobility. And this is true. However, a plan also increases freedom by maximizing the time and energy that can be devoted to substantive issues instead of process issues. I made the choices about how and when decisions would be made and tested them with the Board for its approval. When the Board gave its approval, its members were released to concentrate on substantive issues. The Board members did not, at the time, appear to need to challenge the obvious limitations on their freedom inherent in the plan, perhaps because they knew they could always subvert those limitations later if they needed to. As time went on and the "paper" procedures held, they gained more and more confidence in the plan and relaxed still more from their need to check on me and each other.

A third, somewhat more peripheral fear associated with planning is that in offering a plan in public, one is flying in the face of the knowledge and expectations of others that planning does not work: that plans are made to be broken. Indeed, as the search moved along, I myself was surprised at how well the plan held up and how we stayed within it. Many experienced old hands, including the acting superintendent, told me that they never believed the plan would work or that the system would make a decision according to the procedures or timetable of the plan. Faced with these expectations for failure, a part of me felt foolish in offering a plan and asserting its finality.

The Structures Used in Managing and Exchanging Information

The concept of rigorously managing information so that people could trust it and of improving its quality through carefully designed structures continued to dictate all the critical phases of the search process.

Information Packet

After I presented the entire plan to the entire Board, I mailed a typed packet of all materials from the presentation to each member of the Board. That packet consisted of:

1. A calendar of significant events
2. A time line showing steps in the search process
3. Six pages delineating roles and functions of the Board, subcommittees, and the consultant
4. A schedule of the consultant's planned visits

It also contained my first consultant report. In the covering letter of this total packet, I explained the reason for a consultant's report as follows:

> I had not originally envisaged writing regular progress reports, but since one of my goals is to make sure everyone knows what is going on and that information flows systematically, it seems to me that this kind of report will be useful.

The consultant report described the activities and decisions of the first subcommittee—Recruitment; it provided the copy for the newspaper advertisement, listed the dates when the ads would appear, and presented the procedures and timetable for developing the position circular. All these written steps were taken in the interests of making sure everyone received the same information at the same time.

The importance of this practice of rigorously managing the flow of information by writing down all matters of importance has been stressed retrospectively by a number of Board members. They felt that this technique was central to the development of a sense of trust among the Board members who came to feel that they would be fully informed about what they needed to know and because they did not fear exclusion, that they did not have to invest energy in developing their own sources of information. Since the information was written down, individuals could trust that they were being given the same information at the same time as everyone else.[3] This appeared to combat the tendency (an extreme one in this region) for individuals to share different kinds of information with different people, thus leading to an atmosphere of mistrust in which no one was entirely certain what was being withheld from them or who was being told what.

Recruitment Subcommittee: Initial Steps

The related principle of getting good information by giving it was followed in the Recruitment subcommittee's development of a position circular. The committee decided to be candid about some of the system's tensions and challenges and to read applications in terms both of candidates' sensitivities to those tensions and of candidates' capacities to give good information about themselves relative to the information they had received about the system. This information was requested in an essay asking candidates:

> Why do you want to come to this area? What in your past experience indicates to you that you would be capable of understanding, enjoying, and contributing to this kind of isolated community?

Some candidates wrote stock responses about themselves. These were generally viewed unfavorably. Candidates who stood out were able to respond to the information about the geography, economics, and social conditions of the area; pose insightful questions about it; and discuss their experiences and expectations in a way that showed how they related themselves to what they had read. This conveyed to the committee a capacity on the part of the candidate to view leadership as a process of exchange within a particular context rather than as an assertion of ideas and stances regardless of the context. Thus the essays, in addition to describing a candidate's experience, conveyed information about her or his perception of leadership.

In this sense, giving good information about the community produced a higher quality of information about the candidates' capacities to receive, process, test, and respond to candid material. To obtain such information required a structure—the essay question.

Collecting Constituency Input

Structures were also used to obtain good information from the relevant constituencies in the district. The first was a series of one-hour interviews

[3] See Appendix II-2 for a sample of shared information summarizing the completion of the recruitment process.

with all the key administrators. A collation and analysis of the results of the interviews was written up in a ten-page paper and circulated to all the administrators and to the Board and was given later to all semifinalists.

The next step was to collect information from teachers and students. As initially set up, my visit to five schools to collect teacher input was going to be very much like a political tour; I was going to whirl in and whirl out talking with individuals on the run, between classes, over lunch, in the playgrounds. If I were charming, they would probably feel good about the process, particularly since the people in their region placed a special value on personalities and relationships. But this whirlwind campaign would offer few systematic ways to feed back to them what I was hearing or to know, in any good way, what they were hearing from me. I, therefore, determined that in order to give and get better information, I would do something that was probably novel but that, I hoped, would clearly communicate the value I placed on listening to them and telling them what I heard.

On the basis of my earlier interviews with all the system's administrators, I developed a short two-page questionnaire.[4] I asked everybody with whom I met in the schools to fill out those questionnaires even before we talked, so that if we were interrupted, I would have a record of what they said. Another purpose of distributing a questionnaire in advance was to provoke prospective interviewees to think a bit about the superintendency before we talked. This, I suggested, would improve the quality of our subsequent discussion. Approximately 126 of these questionnaires were filled out. They were then collated and written up. The results were distributed to all the schools and to the Board.

The structure employed here—the design, implementation, and analysis of a questionnaire—enabled the system to confront the importance teachers, students, and citizens attached to personality and human relations skills.[5] This general conclusion surprised no one; however, its quantification placed the importance of personality in front of Board members in a way different from individual perceptions and made them examine whether that indeed was the basis on which they wanted to hire a superintendent. By the end of the search process, the Board's criteria had shifted (as will be discussed in a later section).

Determining Selection Criteria

Still other procedures involving information exchange were utilized in helping subcommittees function effectively. At the second meeting of the Goals and Criteria subcommittee, the time had arrived for them to narrow

---

[4] See Appendix II-3, pp. 232–233.
[5] See Appendix II-4, pp. 233–234.

down their wish-lists and clarify criteria in a way that had a reality and focus. As a way of structuring that focus, I gave them a set of anonymous résumés and a chart selection of criteria which the subcommittee had been discussing for evaluating résumés (Chart 1.2). The résumés were six actual candidates whose names began with the letter "M." Their names were removed and their résumés were duplicated. This package was then presented to the subcommittee. The committee was asked to take the chart and the six résumés and to attempt to use the chart against the résumés to find out how those particular criteria worked in relation to concrete individuals and how committee members ended up ranking the individual candidates.

This activity produced an excellent discussion. Not only did subcommittee members state who they liked among the six candidates (and found that they agreed) but they were disciplined in helping to work on the harder question of how to use the criteria to judge applicants. In fact, one person changed my mind about how I wanted to use that criteria sheet in initial screening, urging me to get away from an elaborate point system and take a much broader cut. He proved right in this respect and was extremely helpful. His schema became the one subsequently used not only by me but also by the Recruitment subcommittee whose task was to rank some thirty applicants who had already been screened as potentially promising.

The good information I presented in a structured form was a filtered list of criteria and a discrete set of real, if anonymous candidates. The good information generated in response included a workable set of criteria and a schema for their utilization. In addition, committee members felt excited at having encountered some flesh-and-blood rather than abstract candidates.

Interview Team Preparation

The concept of developing a structure to improve the quality of information was also followed by the Interview Management subcommittee in preparing for its job of interviewing the six semifinalist candidates. I strongly suggested that only the nine team members (consisting of two teachers, one administrator, and six School Board members) who had been designated would be the ones allowed to ask questions during the first 1½ hours of the public 2-hour semifinalist interviews, that the nine team members work hard initially in preparing their questions, that they assign specific prepared questions to individuals, and that they rehearse their questions with somebody role playing a candidate.[6]

The rationale here was to enhance the chances of members' being able to pay attention to and hear what the candidate was saying by eliminating the

---

[6]   See Appendix II-5 for the interview questions.

Chart 1-2 A Sample Chart for Evaluating Résumés

CANDIDATE	TEACHER	PRINCIPAL	HIGH OR LOW SALARY	RANGE AND DEPTH OF EXPERIENCE AS EDUCATOR	EVIDENCE OF EXPERIENCE WITH SOCIAL/CULTURAL/RACIAL DIVERSITY	RANGE/DEPTH OF MANAGEMENT EXPERIENCE BOTH IN AND OUT OF SCHOOLS	INTELLECTUAL ATTAINMENT AND PERSONAL LEARNING: DEGREES, ESSAY, HONOR, TYPE OF INSTITUTION	QUALITY OF ANALYTIC THOUGHT; SELF-PERCEPTION AS REVEALED THROUGH ESSAY	CONSULTATION/PUBLICATIONS; EVIDENCE OF LARGER VIEW OF EDUCATION	CENTRAL IMPRESSIONS	HUMAN BREADTH AS INDICATED BY RANGE/DIVERSITY OF INTERESTS	EXTRA
#1												
#2												
#3												
#4												
#5												
#6												

DIRECTIONS: The numbered résumés correspond with numbers on the left-hand side of the chart. Rate each résumé on each criterion listed across the top of the chart, using a scale of 1 to 3 (with 1 as superior and 3 as unacceptable).

NOTE: This chart, with actual candidates' names listed down the left column, was used during the Recruitment Committee's screening of the thirty most promising applications.

nervousness that might attend doing something for the first time, the competition of trying to find space in which to ask one's question, and the confusion of trying on the spot to formulate a question when nervous. I deliberately advanced to the group the metaphor of a team who knew its plays and had practiced them before it went into a competition. This metaphor seemed to make sense to the group and led us to proceed, after three meetings, with a full-fledged dress rehearsal plus time out for feedback. The rehearsal enabled the subcommittee to clarify details like introductions and the time required for each question. It further clarified a procedure of allowing five or so minutes of dialogue after a candidate response before going on to the next question.

While the first real interview was nonetheless stilted, an analysis of the tapes (each session was taped) suggests that the subcommittee got better and better at playing their parts. In this case the information the committee offered were their own comparative comfort with and committment to a set of carefully constructed questions asked of each candidate. The data they received in return revealed the differences in candidates' responses to identical questions and the way candidates chose to utilize their time within clearly established ground rules. The structure imposed on committee members limited their freedom to be freewheeling in their interviews but put them in a position to give and get better information.

Interview Team's Collection and Feedback of Public Reaction

The Interview Management subcommittee utilized a structure not only in its internal preparation but in its interface with the public. The subcommittee developed a rating sheet for collecting impressions from the public regarding each semifinalist.[7] This was given to every attendee at each interview and collected immediately afterwards. Similar rating sheets (though with room for comments) were distributed to and collected from each member of the interview team. All these forms, numbering 175, were collated and a chart[8] developed for distribution, showing for each candidate the average rating given by each constituency group: parent/citizens, teachers, guidance counselors, administrators, School Board members, and Interview Team members.

The information given in the form of questionnaires handed out and collected was the Interview subcommittee's way of honoring thoughtful responses from the public. By disseminating the information collected, the subcommittee further conveyed its seriousness. The information received

---

[7] See Appendix II-6, pp. 236–237.
[8] See Appendix II-7, pp. 237–238.

was improved over what one normally gets by virtue of its being systematically collected and analyzed. The average ratings coincided with the Interview Management subcommittee decision on the three finalists from among the six semifinalists, thus reinforcing the idea of the seriousness with which the subcommittee regarded public input. The structures of a rating sheet and of a report facilitated this exchange of information.

Five-Part Design for Semifinalist Process

Overall what we attempted to do with the semifinalists was carefully to structure five different ways—frames—in which the candidates could present themselves. The first frame was the original written application. The second frame for eight to ten people was the interview with the consultant. The third frame, for the six who got that far, was two pieces of writing from them, the first of which was a sample evaluation of an actual but anonymous subordinate, which they were to present as part of their candidacy. The second piece of writing was their written observations after their semifinalist interview in the district in which they presented their thoughts, reactions, observations of their day in the district and of the district schools. This assignment was deliberately open-ended, inviting candidates to respond in whatever way they wanted. The fourth frame was their semifinalist public interview (described above), and the fifth was the finalist interview with the Board and administrators.

CONSULTANT INTERVIEW WITH CANDIDATES

The way in which I attempted to distinguish my interview from the more public ones that would follow was to describe my interview as private and based on the concept of getting good information by giving it. The good information that I volunteered was my perception of their candidacy. To that end, I told them exactly where they stood in the ranking; I indicated as directly as I could questions, concerns, or negative reactions that either I or the committee had about them, and I asked them to respond. Subsequently, I shared with them as much information as I could (and as they were interested in receiving) about the nature of the schools, the politics, and the personalities which I had gathered through my data-collecting activities. I also told them at the time that I had authorization from the Board to share with them—and indeed would be sending them—the two papers I had written summarizing the administrators' perceptions and the teachers,' students,' and citizens' perceptions, as reflected in responses to the questionnaire.

NARROWING THE SLATE TO THREE FINALISTS

The decision-making process of the Interview Management subcommittee in moving from six to three candidates offers an illustration of the concept of rigorous attention to information whose quality people had come to trust. In fact, the decision-making meeting stands out for many participants. What apparently is memorable is the way they were forced continually to go back to concrete pieces of data and reexamine them in the light of what they were currently thinking. Whenever the discussion became abstract, one member later said, "You would stick another piece of paper under our noses and ask us what it meant to us in light of something we'd just said." Those pieces of paper, some of which have already been mentioned, included:

— University dossiers and letters of recommendation
— Candidate essays in response to the question
— Candidates' written evaluations of difficult subordinates (anonymous)
— Consultant profiles on each candidate, including results of at least a half dozen telephone calls to people who had worked with the candidate in a variety of roles plus my impressions from the private interviews
— Candidates' written statements about their visit to and impression of the district
— Tabulated evaluation results from the public and the interview team on the semifinalists

A number of those present felt that those five hours of being forced to confront the discrepancies between the written data and their abstract opinions broadened their viewpoints and changed their minds.

One test of the effectiveness of that experience was that when the Interview Management subcommittee chairman presented the results of the subcommittee deliberations to the Board (using the presentational techniques discussed earlier), the full Committee unanimously voted the recommendations of the subcommittee, much to the astonishment of many, particularly the chairman.

In fact, throughout the process, no subcommittee decisions or products were challenged by other subcommittees or by the whole Board.

EVENTS LEADING TO FINALIST INTERVIEWS

I had operated from the assumption, articulated from the beginning, that once the semifinalists were selected, I would disappear from the scene. As time wore on, it became clear that people were unclear how the finalist interviews were going to be conducted. In fact several Board members came up with a preliminary design which then began to be questioned by other members as giving too much weight to teacher input. I asserted the view that the superintendent should spend a major amount of time on the final day with the people with whom he would spend the major amount of time on the job: School Board and administrators. That view suggested that the School Board interview the candidate and that the principals interview the candidate. This was met with reservations because it appeared that the School Board did not fully trust what would happen between the candidates and the administrators if they, the School Board, were not present.

In response to that, I suggested a design which involved the principals' interviewing the candidates in front of the School Board, and then the School Board interviewing the candidates in front of the administrators. This was agreed to, but with strange unease. People seemed anxious. As we attempted to probe this anxiety, it began to become clear that people were afraid. They were afraid at an individual level that they might make fools of themselves in front of another group, but they were also afraid at a collective level that some of the tensions that divided them and hostilities that lay barely buried would erupt. Finally, I posed the question whether part of the problem with the proposed finalist design was that there was nobody whom they could trust to lead it and to keep the peace, whether—to put it another way—they lacked at the moment of interview the very leadership qualities they were seeking in the interviews. That suggestion met with an enormous sigh of relief, that, yes, that was indeed the problem, and with a request that I return to referee the finalist interviews.

This is what I decided to do but with some trepidation, because it was not the usual role for a consultant. But the Board was quick to point out that nothing about them or about the process to date had been usual and that they really hoped I would go forward with this procedure. Part of my reason for doing so was my sense of how far the Board had moved in recognizing some of their old traps and in seeking to avoid them, if necessary with outside assistance.

THE FINALIST INTERVIEWS

The finalist structure which emerged from this decision was as follows: the morning of a one-day visit was open to the candidate to design for himself by writing in advance a one-and-a-half page statement of his concerns or questions and how he would like to address them. The Board then attempted to implement that request. The afternoon consisted of a luncheon meeting with a three-member contract subcommittee to discuss the terms of the proposed contract and to attempt to establish the salary requirements of the candidate. Following that, there was a formal three-hour session with School Board members and administrators, and following that there was a dinner to which the candidate and his family were all invited with School Board members

only, after which there was some business discussion of remaining issues
before the completion of a long day.

The three-hour afternoon session began with my statement of the process
to date, a recapitulation of the rationale just provided, and the ground rules,
which stated that for forty-five minutes the principals would interview the
candidate and that we would then have half an hour during which the administrators would be asked to give the candidate feedback on how they
perceived his answers or how they regarded his qualifications relative to
their concerns. At that point there would be a fifteen-minute break. Then
the School Board would ask the candidate questions, observed by the administrators, and at the end of forty-five minutes, they, too, would be asked
to offer the candidate some feedback. In each case the candidate would be
offered the opportunity to respond to their feedback.

There is some question in my mind as to whether this structure did indeed
improve the quality of information about the candidates because I did not
have a chance to collect feedback in any systematic way. Certainly, it did
accomplish a number of not insignificant things:

- Both the administrators and the Board were told the same things by each
  candidate.
- Both the administrators and the Board could hear each other's questions
  and observe each other's reactions.
- Both the administrators and the Board were asked to be candid in their
  reactions and were, at least to a degree.
- The candidate was put in a position of working publicly with both groups.

EVENTS LEADING TO THE FINAL MEETING

The final School Board meeting, at which decisions would be made on
which candidate would become superintendent, approached and I antici-
pated not being at the meeting. It had been left to the School Board to make
decisions about how they were going to run that meeting; however, divergent views began to emerge together with little shared realization that
members were in disagreement. Once the Board became aware of the
deeply felt disagreements, they invited me to conduct the session. I was uncomfortable with this request, not wanting to appear at the moment of
decision to be influencing the discussion in the eyes of outsiders or retrospectively in the eyes of insiders as they thought back on events.

However, my attendance or nonattendance became in itself an issue,
when some members of the Board who most trusted what had been happening and wanted me there as a facilitator of open discussions saw other
Board members as not understanding the importance of having a facilitator. I
viewed the requests for my presence by a majority of the Board as a further

expression of their growth in acknowledging their need for assistance in maintaining their new, more collaborative mode of participation. It became clear that the only way for me not to become an issue was to attend at least part of the final meeting.

DESIGN FOR THE FINAL MEETING

The design for the final meeting was another example of a rigorous structure offered to improve the quality of inquiry and information exchange. Perhaps the best way to illustrate this is to quote what I said that night and include the design in the form of an agenda:

> The design for tonight is before you, and I would like to spend a moment leading you through it so that people know ahead of time what to expect.
>
> Hopefully your mind is not totally made up. You see reasons for selecting more than one person. One way to help get clearer is to get additional information. A good way to really hear additional information is to take a stand—which you will not be held to—and find out how it feels and test the new information against it.
>
> In order to facilitate getting new information, I am asking you to play a kind of game. The game involves taking a stand, on a trial basis, namely, voting and then getting additional information and then taking a stand again. The actual nonbinding vote is an attempt to get at your gut level reaction before you hear new information.
>
> I'm not asking you to vote for real; I'm asking you to play a game to produce a higher quality vote later. To take the initial vote in public produces a higher quality game, but I won't insist on its being public if some of you feel strongly. It's still a good game if done secretly.
>
> Then after receiving some additional information from other sources, I will ask you to share with us what led to your choice and what led you *not* to choose the other two. This is at a gut level. I will record all you say on large sheets of paper on the wall.
>
> After that I will ask you to vote again—this time for two candidates. This vote is less a game because its effect will be to narrow the field by eliminating one person. But at another level this is still not a final vote for your new Superintendent, so it gives you some room to maneuver inside.
>
> At that point (step 6) on the Agenda, I will ask you again to examine some additional information. This time the information will be a rational analysis as contrasted with a gut-level response. I'll ask you to go through the evaluation criteria and rate the two remaining candidates.
>
> Then you will be asked individually whether your rational analysis confirmed or disconfirmed your previous gut-level choice.
>
> At that point I will attempt to summarize what I think has happened to date, what I hope you can do together, and I will leave.

The agenda before the Board as I spoke was as follows:

AGENDA

1. *Explanation of Agenda, Process, and Joan Wofford's Role*
2. *Reports*
   - (*a*) Contract Subcommittee and salary
   - (*b*) Follow-up calls
3. *Initial Straw Vote*

   (If you had to choose now at a "gut level," without benefit of hearing additional information, who would you choose?)
4. *Additional Information*
   - (*a*) Results of straw vote
   - (*b*) Administrators' views in terms of their rankings
   - (*c*) Individual School Board members' views on what led each person to choose one candidate and not to choose the other two candidates.
5. *Vote to Narrow the Field*

   (Vote twice for two candidates out of three, with the intent of narrowing the slate of two finalists.)
6. *Additional Information*
   - (*a*) Analysis of two candidates in terms of established, written evaluation criteria
   - (*b*) Analysis of two candidates in terms of additional evaluation criteria which emerged during finalist interviews
7. *Summary by Joan Wofford*, after which she departs
8. *Break*
9. *Nonbinding Vote for One Candidate*
10. *Those in minority restate their views* of what factors majority is overlooking
11. *Final Vote for One Candidate*
12. *Recommitment to a Unanimous Final Public Vote*

When the time arrived for me to offer my summary and leave, I said:

If the process has worked to date, it has generated a higher level of trust among you. Many of you assert that that is true. But let me assert that trust does not mean agreement. You will continue to disagree. What I hope trust means is that you can take each other a little more into account as you work together. What does that mean? That everyone would leave tonight feeling he or she has been fully heard. To do that, each of you will need to exercise the self-discipline to stay with the discussion so that individuals feel acknowledged and recognized for the legitimacy of their views. That means that the majority has to initiate reaching out to those in minority and hearing data that disconfirms their position. For that reason I have inserted step 10.

In many ways this final structure did not work at the level of giving people room to move around and change their minds. Members came to the meeting with their minds made up, and no one wavered. Those who supported the third candidate who was eliminated switched to one of the other two and stayed there. After I left, they debated for many hours before asking me to rejoin them. There was little I could do then, as positions had solidified.

At another level, that of listening to each other and respecting each other, the design did work, as the newspaper quotations near the beginning of this chapter attest. One old-timer said at 3 A.M. as the meeting finally broke up, "My opinion of no one has been lessened and my opinion of many others has been raised."

The Value of Collaborative Participation

The previous sections of this chapter have depicted a relationship between information management and exchange and collaborative participation; they have illustrated some of the structures used to increase the quality of information and produce satisfying participation in a superintendent search process.

At this point, it is useful to ask: Why is this kind of collaborative participation better than the kind of School Board participation experienced earlier in the district?

Clearly, previous School Board behavior was participatory in the sense of people being involved in making decisions and in the process leading to decision. Indeed, as already described, at the consultant interview session, there were School Board members actively present who were not officially designated members of the consultant selection committee. Furthermore, this kind of behavior was officially sanctioned by the School Board's regional structure which, while officially calling for nine regional members at any one time, actually assumed through its system of yearly rotation that all eighteen local members should be informed and regularly attend meetings.

Certainly, these two examples illustrate a mode of participation beyond that normally expected of School Board members. It is, however, a mode of participation built on mistrust. Busy people attend meetings they do not officially have to attend principally because they do not trust what might happen at the meeting nor what they will be told afterwards about the meetings. This sort of participation is exhausting. One must always be on the lookout for news of a meeting that might occur. There is in this behavior the assumption that only by personally being present can one trust what goes on. This emphasis on the trustworthiness of self and untrustworthiness of others is the essence of competition. It can only lead to conflict. This pattern of participation was evident in the early "zoo" experience of search procedures where there was large-scale participation, mistrust of other groups, and conflict over the decision.

This pattern of participation was broken in the superintendent search process described here. Board members came to trust that subcommittees of which they were not members were acting responsibly. Not only did they state that they felt trusting but they also evidenced this trust in their behavior by voting to accept subcommittee actions and reports even on enormously sensitive issues like the narrowing of the finalist slate.

The collaborative form of participation is preferable to the earlier mode because at an individual level people felt exhilarated, not exhausted. They gained insights, perspectives, and developed new skills. At an organizational level, this form of participation was preferable because at a collective level people gained new knowledge about the system and their roles in maintaining its fragmentation. The new knowledge led to a commitment to support the whole system, not just their own part of the system.

The significance of this organizational learning is based on five assumptions about organizations:

1. That organizations, like people, often lose their way and that this takes the form of confusing the original mission with peripheral matters like roles, territory, and status. Periodically the organization has to rediscover and reconnect itself to its primary intent.

2. That contexts change, and periodically organizations have to look at the fit between the present context and their goals, strategies, and assumptions.

3. That it is important for organizations to use a real-life and crucial need (like a superintendent search) to legitimize and make possible the difficult activity of self-examination.

4. That inquiry and reexamination are crucial because one of the things that happens over time is that participants tend to see themselves not as part of the problem but as part of the solution; they tend to disassociate themselves from their roles in the system and to blame others or *the system*.

5. That a reassumption of responsibility by the participants is crucial to the success of any new person, because success is dependent not just on

what that person brings to the job but upon an exchange between the system and the person. There is necessarily a shared responsibility for making the whole system work and that depends as much on the people already there as upon the new person coming in.

From the perspective of these five key assumptions, one of the central organizational lessons learned from the previous "zoo" search process was a confirmation of the distrust among the parts, and this provided the factions with a further impetus to move back into the parts of the system and away from a shared responsibility for the whole system.

The central metaphor that came to represent for me the dynamics of the system was that of feudal barons coming together, reluctantly, to anoint the King and then rapidly dispersing back to their feudal lands, leaving the King responsible for the whole country while they immersed themselves in and fought for their part of the system against the other barons and against the new King.

The Board's new knowledge about the system's complexity and its own role in maintaining the feudalism led the Board members gradually to shift their criteria for selection from external characteristics like credentials and personality to criteria involving the capacity of candidates to develop methods to help the parts of the system work together.[9] In addition, Board members expressed their commitment to the whole system, as opposed to their part, by indicating their interest in a subsequent examination and alteration of the current Board structures in order to minimize the system's fragmentation.

Conclusion

Given this consultant's commitment not only to the task of finding a good superintendent but also to the task of helping facilitate a different style of participation, the kind of behavior described above is hopeful. It will be hard—even impossible—to sustain. Old patterns will quickly emerge, the conflicts will resume, individual Board members will jump to conclusions before another member finishes speaking, and fragmentation will begin to dissolve the sense of unity the Board now has. Yet each participant in the process has experienced what it *can* feel like really to listen to each other, to collaborate, to inquire into what another is saying rather than contest it out of hand, to feel respect rather than contempt for someone else's point of view, to feel "a member of a team" and "proud of each other," as one member was quoted in the paper as saying. And that experience of a differ-

[9] See Appendix II-8, p. 238.

ent way of thinking and feeling and behaving will remain in each participant as an image of hope, a picture that it is possible—extremely difficult, but possible—to behave differently, in the interests not of a part but of the whole enterprise. That image of hope means that they and the system—at least for a while—are no longer the same as they were before the search began. They are, in fact, radically, if temporarily, changed. And that is what this search and selection process gives, not only to the system searching but to the superintendent entering a new job.

Subsequent chapters of this book will delineate some of the ways in which the techniques described here can be employed by an entering administrator in a way that improves the possibility of a system continuing to believe, and to act on the belief, that a different and more hopeful style of participation is possible.

Chapter 2:

Hiring a New Assistant

by PAUL KELLEHER

Hiring a Previous Assistant

Hiring and helping the entry of an administrative subordinate, such as an assistant principal, provides a rare—and undoubtably the best—chance for bringing clarity to issues of role definition and role expectation. My work with a recent assistant principal helped me to understand this truth. I recall one day, long after my former assistant, Glen, had "established" himself, when I overheard him discussing what I will simply call "educational issues" with a group of students in the hall while I worked at my desk tallying a column of budget figures. In that moment of epiphany, I realized that he was doing the work that I wanted to and, more importantly, felt that I should do, while I was doing work that was more properly his. Somehow I had failed to communicate to him what I expected him to do.

Communicating expectations and being clear about role definition seems obvious and simple. What could be more straightforward than telling someone what you expect in job performance? In practice, however, issues of job description and definition which seem clear on paper become complicated, confused, and muddy in the attempt to refine general statements into the nitty-gritty of day-to-day practice. For example, the job description for the aforementioned assistant principal had said that, among other functions, he would "assist the principal in the daily management of the school." What does such a statement mean? Does "assistance" mean the assistant should run to the principal for counsel on every little problem that arises, at one extreme, or does it mean the assistant should assume he knows what the principal wants and rarely consult him at all, at the other? Obviously, much more care needs to be taken in writing a job description to narrow this latitude of definition.

Another major problem which complicates the issue of trying to set clear expectations for a new assistant is that the supervisor's expectations are not the only ones which an assistant has to meet. Parents, teachers, students, and secretaries have their own sets of expectations, often unspoken, about what constitutes effective and responsible job performance. Unless a supervisor can be clear not only about his expectations for an assistant, but also reasonably clear about predictions of what others will expect, an assistant can quickly find himself overwhelmed by sets of conflicting information that make no sense.

In the absence of clear enough information from me about job description—particularly in management areas that involved paper work—my assistant principal, Glen, quickly heard expectations from students and their parents that he should function as a kind of ombudsman for students. This activity, though unquestionably important and invariably performed effectively by him, consumed enormous amounts of his time that in retrospect should have gone into other activities.

Ironically, the more sensitive and intelligent the assistant is, the more likely this problem is to occur. Unless he has clear, specific guidance from his supervisor about what to listen to and how to listen to it, he is likely to make any number of decisions in defining his job in the early stages that will work at cross purposes with what his supervisor wants.

After I realized that Glen had in practice defined his job somewhat differently from what I wanted, I spent much time planning, first, how to confront him with these issues, and then meeting and discussing them with him. As always, he was cooperative and willing. But by that point, the forces at work were more powerful than either of us could control. Expectations of how he spent his time and what he did were set in the minds of all others in the school community. Those pressures made progress slow and difficult in changing the job and his performance of it.

By the time Glen moved on to his own principalship, I had painfully learned that the time to spell out expectations clearly and to define a job was at the start, when the assistant is most likely to hear the signals and most able to take the initiative in structuring the job.

As I began the process of hiring a new assistant, I reflected on the reasons for the confusion about role definition that occurred in my relationship with Glen. A major cause of my lack of clarity in defining the role was my inability to accept the essential loneliness of the principalship. When I hired Glen, I had just completed my first year as principal of this school. I had experienced a difficult and extremely lonely first year as I tried to make sense of the norms of the school, learn about the people, and determine whom I could trust. The bruises and the isolation of that first year made me yearn for an equal as an assistant principal, someone with whom I could share not only the responsibilities of the position but also its sufferings. I looked to find an assistant principal with whom I could share responsibility for running the school on an equal basis, and I described the position that way, both to the interviewing committee and to the candidates.

In my practice of the principalship with a new assistant principal–equal, however, I discovered important limits of the principalship as I experienced it. The first was that no matter how much I yearned for an alter ego, an extension of myself, I was essentially alone. Though Glen was talented, sensitive, willing, and eager, he remained my assistant. In the eyes of the community, teachers, students, and central office people, the buck never stopped with him. In negative situations, no matter how much he tried to take responsibility, people would finally take the bad news only from me.

Second, I was alone in the literal sense that I was one of a kind in my role as high school principal in this district. Glen, however, was one of two assistants who worked for me, and there were other assistant principals in the district with whom he could establish frank and open peer relationships. This kind of sharing for which I yearned seems not to be possible in cross-role groups (e.g., a principal and an assistant principal), but only in like-role groups (secondary principals with other secondary principals).

Finally, the "equal" model did not work for me because I found that I had given to Glen more power to reward faculty members—for example, in allocating travel money—than I was comfortable with or could justify, given the limited number of incentives a principal has to bestow. In short, I had gone beyond my own limits in trying to share the power to reward which was at my disposal.

Through these experiences, I learned that my yearning for an equal assistant could not be met through the organization. In fact, my attempt to establish an equal assistantship only confused and reduced the effectiveness of both my assistant and myself. Others in the organization did not know whom to go to with particular problems.

Writing a Job Description

As I approached hiring my new assistant, writing a job description that clearly defined an assistant role rather than an equal role was essential, in fairness both to me and to the new person. Previous job descriptions I had written were not very helpful. They were neither specific enough in describing the tasks of the job, nor did they make clear distinctions between the decision-making responsibilities of the assistant principal and the principal. These excerpts are from the job description I wrote for the position which Glen filled:

ASSISTANT PRINCIPAL

Responsibilities include:

- Daily operation of the school
- Administration of the school budget and schedule
- Assisting the Principal in observations and evaluations of both tenured and nontenured teachers

In place of this description I wrote a new one which took each of the job responsibilities above—for example, daily operation of the school—and divided it into two categories, *direct responsibility* and *assistance to the principal,* which specify the kind of decision-making power the assistant had relative to the principal.[1] What follows is an example of these two categories applied to the job responsibility of daily operation of the school:

ASSISTANT PRINCIPAL FOR INSTRUCTION

Responsibilities include:

Daily operation of the school

Direct responsibility for:

- Enrollment procedures and record keeping
- Teacher absence procedures and record keeping
- Grade reporting procedures
- Open House evenings

Assistance to the principal in:

- General supervision of the building
- Monitoring student attendance
- Advising and supporting student activities

Direct responsibility means line authority in working with people and programs. The assistant can make decisions in those areas without my prior approval, though, of course, the decisions are subject to my later review. *Assistance to the principal* means that the assistant has a staff relationship to

---

[1] See Appendix III-1, pp. 239–240, for a copy of the complete job description.

the people in programs involved—i.e., he or she counsels and advises me and others but has no direct decision-making responsibility.

This general distinction allows me to map more clearly the boundaries of the assistant's decision-making power. It serves as a format for my assistant and me to discuss and make appropriate changes in his or her role by moving a specific task from the category of "assistance to the principal" to the category of "direct responsibility." These concepts, thus, give both my assistant and me an important working distinction in the ongoing process of clarifying and reclarifying the definition of his role.

A second feature of the new job description is, obviously, a more specific definition of tasks within each area of job responsibility. There were no specific tasks defining, for example, the area of daily operation of the school in the old job description. By contrast, in the new job description, this area of responsibility is broken down into seven subtasks, four under *direct responsibility* and three under *assistance to the principal*.

Setting Up and Running the Screening Committee

The turmoil in schools in the late sixties and early seventies brought about fundamental changes in the scope and nature of administrative authority. One of the most widespread and consistent examples of how various constituencies in schools have gained a share of the power is the use of screening committees to participate in the process of hiring new administrators. Teacher contracts as well as rules and regulations of school boards require that teachers, students, and parents participate in an exercise of authority that once belonged exclusively to the administration. From one perspective, this sharing of authority can both waste enormous time and energy and dilute what used to be an effective exercise of unilateral authority by the administrator.

From this point of view, screening committees can stalemate what once was a prompt and efficient process. In the arena of the committees' deliberations, political factions vie with one another to influence who is ultimately selected to fill an administrative position. Worse yet, the factions may find a consensus that forces the process in a direction that the administrator-in-charge does not want.

Yet participation, when it works well, can lead to better decisions, as any of us knows who has experienced successful participatory processes. Members of the various constituencies in the organization help us—through screening committee discussion—to understand more fully and clearly what the organization needs. Their different interactions with candidates in the interviews and their different points of view on what each candidate can offer the organization expand the information on which the decision is ultimately based. Participation, thus, enhances the quality of the final decision. More-over, participation that leads to commitment to one candidate by the organi-zational representatives increases the likelihood that the candidate chosen will succeed. The new person will have a base of support with which to begin.

As I approached the task of setting up a screening committee to help in the hiring of my new assistant principal, my goal was to structure a process that would strengthen the decision through effective participation and enhance the chances of my new assistant's success. In thinking about the process, I faced a number of questions.

Who Would Compose the Committee?

The rules of our School Board specify that a search committee will aid in the process of hiring new administrators. Those rules do not say how large the committee should be, or who should compose it. I decided, first, that I wanted a fairly large committee—twelve to fifteen members. I realized that a large committee would make accomplishing tasks more difficult. Getting consensus is hard with a group of seven; the difficulties grow geometrically when the committee is doubled in size. However, I knew we would be doing the bulk of the interviewing during the summer; surely absenteeism would occur. But my main reason for deciding on a large committee was that I did not want a group so small that it could be dominated by one or two people grinding their particular axes. I had seen this situation occur before, result-ing in distress for all participants and failure to make good decisions.

I also made the decision at this time to include parent and student repre-sentation on the screening committee. My past experience with these com-mittees had indicated that parents and students not only offer important perspectives but they also can be immensely helpful in helping to break the political logjams that can occur among faculty.

How Would the Committee Be Chosen?

Since the vacancy of the assistant principal occurred late in the year, in the last two weeks of the school year, I did not have time to set up an elaborate machinery for choosing committee members. I approached the teacher union president and proposed that the committee model the structure of the faculty advisory committee, with a representative from each department as well as from the department chairmen. He agreed that this plan made sense and proposed that, since many teachers had already made summer plans, department chairmen solicit volunteers rather than hold an election. I wrote a memo to department chairmen outlining all these ideas and asking their help. Within three days, I had the teacher members of the committee.

I then asked the PTA and the student government each to select two members to serve on the screening committee.

Who Would Chair the Committee?

The decision about the leadership of the committee was a crucial and difficult one. After careful consideration of other options, I decided to sit on the committee as chairman. The other possibilities, selecting a chairman from the faculty members of the committee or asking them to elect one of their number were attractive options. They would demonstrate my commitment to the democratic nature of the process by delegating even more responsibility and authority. Furthermore, if I defined the committee's role carefully enough and precisely enough, such delegation would also save me a good deal of work. I would not have to screen and interview candidates.

Conversely, giving over leadership of the committee involved more risk than I wanted to take. The person we were seeking, after all, would be *my* assistant. No matter how specific the guidelines and limits I set on its operation, the committee in its deliberations could decide upon finalists with whom I could not be happy. To withdraw and allow the committee to take its own course, only to refuse their choice ultimately would risk more damage than to keep the chairmanship.

The special working relationship necessary with my assistant, then, was the primary reason I decided to retain the chairmanship of the committee. Sitting on the committee would give me opportunities to state and reiterate my expectations for the position and the person and to discuss the unique nature of the relationship between principal and assistant in terms of each candidate. I would, thus, be able to advise the committee's work so that its members would help me to choose the best finalists.

In making the chairmanship decision, I realized that I risked criticism that I was "stacking the deck." In order to minimize that risk, I thought it crucial to present at the outset my expectations for the committee, its role, the ground rules under which it would function, and the steps in the process—then invite questions, comment, and revision.

Ground Rules for the Committee

When I met with the committee, I offered these clarifications:

1. That their role was not to do an initial screening, but to interview a group of fifteen semifinalists whom I had identified from 200 applicants.

2. That their function was advisory and not decision making. I explained

carefully that the decision-making responsibility ultimately belongs to the Board of Education. That authority had been delegated to me. I chose to retain this authority for the obvious reason that the assistant's relationship to me was paramount.

3. That their task was to interview fifteen semifinalists, narrow the group to three or four finalists, and then rank those finalists if possible. In discussing this ranking, I indicated to the committee that once we had limited the field to three or four, we would continue our discussion to see if we could reach a unanimous or nearly unanimous opinion about the top candidate. Short of that pleasant surprise, however, the rank ordering of the finalists would end this phase of the committee's work.[2]

4. That committee discussions had to remain absolutely confidential. We discussed various ways to handle questions from other people about our deliberations without violating confidentiality.

5. That committee members would agree to be on time and present for the whole time for each committee session. I passed out a schedule of interviews and other meetings and told committee members how important the continuity of our discussions was. The process was so intensive, so task-oriented, that comings and goings of different people would severely disrupt it.

Apart from a few clarifying questions, members of the committee were relieved to know clearly what was asked of them and eager to begin the task.

Expectations for the New Assistant

I devoted a major portion of this first committee meeting to clarifying for the committee members my two central expectations for the kind of position and person I wanted. I tried to clarify how I saw the position by giving the full job description to the members and, in this context, talking about the distinction between an *equal* and an *assistant* which had been useful to me in clarifying my own thinking. I explained that I was not looking for someone to come in and share equal responsibility with me, a kind of alter ego, but someone who could be an assistant without being a doormat. I wanted a collegial but not an equal relationship.

Apart from my expectations for the position, my effort to state my expectations for the kind of person I wanted focused on the distinction between a *learner* and a *nonlearner*. With the aid of a handout I distributed, I ex-

_____

[2] See p. 167 for a description of the second phase of the committee's work—helping the new administrator begin.

plained to the committee that administrators who are learners try to develop a climate of interaction with others in which not only they but others can test ideas, can take risks as they grope for new understandings, can get feedback from each other on behaviors. This "learning" style fosters growth and change. On the other hand, administrators who are not learners do not listen or change their minds. They restate pat positions, do not let others see what they are thinking, pronounce dogma. People do not disagree, because disagreement is not encouraged. Little feedback occurs, so little learning occurs.

I warned the committee that candidates for administrative positions generally think they are expected to have answers. They think they are supposed to be problem solvers and will conceive of the interview as a test of that problem-solving ability. We would, therefore, have to structure specific questions in our interview format which would help us to discover the developed capacities in our candidates for learning.

In this initial session, we spent considerable time with these concepts. They were new to many people in the group, and puzzling. We had many questions, much discussion, and in general a feeling that my clarification helped people to understand what they should be searching for in candidates.

Planning Interviews

The next major task of the committee was setting up a structure for interviews. We discussed at some length what could be accomplished with a candidate in a one-hour interview. I explained to committee members that at minimum I thought we could expect to determine how well a candidate could use verbal skills in a stress situation with fifteen strangers. Interviews are performances for candidates. Although we may say that a candidate in an interview is deciding whether or not to take the position, in fact a candidate who decides to go through this torture has generally made a commitment to take the job. Therefore, in the interview situation, the candidate wants to perform well by telling us what we want to hear. From one perspective, then, the most successful candidate is the one who is best able to perceive the expectations of the group and to respond to them appropriately.

Beyond this caution, I explained that often the most revealing parts of the interview were not the substance of the candidate's replies to questions. They are, instead, the interactions the candidate has with members of the committees, particularly as the relationship between the candidate and the interviewers grows in the latter stage of the hour.

Several committee members raised the important question of how we could evaluate the experience which candidates indicate in their résumés. I responded that I thought questions that asked candidates to evaluate their experiences are important because they indicate how skillful candidates are at analyzing their own administrative practice—i.e., how much has been learned from both failures and successes. Subsequent to the interviews, we could confirm or disconfirm the candidates' evaluation of their experience by calling others with whom the candidates worked in the past. I explained that this activity would of course occur with the persons' permission, but that it was an integral part of checking out suitability for the position.

Interview Questions

The next step in our process was to consider what kind of questions could be useful to the interview process. I think this was an extremely important step. Members of screening committees lack, generally, prior experience at interviewing and selecting candidates. They simply do not know what kinds of questions to ask. So, I distributed to the committee some possible interview questions I had developed.[3]

I tried to help committee members to see the whole range of questions we could ask candidates—from questions of fact about recent school experience to much more sophisticated questions asking candidates to reveal vulnerabilities. We spent some time describing the purpose and value of these different types of questions. After I felt the committee had a sense of the range of possible questions, the next step was to emphasize the importance of "hypothetical problem" questions. Although I could make legitimate arguments for a variety of different types of interview questions, I thought I should emphasize the value of the one which I believed could be productive for the committee. I explained that the hypothetical problem takes a candidate into concrete experience, away from the kind of abstract generalizations with which facile, glib interviewees can fill up an hour. Our discussion of interview questions led to committee decision about what questions to ask in the interview. Committee members chose some of the questions I had developed, revised others, added their own. Finally, the committee decided who would ask which questions.

Committee Deliberations

Over succeeding days, the committee interviewed intensively, deliberated, and finally narrowed its list of candidates. In the process, I had

---

[3] See Appendix III-2, pp. 241–242.

confirmed to myself the value of my taking the leadership of the screening committee. In the schedule of interviews, I had left enough time between candidates so that the committee would have a chance to talk and share immediate perceptions. These times were critical to the committee's progress in understanding my expectations, and those of others, and in moving in a cooperative direction toward finding an assistant principal who would meet them. Members of the committee continually asked me to reiterate aspects of my expectations. I was, thus, continually reminded of how valuable was the personal examination I had done privately to arrive at a clear picture of what I wanted in an assistant principal.

In another way, too, the committee kept turning to me. People wanted to know whether or not I could work with particular candidates. I felt in a particular bind in responding to that question. First, I could understand why my response would be important to committee members in evaluating candidates. However, I thought my legitimacy as the leader of the group depended in part on not establishing an advocacy too early in the committee's deliberations. What I found myself doing was answering that question in only one or two instances in which I had strong negative feelings. Otherwise, I simply said I would rather withhold my opinions until the end of our deliberations. Yet, in both these ways, the committee continually indicated that they valued and needed my presence.

The discussions among committee members as they struggled to weigh the strengths and weaknesses of various candidates identified important expectations that members of the committee held for an assistant principal, expectations that I know are shared by many others in the school community and beyond. One assumption on which committee members acted as they tried to sort through the candidates was that, among his other attributes, the new assistant principal should be creative; more important, that creativity should be expressed in some program advocacy. A significant number of committee members were looking for a new assistant principal who had the imagination and inventiveness to bring new programs to our school.

The discussion gave me opportunity to help committee members to question their own assumptions. I suggested to them that in an established and a successful school, such as ours, program does not lend itself easily to change. Basically, people are satisfied with the program as it presently exists. Although we pay lip service to the need to change some aspects, almost everyone has such a heavy investment in some part of the present program that any recommendation for program change produces considerable resistance. I also pointed out to the committee that in this period of declining resources, program change is less a function of new ideas and more a function of trying to work with others to find new ways to use old resources and to change prevalent attitudes. In this time of decline, creativity can more likely be exercised in what I called "high-quality maintenance" activities rather than in "change" activities. High-quality maintenance activities involve communication, conflict resolution, careful structuring of processes that involve many people, and staff development. They, thus, demand a high degree of interpersonal skill.

Selecting Finalists

At the end of its interviews and deliberations, the committee began to narrow the field. In that process, the committee and I discovered the difficulties of trying to find anyone who measured up to our ideals. Yet we did have some good candidates and the committee was able quickly and unanimously to agree on the top four candidates. Because the committee worked so well—trying to integrate their own perspectives on the job with mine—I was able to act as a facilitator throughout this process and not take an advocacy position. I tried to find ways to draw everyone into the discussion and to be certain that people's contributions got the attention they deserved. In trying to help the process move forward, I suggested to the committee that we should keep a candidate under consideration as long as any one member of the committee wanted to argue for that person's inclusion among the finalists. When I sensed that the committee felt negatively about a candidate, I would test whether or not any one member wanted to argue for the candidate. This technique worked effectively. Committee members discovered quickly when they were in a minority on a particular candidate and then weighed whether or not the chances of success in convincing their colleagues were worth the time and energy. Throughout the process, I thought committee members acted responsibly in making these decisions.

Finally, as their last task, I asked the committee to rank the four finalists. Though no unanimity appeared in these rankings, a clear majority view emerged.

Choosing Among Finalists

As I faced making a choice among the four finalists for the position, I struggled with the task of putting my new knowledge—i.e., that I wanted a learner, not a performer, as well as an assistant, not an equal, in the position—to a significant test. For, as it turned out, each of the finalists—save one—had more experience than I had expected to find. Each of these finalists, also, was close to my own age. Therefore, I was less likely to have a mentor relationship with any of them.

I used the following process to help me in making the decision:

1. *One-to-one interviews with others in the organization.* I asked each of three administrators who would work closely with the new person to spend an hour talking with each of the finalists. Their impressions were extremely helpful in both confirming and disconfirming information about the candidates.

2. *Telephone calls to people who worked with finalists in other settings.* I used these contacts to try to find firmer answers to the more serious questions that the screening committee had raised about each finalist. The give-and-take of conversation ultimately provided much more information than letters of reference generally provide.

3. *Meetings with finalists.* These interviews were the most crucial part of this stage of the process for me. I tried to structure them so that they could serve as models for the candidate of how we might work together in problem situations later. I presented myself as a learner, someone who was trying to figure out the best person to hire as assistant principal, but who was not yet at all certain about his choice.

   I began each of these interviews by reviewing the context—i.e., the steps in the process thus far and the steps to come.

   I then proceeded to give each candidate with feedback—both positive and negative—about how he had been perceived by people on the screening committee and others he had met in this process. One major purpose in initiating this kind of interaction was to watch the candidate's responses to see if I could learn any more about the degree to which each candidate was nondefensive, capable of exploring the feedback about his performance, capable of competent performance in those areas of responsibility which made up the role description.

   I found this activity extremely valuable. Candidates differed enormously in their ability to listen to what I was saying, in their degree of defensiveness, and in their ability to use their own feelings in the situation as a resource in responding to my statements. This part of the process was memorable for me in that in the midst of one of these conversations—naturally with the person I eventually chose for the position—I became convinced of his suitability for the job.

4. *Final meeting with the screening committee.* I met with the screening committee a last time, and I described to them what had happened in the three steps outlined above—what I had learned from the others in the organization who had interviewed the candidates, what colleagues in other settings said about them, what my experience had been interviewing them. Through reviewing that process, I made clear to the screening committee who my final choice was. Their response was

characterized by enthusiasm and delight. They felt they had had an important part in the decision-making process; they felt their work was successful and effective. It was. The differing points of view of committee members on organizational needs, their dialogue with candidates during interviews, and their incisive perceptions afterward all had unquestionably helped us more completely to define the job and to find the best person to fill it.

As I thanked the committee members for their work, I told them that they had achieved the first phase of their work. They had helped me to select the best candidate possible for the position from among the applicants we had. Now they had a further responsibility to help make that person successful in his entry into the school.[4] As I spoke, I watched committee members spontaneously acknowledge and claim that responsibility.

What I said to the screening committee in their last meeting, however, also applied to me. My job was only half done. I had hired a new assistant. Now I had to work with him on the deliberate steps necessary to make his entry into the school as successful as possible.[5]

[4] For further discussion of the screening committee's role in helping the new assistant get on board, see "Building Bridges to Key People in the Organization," pp. 181–185, in Chapter 7, "Supervising a New Assistant Principal."
[5] Paul's supervision of his new assistant continues on p. 75.

Conclusion to Section One:
Hiring

Both of the hiring cases assume the importance of three activities: inquiring into self and setting on the part of those hiring, engaging in careful planning about how to involve participants, and paying attention to the quality and management of information.

Inquiring into self and setting took the form of gathering and feeding back constituent input in the superintendent search process described in the first case and in the second case of the individual administrator's getting clear about his current expectations, previous mistakes, and past and present assumptions.

Careful planning was evident in the development of and adherence to a search plan in the first case and to the development of a job description and attention to committee formation and chairmanship in the second case.

Attention to the management of information was central to both cases in the way in which ground rules were created governing reporting procedures, confidentiality, and the structuring of discussions. Similarly in both cases the quality of information exchanged was enhanced by preparing interview questions in advance, analyzing what the questions would yield, and probing to clarify assumptions about the nature and needs of the system.

In the materials section which follows, inquiring into self and setting, careful planning and attention to information management and quality appear in a variety of methodologies designed to produce a more efficient and satisfying hiring process than frequently occurs.

EXERCISES ON HIRING

Introduction

The exercises on hiring will be divided into two categories: self-help exercises for practitioners and an exercise for an instructor to use in classroom, workshop, or seminar settings. The self-help exercises are divided into the following categories:

- Procedures for a School Board to Conduct a Superintendent Search without the Help of a Consultant
- Procedures for an Administrator to Prepare to Hire an Assistant Administrator

The exercise for an instructor is a simulation or role play designed to have students practice interviewing skills.

Self-Help Exercise: Hiring, Number 1

Procedures for a School Board to Conduct a Superintendent Search without the Help of a Consultant

Purpose

To provide a School Board the basic steps and procedures for conducting a superintendent search without the use of a consultant.

Overview

The exercise is divided into two major parts: *design* and *implementation*. The design portion includes:

- Preliminary decisions
- Planning the process
- Presenting the plan

The Implementation portion includes:

- Collecting Constituent Input
- Recruitment
- Screening
- Interviewing
- Designing the Finalist Phase
- Making a Decision

Directions

Read through the entire set of exercises before taking action relative to any part.

After reading through all the materials, proceed to follow the activities in the order in which they appear.

For further assistance in designing and implementing a superintendent search, see the excellent booklet put out jointly by the American Association of School Administrators and the National School Boards Association entitled "Selecting a Superintendent," available through the American Association of School Administrators, 1801 North Moore Street, Arlington, Virginia 22209.

For those interested in identifying and encouraging women candidates, the AASA also can provide help through its Office of Minority Affairs' Coordination of Project Aware, a consortium of six regional organizations whose primary objective is to promote and support women in educational administration.

PRELIMINARY DECISIONS

Who's responsible? Prior to proceeding as a Board to design and implement a search process, it is important to choose a single member or a subcommittee to do the basic design work. Present that individual or subcommittee with a charge and have that individual or subcommittee present the plan that is developed to the entire Board for review. Do not as a full Board attempt to manage the design and implementation activities but be sure that all members of the Board feel that they have fully participated.

Extent of search. Also decide at the outset whether or not you intend to hire from within the system. If you do, there is no point in undertaking a nationwide or regional search; indeed such a search could prove embarrassing to both the Board and the new superintendent.

Do not neglect to consider the implications of the Title IX guidelines of the U.S. Office of Civil Rights if hiring from within. These federal guidelines cover the promotion of women and minorities and could provide the basis for an effective challenge of the Board selection by a qualified woman or minority candidate.

Budget for search. Once you have settled on who will manage the process and whether or not it is to be districtwide or national, determine a budget for the search process. Include money for:

- A consultant (if you have one)
- Telephone (arrangements, reference checks)
- Postage (at least two letters per applicant)
- Secretarial assistance
- Advertising costs
- Printing costs (brochure)
- Travel costs to visit candidates or for candidates to visit district
- Entertainment costs if Board intends to "host" a series of dinners
- Legal fees (to draw up superintendent contract and, possibly, to give advice on search procedures)

PLANNING THE PROCESS

It is essential that a plan be developed which places the different components of a search process on a time line. To create a time line:

- rule off a large piece of paper, placing the present date on the far left and the projected date of employment on the right (allow five to six months for completion of a superintendent search).

• place on the time line the components listed below as an overview. Then revise to allow either for feasible overlap (a screening committee can be set up while constituent input is being collected) or to eliminate unanticipated overlaps in activities (there's no point scheduling interviews during spring vacation).

Allow time to collect constituent input. Allow time to choose an individual or group to formulate questions, interview individuals, collate and interpret the data, and feed data back to interviewees. Allow time for the Board to review data, determine the needs of the system, and establish criteria for selection.

Allow time for recruitment. Include:

• Time for newspaper advertisements to be placed, to appear, and to generate a response by mail
• Time for a brochure to be drafted, designed, printed, and mailed
• Time for candidates to receive the brochure and respond (allow more time if the application process is demanding)
• Time for the announcement of your opening to appear in the local and national job-bulletin flyers, such as that put out by the AASA every six weeks (which requires that their form be used and that it be received two weeks prior to the date of publication)

Allow time for preliminary screening of candidates. Include time to:

• Set up mechanism for receipt of preliminary inquiries and completed applications
• Set up screening mechanism (a citizens committee, the entire Board, a subcommittee of the Board?)
• Make decisions about criteria to be applied in screening
• Make decisions on how many applicants will be recommended and to whom

Allow time for interviewing. I include time to:

• Determine how many people will be interviewed, for how long, with what kind of time between interviews, and how often (will semifinalists be reduced to finalists and then finalists asked to return?)
• Determine whether the interviews will be public and at night or during the day
• Allow time for public notice of interviews to appear

- Determine by what means candidates will be interviewed, and, if a committee, how long it will take to select and collect members and help them prepare for the interviews
- Determine whether data will be collected from the public on their impressions of the candidates and how that data will be collected, analyzed, and fed back
- Allow time for data analysis and feedback

Allow time for finalist process

- Allow time for Board visits to home "turf" of finalists, if desired
- Alternatively, plan a finalist design which does not simply repeat semifinalist interviews

Allow time for making and executing the decision.   I include time to:

- Map out the time and process by which a decision will be reached
- Place the board meeting date on the time line
- Allow time for the selected candidates to make a decision
- Alternatively, ask them to commit selves ahead of time to the job if offered
- Allow time to turn to your second and third choices if the first-choice candidate turns you down

PRESENTING THE PLAN (TO CONSTITUENT GROUPS AND MEDIA)

Present the plan to the Board (and other constituencies), revising it in line with feedback.

Once revised, share the plan with all parties. Also share the plan with the media so that they have full knowledge of timetable and procedures. Indicate times of the plan when you will have specific announcements for them. Such times and announcements would include:

- Completion of application process—number of completed applications received
- Completion of first-phase screening—overall profile of applicant pool
- Completion of phase that produces semifinalists—who they are, where they come from, when their interviews are scheduled (make your intentions to announce their names at this point known to the candidates so that there will be no surprises)
- Beginning of finalist process—names of finalists and reiteration of finalist design
- Time you appoint superintendent—press release announcing decision (which new superintendent has seen and approved)

Implementation

COLLECTING CONSTITUENT INPUT

The implementation phase is critical if the system is going to look inward at itself as well as outward toward likely candidates. The phase was central to the sort of organizational change that occurred in the case entitled "A Superintendent Search Process" (see Chapter 1). However, it is extremely difficult to manage effectively without an outsider. If the system values this kind of organizational inquiry, it would do well to have an outside consultant solely to manage this aspect.

If a consultant is not to be hired, this phase might best be dropped unless there is within the system someone who is trusted across hierarchical lines and skilled in interviewing and managing data.

For more specific help in interviewing techniques, questions, collation and feedback of information, refer to the Index.

1. Designate someone or ones on the Board to conduct a series of interviews with the relevant constituency groups regarding their sense of where the system is now, what it needs in the way of leadership, what critical issues face it in the next five years, and what kind of person they would like to see in charge.

    Selection of that person is key, and it ought to be someone who can listen well, is trusted, and is not strongly identified with a view point which the person would be suspected of pushing.

2. Write out and circulate the interview questions ahead of time together with a copy of the search plan. Interview:

    *   Other Board members
    *   Outgoing superintendent
    *   Other central office staff
    *   Principals
    *   Teachers (Teachers' Association, Advisory Board, randomly selected groups)
    *   Citizens/parents (this could be in a meeting at which some district models were presented for people to react to)

3. Collate and analyze interview data.

4. Present data to the persons interviewed, indicating areas of congruence and agreement and also indicating areas of disagreement.

5. Collect reactions to those to whom data were fed back.

6. Have the Board review the initial constituent data and the interpretations of the data, and make a statement summarizing:

(a) The prioritized needs of the system as reflected by the data from different parts of the system

(b) The implications of those needs for the kind of person sought

(c) The criteria by which selection of a new superintendent will be made

RECRUITMENT

Decide how broadly the system wants to advertise its opening and place ads in appropriate newspapers.

1. Decide how the system/community is going to present itself. Will it use a brochure specifically designed to announce the opening and describe the community? Will its aim be to present the community solely as it likes to think of itself, or will there be an attempt to reflect on some of the tensions, issues, and dilemmas the community currently faces?

(a) If a brochure, it should include the following information:
   • Reason for opening (retirement, death, etc.)
   • Application procedure and timetable
   • Salary range and contract provisions
   • Experience and preparation (Will you require a doctorate, or give preference to one? Ought the candidate have previous experience in the same role? Will the new superintendent need to live in the community? What personal qualities are desired?
   • Facts about the school district (size, cost per pupil, budget, etc.)
   • Description of the community
   • Members of the Board of education
   • Whether the district is an affirmative action employer

(b) If there is no wish to design a brochure, are there existing documents which collectively would present a reliable portrait of the job, system, and community?

2. Decide whether all applications are to follow a standardized, and hence comparable format, or whether résumés are acceptable in whatever format candidates choose. If a special form, you can ask candidates to list names, addresses, and current phone numbers of people whom they have worked for, have worked with, and who have worked for them. These people can be telephoned as part of the check-out process.

3. Decide whether candidates will be asked to write an essay specifically about the position they seek in your system. If so, design a question which requires them to be specific about something (their appropriateness to the district requirements of your system, an analysis of an administrative action they once took which they deem a mistake, etc.).

General statements of educational philosophy make dull reading, sound alike, and do not serve a useful screening purpose.

4. Notify appropriate university placement centers and schools of education of the opening in your system by mailing a letter enclosing a number of brochures and application forms.

5. Send a similar letter and a copy of the brochure to noted educators and superintendents in your area asking them to nominate two or three individuals whom they feel would be appropriate.

6. Decide what will constitute a completed application and state the terms in the section on application procedures:

    - A formal letter of application?
    - A completed application form?
    - An up-to-date résumé?
    - An up-to-date set of credentials from applicant's college or university? Who is to request those—the committee or the candidate? (Recommendation: The candidate is responsible for getting those documents to the committee in time. It's useful on the application form to have the applicants assert that they have made the request from such and such an institution on such and such a date and sign it).
    - Evidence of certification in appropriate state for specific job?

SCREENING

1. Decide who will receive, log, file, and respond to letters of application with the appropriate information.

2. Decide who will receive résumés and dossiers and determine application's completeness. What will that person do with completed applications?

3. Decide who will read and screen the completed applications:
    - A screening committee of citizens whose function is to screen all applications and pass on 10? 20? 30? to the School Board for their further screening?
    - A subcommittee of the Board?

4. Decide by what criteria and by what methods these decisions will be made.

5. Utilize a form such as the one illustrated in Chart 1-2 on page 29, writing preliminary criteria into the columns across the top and using anonymous résumés from the personnel files to discover how the proposed criteria "work":

    (a) Do the criteria discriminate between potential candidates?

(b)   Do they reveal the information that is needed?

(c)   How can they be revised to reveal more pertinent information?

6. Determine how many phone calls will be made per candidate to check out the recommended individuals with individuals who have worked closely with them as subordinates, peers and supervisors, and can speak to both their strengths and weaknesses.

7. Decide who will make the phone calls and how they will report the results.

INTERVIEWING

If an interview team, like an athletic team, knows its plays, has practiced them, and knows what to expect from each other and from others in response to various moves, it is in a better position to handle itself well in competition. This model suggests the importance of selecting a team, having them develop their questions, and insisting they rehearse (or role-play) an actual interview before they conduct one.

1. Determine what constituencies should be represented on the Interview Team.

2. Determine how many people should constitute the team (probably no more than nine).

3. Determine the chairmanship.

4. Determine how long the interview will last (1½ hours?)

5. Determine at what point, if at all, the public will have an opportunity to ask questions.

6. Determine the method by which the public will be asked to share their reactions:
   • An evaluation checklist?
   • An open-ended request for written reactions?
   • Informal conversations?

7. Determine the questions to be asked (probably no more than one per interviewer).

8. Draft and redraft the questions.

9. Answer the questions to see what they produce.

10. Redraft, making the questions more specific and concrete.

11. Determine the order in which the questions will be asked.

12. Role-play an actual interview (tape-recording it as you go) with some-

one performing as a candidate and with each individual asking a specific, predetermined question in the order which has been predetermined.

13. Have the chairman practice stating the ground rules of the interview:
    *   How long the interview will last
    *   Who will speak (introductions)
    *   How long each question is to take
    *   How evaluative data will be collected and what will be done with it

14. Have the chairman time each question to see how it is fitting into predetermined time allocations. (One good approach is to allow five minutes for each answer and another five minutes for the mutual give and take which flows from the question and answer before calling time and going on to the next set question.)

15. Discuss, either at the end of the interview or after each question, problems and proposed revisions.

16. Tape-record the actual interviews for subsequent use by the team as a self-assessment, a record, and for those who missed the interview.

DESIGNING THE FINALIST PHASE

The finalist process may consist principally of a visit by the Board to the individual's home territory or it may consist of a return visit to the district by the finalist candidates. Assuming it is the latter, care should be given to design ways by which the candidates can reveal more parts of themselves to the Board as well as seek answers to questions they must have about the district.

Some options for the finalist visit include:

1. Simulations in which the candidates are asked to engage with others in tackling specific but typical problems such as
    *   Budget
    *   Personnel policy

2. Simulations in which candidates are asked to demonstrate their approach toward
    *   Supervising a subordinate
    *   Evaluating a subordinate

3. Written exercises in which candidates are asked within a prescribed period of time (twenty-four hours) to address in writing a specific issue.

4. Informal sessions (such as a dinner) with the Board.

Candidates should also be given an opportunity to meet with a contract subcommittee, which has developed a model contract, to go over its provisions and raise questions, so that the Board can be reasonably assured that their terms will be acceptable to all finalists before the Board makes its final choice.

At the end of the finalist phase, the Board may wish to ask all finalists to state whether or not they will accept the position if offered.

MAKING A DECISION

How the final candidate is selected is almost as important as who the selection process chooses. A seriously split vote, leaks to the public of how the votes lined up, breaking of confidentiality about candidates, hard feelings among Board members—all these can easily occur and can adversely affect the new person even before the contract is signed.

1. Decide ahead of time to meet in executive session to be able to discuss candidates openly. (Vote in public session.)

2. Decide ahead of time by what kind of vote a decision will be made (majority, 2/3's, consensus).

3. Decide ahead of time whether to take straw votes before a final vote.

4. Decide ahead of time how the discussion will be structured.

5. Decide ahead of time by what means all Board views will be heard.

6. Decide ahead of time what weight will be given to the views of various constituent groups regarding the finalists.

7. Decide ahead of time by what means the winner will be contacted, finalists notified, and who will make that contact.

8. Decide ahead of time by what means and when a contract will be signed.

9. Decide ahead of time when a public announcement will be made.

10. Decide ahead of time by what procedures a second or third candidate will be selected in the event the first-choice candidate declines the position.

11. Decide ahead of time who will retain all application materials for two years as required by EEOC regulations and who then will be responsible for destroying them to assure confidentiality of all candidates.

Self-Help Exercise: Hiring, Number 2

Procedures for an Administrator to Prepare to Hire an Assistant Administrator

Purpose

To provide a set of questions which will guide an individual administrator in preparing to hire a subordinate.

Overview

The exercise only deals with internal preparation. Once that is in place, the administrator will need to choose which of the steps in the previous exercise ("Superintendent Search") are applicable and on what scale.

Directions

The questions listed here should be answered *before* an administrator sets in motion any of the normal screening and hiring apparatus. For a complete picture of how this sort of preparatory work can create a satisfactory hiring process see Chapter 2, "Hiring A New Assistant."

1. Ask yourself:
   (a) With my last assistant, what worked satisfactorily and what did not?
   (b) In what ways was I responsible for the things that went wrong?
   (c) What assumptions about myself and my role and about the other person and role did I make that influenced what went wrong?
   (d) Have those assumptions changed? How?
2. Use the following headings to define in writing:
   (a) My new assumptions about:
      • Myself
      • My role
      • The relationship I want with a new assistant
      • The kind of work I want the new assistant to do
      • The kind of person I want the new assistant to be
   (b) The expectations I believe others hold for the new assistant:
      • Teachers
      • Other administrators
      • Parents
      • Secretarial staff
      • Students

3. Take out the old job description for this position and divide each area of responsibility on it into the two categories, "direct responsibility" and "assistance to."

   • *Direct responsibility* means line authority and indicates that the individual can make decisions in those areas, without prior approval though subject to later review.
   • *Assistance to* means that the individual has a staff relationship, i.e., (s)he counsels and advises but has no direct decision-making responsibility.

4. Use this initial delineation of responsibility to tease out subtasks which do not appear in the old job description but which should be there.

5. Using the job description (Appendix III-1, pp. 239–241) as a model, write a new job description.

6. Test the new job description by reviewing in detail three incidents of conflict between you and your past assistant; see whether the new job description would have clarified the areas of conflict in each incident.

7. Further test the job description by asking two other administrators in the building to indicate whether the job description adequately covers areas of vagueness or potential conflict in their spheres of responsibility.

8. Be prepared to present to a screening committee both the new job description and your list of expectations about the kind of position you want to fill and the kind of person you want to fill it.

9. At this point proceed to set the machinery in motion for selecting a screening committee, choosing a chairman, issues, and developing ground rules (see pp. 45–48 of Chapter 2); also utilize appropriate procedures from the Self-Help Exercise, Number 1, pp. 58–67.

Instructor's Exercise: Hiring, Number 1

Practice Interviewing Skills

Purpose

To put job seekers in the position of interviewer with the intent of forcing them to think and feel the "world" as it exists from the interviewer's side of the table (insights should be translated into better performance in actual interview situations).

Directions to Instructors

1. Decide what position in what kind of organization the interview will be aimed at filling.

2. Describe the following exercise to the class and encourage them to flesh out the scenario; e.g., Assistant Superintendent for Instruction in a large suburban school system with declining enrollments where the central concern is accountability and test scores and the interviewers are the Board of Education,

    or

    Director of a small community-based day care center where interviewers are a mixture of parents, Board members who are also parents, other staff members and where the central issues are the handling of parents.

3. At the initial meeting divide the group into teams of no more than eight persons. Tell them their job is:
    (*a*) To develop a list of questions to be asked, and why
    (*b*) To assign questions to individuals
    (*c*) To appoint a chairman who will be in charge of introductions and time allotments
    (*d*) To agree on time allotments for individual questions and total interview

4. At the second meeting, designate three persons as interviewees, and have each interviewed by the interview team. (If there is more than one team, you may wish, depending on time, to have parallel interviews occur.)
    Ask observers to rate the interview teams on:
    (*a*) Quality of information elicited by questions asked
    (*b*) Differences in candidates brought forward by the format
    (*c*) Smoothness of team's function in relation to putting candidates at ease
    Ask the three candidates to offer feedback to the team on their reactions to the interview.

5. Ask the observers and the team members to offer feedback to the interviewees on their performance. (This is the natural first step, given most people's eagerness to receive feedback on how they did as interviewees. We suggest it be placed last in order to emphasize the purpose of this exercise: to improve interviewees' skill by having them experience the role of interviewer.)

Section Two:

ENTERING

INTRODUCTION TO THE SECTION

The new administrators are, or should be, centrally concerned with obtaining, evaluating and acting on information about the organization they are entering and about themselves. In this section on Entry, we see two administrators—one who ignores his need for information about the setting and acts instead on the prior information in his head and the other who carefully tests the information in his head and systematically employs structures to gather and test information about his new setting from the participants before he acts.

"A Bad Beginning" shows Paul Kelleher's well-intentioned failure to make change fast in a school where he took a new job as principal. It shows why we believe new administrators should aggressively seek information about the new setting and expose their own beliefs to public testing before reflexively acting from them in efforts to make change.

In contrast, the second case-story, "A Good Beginning," by Dan Cheever, shows how Dan implemented a plan of entry activities which kept him from jumping in too quickly to solve problems or make change. Dan's plan forces him to engage people from all levels of the school-system hierarchy in information gathering and analysis. Systematically collecting information about the system, Dan builds trust in his authority by basing his decisions on the information collected from members of all levels of the system's hierarchy, information which he validates by feeding it back publicly to all key groups in the system.

Following the two chapters in this section is a set of exercises for individual practitioners who want step-by-step guidance in designing their own entry plan. As well, there are exercises on entry for instructors to use in classes, workshops, and seminars.

Chapter 3:

A Bad Beginning as Principal

by PAUL KELLEHER

Introduction

When the superintendent called me in May 1973 and offered me the principalship, I felt as if a dream had come true. I had taught for five years and then served as a junior high school assistant principal for two years in a prestigious, suburban, affluent school system. I was only twenty-nine years old, but I felt impatient. Two years as an assistant principal were enough. I had already applied for principalships at various levels within the system and had come up second best. Though I would have to leave the school system in a community that had been good to me and travel fifty miles to a new place, I was ecstatic. I would have my own school. Even more exciting, I would have a new school.

My new system was expanding, adding a second middle school. Though it would be housed in an old building, I would have the chance to hire almost half the staff. In addition, I would be working with a superintendent whose ideas I liked. The year was 1973, but my new boss espoused a commitment to the liberal ideas of the sixties that I still loved—openness, freedom, spontaneity, individual growth. He wanted to make the new middle school a place to help adolescents grow and flourish. What could be better!

In less than two years, my dream turned into a nightmare. I discovered

that the fifty miles I traveled from my old system to this one might just as
well have been fifty thousand miles as measured by the differences in community ideas about education. On a rainy April night in the spring of 1975, I
sat beside my lawyer while the School Board announced that it would not
reappoint me.

Differences Between the Old and New Systems

What happened? The causes of my fall from grace were as complex as they
always are in situations involving many different people with different ideas
about education. But the essential element in my failure to win School Board
and community support was my inability, right from the start, to take into
account how different my new school, school system, and community were
from those I was leaving. I made a bad beginning because I did not fully
realize that although these communities were only fifty miles apart, they
were, in fundamental ways, fifty thousand miles apart in terms of how they
worked. Community ideas about schooling, about children, about life itself,
were incredibly different. And so the norms that controlled life in school
were different.

The community in which I had learned to teach and to become an administrator was in some ways a stereotypical liberal, affluent suburb. Many of the
people who lived there felt secure that they had indeed arrived in the upper
middle class. A large percentage of the population was Jewish. Thus, the
community and the school system had the benefit of the concern for education that Jewish culture often brings. Because people were economically
secure, the population was stable. Most students had attended the system's
schools from kindergarten on. The community was large enough and
heterogeneous enough so that not everyone was wealthy. But only a small
portion of families had incomes that fell below federal poverty levels; only a
tiny percentage of the school population was eligible for the free lunch
program.

My new community contrasted sharply with this image of suburban, liberal tranquility. It was exploding with its own growth. In the late 1950s, it
had been a sleepy country town on the beach fifty miles south of a metropolitan area. It was too far away, then, to be a suburb from which people could
commute to the city. However, an event then occurred that affected the
lives of everyone in the town from that time on and influenced events right
up to my firing. A highway was built. Suddenly people began to think they
could commute to work from the beach. Beginning after World War II, Irish
and Italian working-class families had purchased little summer cottages on
the beach. With the new highway, they began to dream of permanently

escaping from the city. They started to renovate their cottages and to make them into year-round homes. The year-round population of the community began to swell—from 2,000 in 1957 to something over 20,000 in 1972.

Strains in the community and the school system were, of course, enormous. New schools were built. The old-line Yankees and the new insurgents fought battles in town meetings over community services. The town and its schools had to cope with a whole new population of people, some of whom wanted desperately to escape from the tenements of the city but who had inadequate or barely adequate resources to realize their dreams. In 1973, fifteen to twenty percent of the population had incomes below the federal poverty line; their children were eligible for free lunch in school.

Sometimes their dream of exurban paradise turned into disaster. At least once per winter, a fatal fire consumed a renovated summer cottage with an overtaxed heating system that could not handle the burden of keeping a family warm through the winter. Even those who had the resources adequately to heat, feed, clothe, and shelter children for the winter on the beach sometimes could not succeed. A divorce, or a father who lost his job, meant a family must return to the city. The school population was, thus, highly transient. Very few of the students in sixth grade had begun their schooling in the system's kindergarten. The community was both literally and symbolically built on sand. People had few roots there. The fabric that knits families together in a more stable community was missing. So the town was widely divergent on all objective indices—including wealth, religion, and attitudes toward school.

The attitude toward children in school was the most marked and important contrast between these two communities. For the parents in my liberal suburb, Drs. Spock and Gesell were the authorities to whom to turn. These parents organized their homes and family lives around their children's growth. They believed the children would grow and flourish if they were allowed to express themselves. And they expected the schools to be organized on these same child-centered principles. For the parents in my new community, the Catholic church and their own parents were the authorities from which they learned about the upbringing of their children. Children were "to be seen and not heard." These parents believed that the children would grow and flourish if their impulses were controlled.

I walked into the job of creating a new school in this community without taking these differences into account. I was smart enough to recognize that the new community to which I was moving was different from my old one. But those understandings remained vague and unexamined at the start. I did not understand how those differences affected the expectations of the people about their schools. Caught up in the excitement of beginning, I did not fully know that incredible differences separated my new community from my old one in terms of the explicit operating principles governing how the schools worked and in the implicit norms governing the behavior of the people in them. I viewed myself as holding a mandate from the superintendent to change middle school education in this town. Right from the start, I set out to accomplish that goal. In the first months of the job, I made no effort systematically to learn the expectations and aspirations of parents, teachers, and students. Only later did I begin to learn and take into account the attitudes and norms of the community and its people. That learning came too late to help.

I Ignored the Systems's Norms for Hiring

One of my first and most important tasks as a new principal was to hire the staff needed to open the new middle school in the fall. I did not try to learn how the system chose teachers in the past, what the expectations of parents and education were for teachers, or who were successful teachers in the system. Rather, I naïvely and simply set out to find new teachers who would have succeeded in the environment in which I had previously worked. I sought people who had the best academic backgrounds I could find. Thus, the staff I eventually hired was sprinkled with people who held Ivy League degrees. I sought teachers who were committed to the same liberal ideas that I was. And I sold them on the mission of changing middle school education in this backwater town. Thus, the staff I finally put together for that first year included a number of people whose liberal attitude and life-styles attracted them to the communities around the universities in the metropolitan area and who, therefore, planned to commute the fifty miles to work. A number of them were Jewish.

In these staffing decisions, I violated a host of system norms. As I discovered later, most of the teachers in the new system had graduated from the local state teachers college. Most of them lived locally and understood, even if they could not articulate, what the community expected from its schools. Many of them were Irish and Catholic. Finally, and most important, they understood that discipline and order were paramount in what the community and the school system valued for children. No matter what students learned, the first criterion of good teaching was a class of students sitting quietly.

Understandably, my young liberals had a difficult time surviving that first year. Children whose school experience taught that a teacher will rule with an iron hand in class have difficulty understanding a teacher who is committed to openness, individualization, and freedom of expression. Some of my teachers must have seemed like strangers from another planet to these children. A teacher's invitation to them to participate was viewed as a license to rebel. Some of my imported teachers found the students unmercifully cruel as they took out their frustration and hostility on the first adult who allowed such behavior.

Relationships with parents were not much better. Again, the problem was that both the new teachers and I assumed that parents shared our beliefs about education, shared our aspirations for their children. They did not. They viewed our attempts at individualizing instruction as an unproductive impediment to the class's moving smoothly through the textbook. They saw our attempts at making their children happy and comfortable in school as unnecessary pampering that only brought disorder and distraction to learning.

Because of these problems, one of my teachers did not even survive that first year. With much sadness and pain, she simply had to quit. And one group survived the year but simply could not see themselves working in the school or the community another year. Ironically, amid all the larger problems we faced, one constant, routine irritant for these young teachers was the fifty-mile commute. The distance these committed young educators trekked each day remains for me a painful symbol of the distance between all of us and the community we purportedly served.

One of the most painful feelings I have about this whole episode in my professional life is the guilt I feel about these young teachers. Without intending to, I naïvely misled them into thinking that what they wanted from teaching and what they believed in for children was possible in this new middle school we were creating. If I had the process of teacher selection to do over again, I might make the decision to violate staffing norms in the ways I did. However, I would not make that decision without: first, developing a clear picture for myself of what the community, the parents, and students expected of teachers; then, informing the new teachers of this picture; and, finally, developing a clear plan for helping everyone to make sense of the different teaching they were experiencing and witnessing in the school.

I Ignored the System's Norms for Cafeterias

Another area in which I naïvely and ignorantly violated norms was in the organization of the school. Ironically, what I viewed as a tremendous opportunity—the possibility of creating my own school and school climate—produced the worst consequences for me. Even assuming the same community climate, perhaps I could have been successful in my new job if, instead of moving into a new school, I had moved into an established one with a clear set of operating procedures, rules, and traditions. In the vacuum of the new school, I simply made more mistakes.

A painful example of those mistakes occurred around, of all things, our cafeteria procedure. In the nurturing environment of my old child-centered school, I had viewed the lunchtime as an opportunity for restless twelve- and thirteen-year-olds to let off steam. After they purchased their food, they could sit wherever they liked, presumably with their friends. They did not have assigned seats. Students could move around the cafeteria as they wished. In good weather, they could go outside and play together. Other than forbidding the throwing of food and hitting each other, I established no other rules.

In my old school, lunchtime, of course, verged on mayhem. The cafeteria was always a mess. Although students were "encouraged" to clean up and throw their waste in the baskets, without a systematic seating arrangement, that policy was hard to enforce. In addition, there was much shouting and some running, although the adults present—I, usually—tried tolerantly to keep students moderately calm. I remember that I often had a headache after the lunch period, but I viewed the suffering as an occupational hazard. And I believed that the freedom children had at lunch helped to make the afternoon of sitting in classrooms more tolerable for them.

Consistent with my other decisions, I organized the cafeteria procedures in my new school in exactly the same way. It did not take me long to discover my error. First, the students were less able than those in my old school to handle the freedom. They had never had another school experience like this one. After the first few weeks of school, I realized that I had more fights to handle than I had ever had to cope with in my old school. In addition, I discovered more serious crimes—such as extortion—that at least I had never known about in my old school.

In addition to this evidence directly from students, I heard from others that the cafeteria procedures were not working. Teachers who had been transferred to my new school from other schools in the district began to complain about what they viewed as the disorder and anarchy in the cafeteria. One of them even threatened not to take cafeteria duty if I did not do something about the problems there. What motivated me to action, finally, was the visit of my superintendent and some of the "liberal" members of the school committee in October. After the visit, my boss extravagantly praised the atmosphere I was creating in the school. But the president of the school committee, ironically one of my strongest supporters later on, thought I should do something better to "organize" the cafeteria.

The consequence of this negative feedback was that I began to be interested in how cafeterias were run in other schools in the system. I discovered, to my dismay, that the experience that I was giving students and teachers at lunchtime could not have been more different from what they were used to in other schools. Students in the other middle school, for example, came to lunch in line, marched down the hall by their teachers. In my school they came in mobs, usually running, and unsupervised. In the other middle school, after children filed through the lunch serving area, they had assigned seats. When they finished eating, they had to sit quietly at their tables until they were allowed by the adult in charge to return their trays and throw away their waste, one table at a time. When that task was completed, they had to return to their tables, again to sit quietly until dismissal. When the bell rang, they were dismissed one table at a time to the hallway.

I was distressed by the idea of running a school in this kind of repressive fashion. If we could not allow students to have some control over their lives and some time to themselves without adult supervision at lunch time, when could they? Nevertheless, I began, with the help of the staff, to try to pull back from the openness and freedom I had given students at lunchtime. Yet the cafeteria remained a source of continued frustration both for me and the staff for the rest of the year. The statement that teachers should start off strictly and loosen up as the year goes along is repeated frequently because it is so true. Once students had a taste of the freedom of lunchtime, we had great difficulty trying to become more strict.

As I look back, I think that this relatively minor area of concern was a major source of the bad feeling that developed between me and the members of the staff who entered the school from other places in the system. Again, if I had to make the decision about organizing the cafeteria, I might set up procedures that were much looser and more permissive than those in other cafeterias in the system. But I would know that before I began, because I would have systematically sought out other principals and determined how they ran their cafeterias before the year began. My failure again was in the assumption that the norms governing student lunchtime were the same in my new school as they had been in my old one.

I Ignored the System's Norms for School Discipline

Another important area in which I unwittingly violated norms was in school discipline. As assistant principal of my previous junior high school, I had seen myself as a counselor for those students who were in one kind of trouble or another. I spent long hours talking with pupils who were sent to me for misbehavior in class. In those conversations, I tried to help my restless and at times unhappy young charges become more aware of their responsibilities to their classmates, to their teachers, and, finally, to themselves and their own learning. And I had some success, even when I had to mete out some punishment or other. Students liked me. In some instances, their behavior even improved.

In my new school, without questioning the expectations of staff, students, or parents about discipline, I set out with the same approach. I found very different results, however. Shortly after the school year began, I felt overwhelmed with too many disciplinary problems and not enough time to work with them. My new school had a disciplinary "bench" right outside my office to which teachers regularly and routinely sent class miscreants. Particularly after lunch, the "bench" always seemed to have four or five people, especially boys, waiting to see me. No matter how I tried to speed up my counseling sessions, I rarely was able to confer with all the students. When I opened my office door, and saw no one sitting on the bench, I rejoiced at my temporary reprieve.

Rather than trying to understand the concept of the bench and the teachers' attitude toward school discipline, I determined to solve the problem by essentially helping them to change. I set up "counseling sessions" for the teachers who seemed to be the worst offenders in terms of sending pupils to the bench. But in those sessions, what I failed to do was to elicit from the teachers their sense of what the "bench" meant to them in their work with pupils. Only some time later did I consciously realize how important order and quiet were in the values these teachers held for their classes. The system had taught them that any deviation from classroom regimen on the part of pupils led only to chaos. Some of them truly believed that if they risked trying to handle these problems in class, they would lose their authority over the other pupils. Powerful forces, thus, worked on these teachers and impelled them to send pupils to my "bench."

In the early weeks of my job, I simply failed to realize what I first became consciously aware of much later in the year, that one of the system's main disciplinary responses was to send trouble elsewhere. I had a memorable conversation one afternoon with one of my staff members who, in a rare moment of candor, criticized my disciplinary practices. This man was a member of the "old guard" in my school. He had served the district for many years in a number of roles and was a spokesman for those on my faculty who had transferred from other schools in the district. He told me that afternoon that what a principal should do was to suspend from school every one of the "troublemakers" who were causing disorder in our school. He said, "And you should keep on suspending them, until their parents or some community agency finds a more appropriate place for them to get their schooling." By that time, his attitude did not surprise me. Still, I was troubled with the realization that probably many people in the school and in the community felt just as he did. Order and quiet were the paramount responsibilities of the school. Those who could not comply should be put out on the street.

I Ignored the System's Norms for Tracking

The most important area in which I violated the school system and community norms, again without consciously understanding what those norms were or how egregious were my violations, was in organizing pupils into classes for instruction. From my background and experience, I believed that as much as possible, educators should group students of varying abilities into classes. My arguments for heterogeneous grouping were the usual ones: less able students would progress faster in a more challenging environment; they would feel greater self-esteem when grouped with more able students; more capable students, conversely, would deepen and enrich their own learning; teachers could organize activities that would allow bright students to help their less able peers; finally, participation in a democratic society means people of widely differing abilities and interests learn to work together.

My old school system espoused these principles, at least tacitly, in the grouping of youngsters in elementary and junior high schools. Parents seemed enlightened to the advantages of heterogeneous grouping, aware of the importance of not separating the best students into an elite which had the best teachers and the best learning situations.

I was shocked to discover in my summer of preparation for my new job that my new system routinely "tracked" students into ability groups from first grade. As I studied the schedule that counselors had developed that first year of my new school, I saw that not only did the top groups have reportedly the best teachers but also they had the smallest classes. I believed that these were very unfair advantages to give to an already advantaged group of students.

I did not, however, immediately move to change the schedule assignments or to reorganize the classes for that fall. I considered that possibility, but, fortunately, there simply was not time to reschedule. Instead, shortly after the school year began, I embarked on a campaign with the staff and the community to bring about educational enlightenment. I assumed that the tracking policy derived from ignorance and that if I could show people the educational and social assets of a heterogeneously grouped school, they would embrace the concept.

School Norms Reflect Community Norms

What I failed to realize was that the school system's norms for grouping students reflected deeply held assumptions about the nature of schooling and the nature of society.

People in my new community were not yet stable and secure with the rung they had achieved on the socioeconomic ladder. They were still climbing their way up. Predictably, the most active people in school affairs in my new community were the parents of those students who did relatively well. Those parents wanted every advantage they could get for their children— the best teachers, the lowest class sizes, the advantage of being in a stimulating class with other bright children, and they fought tenaciously for those advantages. Quite literally, my old community could afford to be egalitarian; my new community could not.

In these terms, my old community was homogeneous enough that the range of social and economic stratification was narrow. By contrast, my new community was much more heterogeneous and much more stratified. The economic and social life-styles of the working-class Irish and Italians were markedly different from those of the old Yankees, or of the new technocrats who inhabited the new homes on one-acre lots in town. Although I thought that the parents of the less able children, who not coincidentally tended to come from the lower classes in town, would knock down the doors in protest over the school system's homogeneous grouping policies and in support of new changes, they did not. They accepted and believed in the stratification of the community and in the tracking of the school system. They believed, if they had an opinion on heterogeneous versus homogeneous, that their children should be set off in separate groups where they could be more "comfortable" and get "special help."

As I naïvely moved forward during my first school year with the plan to change the grouping policy, I did not realize that I was in fact suggesting a change in the social structure of the town. Because of my own deeply held educational beliefs, I might have moved ahead with my heterogeneous grouping idea even if I had recognized these complexities earlier. But the point is that as I entered the job, I did not attempt to find out what community norms and expectations lay behind the system's tracking policy. And I, in no way, understood how powerful and deeply held the assumptions were that underlay those norms.

Throughout the rest of my first year, I continued to promote evangelically the benefits of heterogeneous grouping in every parent, teacher, and school committee forum I could. In the spring of the year, I announced my intention to group all students heterogeneously in classes for the following year, with the exception of one class in eighth-grade math and one in science. Teacher reaction ranged from ardent support among my young liberals to passive resistance from the old guard. They knew, by this time, that there was not much hope of changing my mind, so they did not actively protest. Community reaction, though, was somewhat different. Parents went to the School Board, which late in the spring scheduled a special meeting to discuss the merits of heterogeneous versus homogeneous grouping. After my presentation, the audience shared strong and conflicting responses. A minority of parents supported the plan, while School Board members wrangled among themselves. Finally, the School Board, by a split vote, voted to allow me to group the school heterogeneously for the next year *except in math and science*. I interpreted that vote to mean *except for the math and science* I had already exempted from heterogeneous grouping (*in the eighth grade*). So did my boss. During the next school year, the School Board, at least its majority members, began to make clear that their interpretation of their vote the previous spring was somewhat different. In October, when it was obviously too late to change the schedule, they informed the superintendent that they meant all math and science classes should be homogeneously grouped. In the spring of the year, this incident became the main reason they wanted to fire me. They believed I had deliberately disobeyed their policy.

To Discover Norms Requires More Than Usual Entry Activities

One response to this story may be, "Well, I certainly know that when you begin a job you need to meet with the various constituencies whom you will serve to discuss their expectations and yours. Too bad he did not know that."

As I entered the job, although I was naïve about the norms of my new school and community, I did undertake the usual meetings with teachers and community members. But the "usual" introductions to parents and staff tend to be little more than social ceremonies. New administrators have the chance to test and demonstrate the ability to remember names. School and community members have the chance to size up the new person and determine whether the new person jogs or plays tennis, goes fishing or tends a garden. In these informal, polite circumstances, nothing more than conversational attention can be paid to issues of substance. These usual introductory meetings, then, do not give either enough or the right kind of information to the new administrator.

In order to learn the norms of a new school and community, new administrators need to structure a formal set of meetings which focus their attention on the exploration of these norms. For example, in order to acquire the information I needed to avoid violating cafeteria norms, I should have interviewed—in some rigorous fashion with a carefully developed set of questions—other principals in the district. If I had asked the right questions, these interviews could have helped me immeasurably in coping with the problems I had to face.

I didn't, obviously, meet my colleagues with this formal agenda before I began my job. If I had, perhaps I could have avoided what ultimately happened. But few new administrators in my experience take the time to plan a set of meetings rigorously designed to ferret out information about the norms of their new school and new community. One of the reasons such a plan of formal meetings is so unusual is that it is so difficult to accomplish. In itself, a set of formal meetings designed to help the new administrator's entry violates norms. In most entry situations, both the new administrator and those who work in the new setting expect that the first task will be to move in and get work accomplished. So that is what we do. Making untested assumptions about how our past experience applies to our present circumstance, many of us have begun new jobs by quickly making changes and solving problems without enough knowledge of how our new environment works. And some of us have suffered with the consequences of such an unplanned entry.

Chapter 4:

A Good Beginning as Superintendent

by DANIEL S. CHEEVER, Jr.

Introduction

"Now that you've got the job, when are you going to plan how to begin work?"

Flushed with my success at having been picked for the job, I reacted angrily to the question. The previous evening I had been appointed superintendent of a suburban school district, after a grueling three-month selection process which culminated in a public interview with the School Board before 200 citizens. I hadn't even finished celebrating, and here my consultant was telling me to get back to work. More important, the question evoked the fears and self-doubt deep within me. "*Plan* how to begin work?" I had never thought of starting a new job in quite that way. How do you do it? Could I do it? If not, would I fail before I began? During the next two hours, we talked about different ways of starting my new job, and gradually I realized that neither of us had a clear idea of what it might mean to begin work in a different, planned way.

Some points did become clear, however. First, we recognized that I was afraid of starting work. The district, although a good one, had suffered serious problems recently and I was not confident I could succeed. There were several strikes against me: I was young, I had never been superintendent in a district which included a high school, I was appointed on a split School Board vote without full support from the faculty, and my appointment came after a year-long search in which the School Board had fired its original consultants and started the selection process over again.

Second, my view of how to begin work was to do just that, to begin working on the problems piled up on the desk. One of my written recommendations had described me as "a bear for work with a New England conscience," and the description fit. Later, the consultant and I labeled this tendency to jump in and be helpful as my "jump reflex." The school district had a lot of problems, some of them serious, and my tendency to want to be helpful—coupled with my insecurity about whether I could handle these problems and my desire to prove myself worthy—created a powerful drive to tackle every problem in sight. The idea of taking time to "plan how to begin work" seemed like a waste of time, or at least like an interesting but unnecessary diversion from the real task at hand.

Finally, that discussion with my consultant uncovered a hitherto unrecognized fear. The school district *expected* me to jump in and start solving the problems which had piled up during the lengthy selection process. The district expected me to solve these problems with magic; a few incantations, the wave of a wand, perhaps a little elbow grease, and "poof," everything would be fine again.

This last realization particularly troubled me. I did not mind setting high expectations for myself because I could endure in private the sense of failure if I did not succeed. But if the district, especially the School Board, had unrealistically high expectations for what I could accomplish, then I was risking public failure. This possibility frightened me. I labeled this fear my "White Horse" syndrome. That is, the district's image of its new superintendent was that of a "man on a white horse" who could charge into town and, through his skill and daring, drive out the hostile forces which had plagued local citizens. It was a compelling image.

After two hours of discussion with my consultant, we agreed these issues made a strong case for my stopping to plan my entry. At worst, I would not like the plan, decide not to use it, and lose only the time it took to develop it. Many meetings and many months later, we had designed and I had carried out an entry plan. My fears had not become reality, and the backlog of problems which had piled up on the desk were largely resolved. Looking back, my entry plan had proved to be my most important activity as superintendent of schools.

Definition of Entry

From my experience emerged a definition of entry as a planned set of interviews, feedback sessions, and school and community visits through which:

1.   The new boss and members of the organization get to know each other as fully as possible in a brief period of time outside the day-to-day context of crisis and problem solving.

2.   The organization and its new boss examine key issues in the organization's past, in order to "make sense" of how such issues are handled and to identify the norms which affect how the organization functions in the present or may function in the future.

3.   The new boss and members of the organization identify tasks to be done, and rank these in order of priority.

4.   The new boss establishes how these tasks shall be accomplished, after a process of consultation among individuals and, later, the organization as a whole.

The third of these four goals concerned the "whats" within the organization; that is, information about what tasks needed doing and the key individuals who would do the work. The first, second, and fourth goals concerned the organization's "hows." The "hows" had to do with the problem-solving and decision-making processes by which key issues would be addressed, as well as the norms which governed how people interacted in these processes, particularly as regards the sharing or withholding of information. Thus, I conceived of entry as a process in which I and members of the school system would examine the "whats" and "hows" within the system, arriving at an agenda of tasks which set our direction for the future.

Entry Design

Entry design[1] was the period of time when I developed a carefully orchestrated sequence of events in order to identify and interview key personnel, analyze the interview data, feed back this data to groups within the system, visit schools for several days at a time, and meet with key community groups and leaders. This plan was written in chart form, including time lines for conducting and completing these activities. In effect, it pictured how I would spend my time during the first few months on the job.[2]

My plan also identified those parts of my job for which I would be responsible during the entry program and those parts which I hoped to assign temporarily to others or defer until completion of the plan.

Upon seeing my entry plan committed to writing, I felt uneasy. When, I wondered, would I get around to doing the job for which I was hired? My

---

[1]   From Barry Jentz, Daniel S. Cheever, Jr., and Stephen B. Fisher, "Got a New Superintendency? Here's How to Make a Grand Entrance," *Executive Educator*, vol. 2, no. 5, May 1980.

[2]   See Appendix IV-1, pp. 243–254 for an entry plan used by another superintendent.

entry plan addressed this question through the development of a "work plan" approach to delegating the list of seventy-one tasks which awaited me when I began my new job.

Getting the Plan in Place

After designing my entry plan, I sought the Board's help in improving the plan and its approval of particular parts of it—such as extra compensation for an assistant carrying some of my duties temporarily. This official sanction gave me the security to turn aside subsequent demands on my time—some of them from the Board—which might have interfered with entry. Likewise, I consulted with others in the organization whom I intended to have participate in the plan, seeking their help in improving it and their support in making it work.

Informing Others

Having received approval for the entry program, I let others—teachers, administrators, other school employees, the community—know in writing how I would spend time during the entry phase. I did this by means of a brief memo to all staff with copies to the press.

Interviews and Feedback

After developing an entry design, getting the Board's sanction for these entry activities, and informing all staff, I began to gather information about the school system, analyze it, and feed it back to the organization in a systematic way.

I structured my interviews carefully and sent out in advance the questions to be addressed. After the interviews I analyzed the information and reported it back, along with conclusions I had developed from the data, and any implications for action which I saw. I was testing the validity of my information during this feedback process, altering my conclusions and developing implications for action as a result of the dialogue provoked by my feedback presentation.

School Visits and Feedback

Up to this point, entry activities had involved only me and those with whom I would work most frequently—the School Board, key staff, representatives of major union groups. School visits were a way to get to know all faculty, not only by name or in their instructional roles, but also to find out how they saw their work and felt about it. School visits also gave me an opportunity to present myself, test some of my impressions and assumptions, and acquaint the faculty with my ideas about leadership in a time of declining resources.

Community Visits and Feedback

Orientation to the community can take several forms. In my case, the two most important forms were individual interviews with key members of the community and neighborhood coffees sponsored by the PTO, in which I made a brief presentation based on my entry interviews and feedback meetings. Then I asked for comments and concerns from parents. Other components of this orientation included a similar presentation to the PTO Board, to leading community groups such as the churches, Rotary and Kiwanis Clubs, Town boards and officers, and private interviews with the press.

Handling the "Regular Job"

My commitment to using the entry plan outlined above was tested right from the outset. When I began work, I found a list of seventy-one unfinished tasks on my desk. The School Board chairman and acting superintendent had developed the list "to help you know what you should do in the first few weeks."

Their expectations for my start up played into my own weakness for singlehandedly solving problems as they came at me. With some trepidation, I questioned the chairman's assumption about how I should begin—by going to work on the seventy-one unfinished tasks—and she replied only partially in jest, "Of course, that's what we hired you do do!"

It was at considerable risk on both our parts that we talked further about how I could begin in this way while, at the same time, "getting to know the system" which was one of the board's seventy-one items and at the heart of my entry plan. Her willingness to consider and then support my different approach to getting started meant a great deal to me. The idea of an entry plan was new, and for all of its appeal I had no firsthand experience in making an entry plan work.

After my talk with the chairman, I was convinced that before I proceeded with my entry plan I had to address the seventy-one tasks somehow. I settled on an approach which I called "work plans." This approach consisted of asking all administrators to rank the seventy-one items according to two criteria. The first criterion asked for a ranking according to importance:

which item was the most important to resolve, which was next most important to resolve, and so on. The second criterion asked for a ranking according to due dates: that is, when did each item have to be completed. This approach would give me a clue as to which tasks could be postponed awhile.

From these two rankings I built a composite list of the seventy-one items in priority order. Working with administrators, I divided the list among all of us—including myself—assigning each item to the person whose position made him or her the most logical to assume lead responsibility for the issue. I then asked each administrator to develop a work plan for each item which:

1. Defined the task to be done

2. Indicated whether the task was a high, medium, or low priority to the superintendent, School Board, himself, and the school system

3. Identified key steps, dates, and people who would be involved in resolving the issue

4. Specified the expected outcome

Chart 4-1 is an example of a work plan for developing the negotiations strategy.

As each administrator developed drafts of their work plans, I reviewed them and modified them as necessary. When all were ready, the Administrative Council (composed of all administrators) reviewed the entire package and again suggested modifications. As a result, every administrator knew what was going to happen and how it would occur. Every administrator had participated in developing these plans and, in so doing, had also developed a commitment to them. Even though they did not like doing this catch-up work, the prospect of being caught up was appealing.

This work plan approach combined an emphasis on *what* needed to be done with *how* it should be done, which, of course, were objectives of my overall entry program. Through this approach we developed specific plans for completing old work; eventually, all this work was done. Equally important, the process of developing work plans—in other words, the process of how I accomplished a particular piece of work—established several important norms. Among these were:

1. That the new boss cared about getting caught up and would not let things continue unresolved.

2. That it was important to spend time carefully planning how to accomplish a task, rather than jumping in without forethought.

3. That those who were supposed to be responsible for a particular job would, in fact, be responsible for it.

Chart 4-1 Work Plan for Developing the Negotiations Strategy

NAME *Personnel Director*

DATE *March*

DEFINITION OF TASK	PRIORITY TO*				KEY STEPS, DATES, AND PEOPLE	OUTCOME AND DATES
	SUPT.	BOARD	MYSELF	SYSTEM		
1. To evaluate the present contract and determine provisions we want to change.	M	H	H	M	1. School Board completes hiring process for a new attorney (May 1).	The Board's attorney will obtain information about areas of concern in present contract, present administrators and the Board with proposed language changes and a strategy for negotiations, obtain reactions to the proposals, and develop a final negotiations plan well in advance of the first bargaining session.
2. To develop proposed language for each desired change.					2. Attorney, superintendant, Administrative Council discuss present contract and identify problem areas or language to change (May 30).	
3. To plan our bargaining strategy.					3. Attorney prepares a written analysis of present contract and suggested negotiations goals (June 30).	
4. To begin negotiations.					4. Attorney reviews analysis and goals with administrators (July 15) and School Board (Sept. 30).	
					5. Attorney prepares final draft of negotiations strategy and goals (Oct. 15), reviews with School Board (Oct. 30).	
					6. Formal negotiations begin (Nov. 15).	

*H = high, M = medium, L = low.

4. That information about these tasks and how they would be addressed should be shared with others, cross-checked for possible hidden side effects, and coordinated carefully.

5. That when decisions about how to handle each issue had been made, the information should be shared with the School Board.

This last norm was established through a final step taken before I firmed up a final schedule for my entry program and informed others about these activities. The School Board needed to be informed of the work plans and invited to help improve them. So doing would accomplish several purposes. First, it would explain how we were going to address the seventy-one tasks identified by the Board as important. Second, it would minimize "Monday morning quarterbacking" after we had finished a work plan because the time to question what we planned to do, or how we planned to do it, would be provided before we began work, not after. Finally, I hoped that sharing the work plans with the School Board would create a sense of confidence in my leadership, and thereby create a favorable attitude among the Board and the school district for my entry activities.

I decided to inform the Board by means of a written memorandum which explained the work plan approach, as well as by giving each Board member a set of the work plans for all seventy-one items. I listed these work plans and the memorandum as an agenda item for a School Board meeting in order to give us full opportunity to discuss the overall approach as well as any of the specific work plans.

This approach worked well. After discussing the memorandum and the accompanying work plans, the Board expressed admiration for how I had organized the school district to tackle these items. More important, the Board seemed to gain confidence in me and my ability. It also agreed to my request that the Board continue to pay a stipend to the assistant superintendent for business so that he could handle some of my regular duties in order to free me up for my entry program. With their agreement on the tasks to be done, I could now schedule my entry activities, inform others, and carry them out.

Interviews and Feedback

Interviewing key personnel, analyzing the interview data, and discussing the implications of this data with those people is the most important step in the entry process. During this part of my entry program, I found I had a rare opportunity to gather information in a systematic, unhurried fashion. I could concentrate on collecting information, searching for its meaning, testing my knowledge and having it confirmed or corrected, and, finally, reformulating my picture of people, programs, and issues within the school system.

Structuring a Set of Interviews

I found personal interviews with key members of the organization to be a crucial source of information about the school system. The structure and sequence of these interviews was important. Because school systems are hierarchical, it made sense to conduct the interviews according to rank. I assumed that people within the system were turf-conscious and concerned with protocol, as in most organizations, and that any other sequence of interviews would promote suspicious speculation. I began my interviews with the chairman of the School Board, followed by other Board members. I then interviewed central office administrators according to rank, officers of the Teachers' Association, building principals, other employee groups, community leaders, and finally the press. In retrospect, I think this order was correct, although I found it acceptable to vary it slightly to accommodate the calendars of individuals being interviewed.

I also assumed that the interviews would most likely succeed if they were highly structured and if each participant received in advance the questions to be covered, in part because people in an organization are predictably suspect, even mistrustful, of new and different behavior. These interviews, let alone my whole entry plan, was new and predictably different from what people expected of their incoming superintendent. I tried to speak to persons' natural and inevitable discomfort not only by announcing the structure and content of the interviews in advance but by taking a firm stand on the issue of confidentiality of information. I promised complete confidentiality for any information which I learned during interviews and explicitly acknowledged the discomfort created by my entry program. At the start of each interview with key people in the system or community, I briefly stated that I would keep confidential any information which the interviewee specifically identified as confidential. At the end of the interview, I reviewed aloud my notes with the interviewee to check those statements which had been identified as confidential.

Questions to Ask in the Interview

Before beginning to interview key personnel or collect other types of data, I determined the type of information to gather and how to use it.

There were four kinds of useful data, each of which was based on certain assumptions and which led to the specific interview questions presented later:

1. Information about *what* key people in the system wanted done. To tap this data, I developed a category of questions which asked them to describe problems which needed to be solved in the system as a whole and in their area, and to rank these issues in priority order.

2. Information about *how* people wanted things done within the school system. My questions in this area tried to elicit how decisions got made, the past precedents and group norms which led to those decisions, and any new ways of acting which people wished could be developed.

3. Information about the *people themselves.* I found that as a person talked in an interview, I obtained a great deal of spoken and unspoken information about that individual. In interviews with others, that person was also described by colleagues within the school system.

4. Information about the *climate for learning;* that is, how self-reflective people could be about their own behavior and its consequences. (The assumption here was that unless people in a system can examine their own practice, the system cannot self-correct, cannot renew itself. I needed to know who could, and could not, step back to examine both their strengths and weaknesses.)

My set of interview questions followed an order designed to progress from "safe, factual" questions to ones which encouraged a person to risk criticizing an aspect of the system or speculate about how things should be. The questions included the following:[3]

—   Please give me a brief autobiographical sketch of yourself, including information which you feel I should know about you.
—   When did you first come to this school system? What have been your responsibilities in it? What impressions have you formed about it?
—   What is the key issue for your own work in the school system? Is this an issue which we need to work on in the next few weeks, or can it wait until a future time?
—   What is the school system's key issue—it might be different from your own—in the next few months? What should I know about this issue? When should it be resolved?
—   Describe a moment when the school system was in great conflict. How did the conflict arise? What people played roles in it, and how did they react under pressure? How was the stress resolved? How should it have been handled and resolved?
—   Describe a very difficult decision you had to make. What was the issue?

---

[3]   See Appendix IV-2, pp. 254–255, for two sets of entry interview questions used by administrators entering other new administrative positions.

Why was it important? How did you reach a decision? What did others think? What would you do differently now.

Interviewing

LISTENING SKILLS

To help these interviews succeed, I found I had to overcome some bad habits and develop new talking and listening skills. For example, when I realized during an interview that I was starting to formulate a response while the other person still spoke, then I was aware of the jump reflex in myself. Often, I jumped in by offering help which was not asked for and which I later regretted having offered.

The following example illustrates a jump reflex action which I subsequently regretted. In my first meeting with a staff member, she complained about lacking adequate materials to individualize instruction. Acting from my jump reflex, I followed the complaint immediately with a commitment to get new materials and find out if other teachers had the same problem. My error was in not inquiring into what lay beneath her complaint, testing whether deeper concerns existed. In this case, for example, I later found that the teacher felt inadequate about her work with many of her students. She felt it was more legitimate to complain about a lack of materials than it was to talk—particularly with a new administrator—about her lack of professional adequacy.

During my interviews, I tried to avoid the jump-reflex trap by learning to restate what the other person seemed to be saying, as a way of testing my own understanding. Gradually, I learned to set aside the content or problem presented in an interview, content which in my past had been the spark that ignited my desire to help. Instead, I forced myself to ask, "What might be the meaning to this person of what has just been said?" By forcing myself to slow down enough to confirm or disconfirm my understanding of the other's true concern, I found I could eventually respond in ways that were more helpful to me and others.[4]

Another urge which I had to control was listening too carefully to the "should, ought, and must" voice within myself. This internal voice revealed my private picture of how I thought the world was supposed to behave: how a faculty should be involved in curriculum decisions; how a central office should support building principals, to cite only two examples. I tended to

---

[4] See Barry C. Jentz and Joan W. Wofford, *Leadership and Learning: Personal Change in a Professional Setting.* McGraw-Hill, 1979, for explanation of this skill of "imaging out loud" or testing assumptions, pp. 123–161.

shape the world of my new job to fit the "should" pictures I had in my mind. But this attempt to shape the world to fit my predetermined picture was bound to get me into trouble if I proceeded without understanding what my "should" pictures were and without testing their validity in the new setting.

I hoped I could avoid getting off to a bad start by learning to listen for these voices in myself—the voice which might scold me by saying, "This shouldn't be happening this way!" or "This shouldn't take so long," or "They should take more initiative." Secondly, I learned to use this voice to test my "should" pictures of the world, instead of simply expecting others to change. Finally, I tried to develop and use ways of listening for the "should" voice in others and then test whether that person was rigid or open to self-reflective questioning and change.

In my interviews as I struggled to listen for and test the "should voices" in myself and others, I also found it important to listen for feelings of confusion, puzzlement, or a sense of something being "off." If an interview or description of a problem didn't seem quite right, I tried to trust this instinct and force myself to wonder why. I found that such contradictions or discrepancies often held the key to important learning by revealing deeper problems which had impeded solution of surface issues. For example, after listening to the president of the Teachers' Association and the chairman of the School Board describe, in separate interviews, the importance of developing a new teacher-evaluation system, I was subsequently puzzled about why each had not talked as openly about this issue with the other. Both people claimed to have made such comments to each other and received little response.

This discrepancy, or sense of "something not quite right," led me to question whether there were underlying forces which had prevented communication about evaluation. I learned that, indeed, there were such issues. Despite a long history of mutual regard, neither side fully trusted the other's stated viewpoint about evaluation. The issue had become bogged down in collective bargaining the previous year as well; therefore, neither side had been able to work collaboratively, much less without adversarial overtones, to improve the evaluation process. The School Board had assumed the Association would press for an evaluation system which would make possible the reduction of tenured teachers by seniority only. The Teachers' Association assumed that the Board had little interest in evaluation as a process for professional growth and was concerned only with reduction-in-force. I was able to test these assumptions directly, and thereby help each side realize its inferences were incorrect. In actuality, the School Board was deeply concerned about an evaluation process which would promote professional growth in spite of declining enrollments and reduction in force, while the Teachers' Association had no interest in an evaluation process that would use seniority as the sole criterion for staffing decisions.

Listening to my own jump reflex, "should voices," and feelings of a "discrepancy" provided me with information in the interviews which I could use to promote inquiry, unravel misunderstanding, and eventually produce better data.

TALKING SKILLS

The more concrete the information exchanged during the interview, the more useful that data will be. Particularly in interview settings, people tend to state problems indirectly or express concerns abstractly. The more abstract the statements, the more likely they may be misunderstood or dismissed as insignificant. Thus I tried to conduct interviews which developed concrete, specific statements.

Eventually, I was able to develop some skill in eliciting concrete information. For example, when one administrator rushed through his description of how a key decision was made, I "played back" to him in chronological order the events he had described. By separating this blur into discrete events and asking how one led to another, I drew out a more detailed chronology. Gradually he began adding new scenes until what had been a series of isolated, disconnected still photographs became a motion picture composed of many frames. At this point he was able to identify which frame, or event in the sequence, was the central source of his concern about the decision. We then enlarged that frame by reconstructing in minute detail the external and internal forces which created his concern, leaving us both far more aware of what had happened than we had been after his initial, brief description.

Once I had a concrete picture of another person's view of how a key decision was made, I shifted my concern to exploring whether or not (and how) this person had shared these views with others. I wanted to find out if the people I interviewed were in the habit of withholding their views or presenting and validating their views with other key people. I find that if people make decisions on their private information and judgments without validating them with others, the quality of decision making suffers because any single person's access to information is limited.

When I could get concrete information from an interviewee which had been shared and corroborated, I could trust and use that information in constructing my own view of organizational reality. The upcoming feedback sessions would force me to share rather than withhold my view and find out if others, collectively, could confirm it or disagree.

Analysis and Feedback of Data

As I gathered data from interviews and written material, I was at first overwhelmed by its quantity and complexity. The use of several procedures to record and analyze the data kept me from inappropriately taking sole responsibility for resolving the complexities by myself. The idea behind feeding back the data was to engage others with me in searching for a collective understanding of the nature and needs of the system.

During each interview, I had scribbled handwritten notes. Following the interview, I transcribed them onto note cards, with a separate card for each major thought or topic. Each card had headings which identified the topic, noted the name of the interviewee, and the date of the interview. Tabulation of the data in this manner allowed me to shuffle and reshuffle cards in a variety of ways: for example, to group together all those cards which pertained to the same incident in the school system, or to group them according to perceptions held by the School Board or administrators, or vice versa.

I found I could analyze this data in a variety of ways. For example, I could briefly review each person's autobiographical sketch and then set it aside. I used other cards to develop an agenda for future work: for example, the statement of key issues facing the school system (as seen by School Board members, administrators, teachers, and the community leaders) helped determine the agenda for my work as the new superintendent.

When I finished my analysis of the data, I was left with two simple charts or grids which followed from my definition of entry as focusing on both the "whats" and "hows" of administrative action. The first of these grids, the "Whats: Key Priorities," is summarized in Chart 4-2: down the left-hand side of one grid were listed a number of issues which had been identified most frequently by different people during my interviews or which I suspected, after analyzing those interviews, were the most important issues for the school system. Across the top of the "what" grid were several columns, a separate column for each major group within the school system, such as School Board, central office administrators, principals, Teachers' Association officers, parents. The grid revealed at a glance the different points of view held by key groups within the school system. These differences subsequently proved important since I had to work with these differences in order to solve the school system's problems. Conversely, the similarities also proved important because, as the summary of my grid indicates (Chart 4-2), there was striking unanimity among almost all groups about the improvement of teacher evaluation as the top priority.

The second grid, the "Hows" grid summarized in Chart 4-3, presented the views of different groups within the system as seen by the School Board or administrators. I chose this way of organizing the second grid because the data revealed clear agreement and differences: agreement that each group felt the other was an obstacle to its doing its job well, and differences on how good the school system was (the "drinking glass" was seen by both groups as

Chart 4-2. The "Whats": Key Priorities

	SCHOOL BOARD	ADMINISTRATORS	TEACHERS	PARENTS
Key issues for your area	1. Rebuild our confidence and public's confidence.	1. Improve communication with School Board.	1. Improve the evaluation process.	N.A.
	2. Be less involved.	2. Improve teacher evaluation.	2. Boost teacher morale and trust.	N.A.
	3. Support our new superintendent.	3. Complete the junior high organization study.	3. Improve communication with administrators, Board.	N.A.
School system key issue	1. Improve teacher evaluation.	1. Improve teacher evaluation.	1. Improve teacher evaluation.	1. Reduce system's defensiveness with parents.
	2. Catch up on seventy-one tasks.	2. Finish next year's budget.	2. Cope with declining enrollment.	2. Improve teacher evaluation.
	3. Study a possible administrative reorganization.	3. Be more proactive instead of reacting to pressure.	3. Begin negotiations with Board.	3. Improve special education.
	4. Finish two program evaluations.	4. Improve confidence and morale.		

Chart 4-3 **The "Hows": View of Others**

	SCHOOL BOARD VIEW	ADMINISTRATORS' VIEW
of the School Board	1. Composed of good individuals; a few internal concerns	1. Good individuals
	2. A good working group which operates by consensus	2. Have faced tough problems successfully in the past; good schools because of the Board
	3. Meetings could be better if there was less talk, more self-discipline, and tighter time schedules	3. Could be much more effective as a group but too involved in administration; want to solve every problem, can't focus on a few; too responsible to a few people, generalize from a few complaints; sometimes not confident in administration; not sure what they want, individuals make requests rather than Board priorities.
		4. "If they'd do their job better, I could do mine."

of the administration	1. Good individuals	1. No consensus: strong individuals; a few internal concerns and factions
	2. Could be more effective as a group but unresponsive to some of Board's requests; unsure of what we want (though we are sure); not enough follow-through on issues	2. Meetings could be better: boring; too much time spent on noneducational issues; hidden agendas get in the way of solving problems
	3. Roles unclear, may complicate solving problems	3. Roles are unclear; may complicate solving problems
	4. "If they'd do their job better, we could do ours better."	4. Time is spent on tasks not in my job description (usually at School Board request)
of the superintendent	1. Two points of view: *he* should do it, he is responsible versus *we'll* do it, each of us has different and overlapping responsibilities	1. Two points of view: *he* should do it, he is responsible versus *we'll* do it, each of us has different and overlapping responsibilities, we want a closer administrative team
of the system	1. Very good, but "the glass is one-quarter empty"	1. Excellent, "the glass is three-quarters full"

filled to the same level, but one group focused on the small portion which was empty, while the other relished the large portion which was full).

My next problem was how to present this data to those whom I had interviewed. I decided to present my major findings in a ten- or fifteen-minute presentation to administrators, followed by discussion of the implications of the data. I scheduled a similar meeting with the School Board for the following week, and with officers of the Teacher's Association for the week after that.

Although I planned the first feedback session carefully, the presentation was difficult. I was nervous, not realizing that central office administrators and principals were nervous as well. I began by reviewing the purposes and schedule of my entry activities in order to establish a context for the interviews. I then explained that our meeting had two purposes: first, to share, as promised, the major information I had gained from them during the interviews, and, second, to test these impressions for accuracy. I made clear that I expected them to acknowledge and "own"—or to disavow or modify—each of the summary statements which I had drawn as representative of their group's position.

The meeting began well. They were quiet and attentive during my presentation, focused on the grids I was drawing on the chalkboard. There were occasional smiles as I wrote down viewpoints held by members of the Teachers' Association or School Board. By and large, they confirmed the accuracy of the data. The most difficult part of my presentation came toward the end, when the question of "what do we do next?" hung unanswered in the air. My grids had revealed one issue—the improvement of teacher evaluation procedures—to be the top priority of every group within the school system. However, at the same time the data made clear that each group expressed distrust of the others' interest in resolving this issue. Each group had formed negative impressions which it had withheld from the other groups.

I asked whether central office administrators and building principals would be willing to work on this issue with me. There was little response, and I sensed that people wanted more information about how I proposed to proceed before committing themselves to help. I asked if this assumption were true, and they confirmed it. I then asked what ground rules or criteria they would like to establish if we were to work collaboratively with the School Board on the one hand and the Teachers' Association on the other. At first they generated a lengthy list of guidelines for successful collaboration. One member then commented on the length of the list and pointed out that its length alone would convey an attitude of mistrust and negotiation, confirming the impression held by others that administrators were an obstacle to progress. These comments shifted the tenor of their discussion dramatically. The administrators decided on almost no preconditions and developed an unspoken determination to prove they were serious professionals committed to working on this task. I was elated.

My elation was short-lived. My second feedback session with members of the School Board was less successful. While the School Board reacted positively to the style and tone of my presentation, its members were less able to discuss the implications of my data without defensiveness. Whereas administrators had been able to examine the viewpoints of themselves, teachers, and School Board members on the grids in an inquiring manner, School Board members tended to point out why administrators or teachers should not hold to the position they did.

This reaction surprised and discouraged me. My initial hopes for a quick resolution of the teacher evaluation problem were fading. While administrators had stated firmly that they would be willing to talk directly with the School Board and Teachers' Association about teacher evaluation, the School Board was divided. Two members indicated interest, although not enthusiasm, one member was uncertain, and two were opposed.

We discussed briefly what to do about this divided opinion. One member suggested that I should address the issue of teacher evaluation by meeting separately with each group: School Board, Teachers' Association, and administrators. When each group had discussed evaluation and developed a position to which it was committed, then perhaps the three groups could come together. Other Board members quickly supported his suggestion and I, unsure of how to proceed and feeling that half a step forward was better than no step at all, agreed as well.

My third feedback session, this time with officers of the Teachers' Association, was similar to that held with administrators. Teachers looked at the data with interest and occasional surprise, and demonstrated an ability to step back from their own position to discuss implications of the data from the perspective of the school system as a whole. Since the choice of coming together to discuss teacher evaluation was now ruled out, due to the School Board's reluctance, I proposed instead that I meet separately with the Teachers' Association to further understand their viewpoint on evaluation and their proposals for improvement. They concurred, and promised to send me several proposals which they had developed in recent years with the previous superintendent and discussed during the previous year' collective bargaining with the School Board.

At the time, I viewed these feeback sessions as only partially successful because I had failed to arrange a joint workshop on teacher evaluation. But the feedback sessions allowed each group to take responsibility for identifying teacher evaluation as the priority—the "what"—for future action. Rather than acting from the assumption that everyone knew this concern was shared, I could trust that the interview data and feedback sessions had produced new evidence of this shared concern. As well, the feedback sessions had saved me from a potentially disastrous step. Because they revealed a lack of readiness among key groups, the feedback sessions had disconfirmed my assumption that a joint workshop would succeed. Had I plunged ahead and failed, I would have had to recover from a significant setback.

School Visits and Community Visits

The school and community visits phase of my entry plan were designed to challenge me to get out of the office and into contact with the new setting. Without frequent contact and firsthand knowledge, I knew I would fall into the trap of developing policies and programs unrelated to the real needs of the district.

School Visits

While school visits did not yield as much detailed data as the earlier interview and feedback stage, nonetheless they provided the basis of my subsequent support among faculty, as well as among parents pleased that the new superintendent was visible to students. My school visits were also fun. More than simply a chance to get out of the office, school visits gave me the satisfaction of getting to know the professional faculty with whom I would be working.

In preparing for my visits, I had asked each principal to plan my three-day visit to the school as he or she wished. Aside from making clear that I wanted to spend some time in classes and some time meeting with and listening to the faculty, I left to each principal the choice of how my time should be organized. I asked each to plan my visit in whatever way (s)he would normally plan a similar activity. Not surprisingly, I found great variety in how the principals carried out these instructions, variety which taught me about each principal's decision-making methods. One, for example, planned my visit entirely himself and announced it to his faculty. In his view, he was protecting his teachers from the time-consuming chore of deciding as a group what to do with the new boss for three days. I suspected he was also maintaining control over what I would, and would not, see. Another planned my visit with his entire staff at a faculty meeting. What he lost in efficiency, he gained in the involvement and commitment of his entire faculty. Most principals were quite businesslike and ended up with a plan that combined observation of classes, formal meetings with each department or team, and attendance at a full faculty meeting. Two planned faculty parties in private homes where we could unwind and relax together. One also had me supervise the lunchroom and take my turn at recess duty "so you really get to know us." He earned high marks in my eyes, as well as in the eyes of his faculty, who seemed to relish the idea of the new boss coping with lunch lines.

Each principal sent me in advance a schedule for my three-day visit. The night before the visit began, I tried to memorize the staff roster, going over every person's name and assignment. I found that by the end of the third day, I could identify almost every staff member. The major part of my time during these visits was spent observing classes. This posed several dilemmas for me. For example, was I expected to sit in the back and merely observe or to participate? How should I respond when, at the end of the class, the teacher clearly wanted some judgment about how well (s)he had done?

I found that I could combine observing and participating in a manner that accommodated each teacher's needs. Some had planned class activities in which I clearly played a role, while others seemed more comfortable with me sitting in the back of the room watching. Particularly difficult was the question of how to respond at the end of the class. I thanked the teacher for giving me the chance to sit in, and complimented what I had seen. Most classes were good. In a few cases, however, I saw problems. Although my bias is to be frank and not withhold information, I decided not to raise my concerns at that time. Given the informality of the context for our discussion and the teachers' unfamiliarity with me, and possible mistrust of my motives, I doubted our abilities to exchange negative information to produce learning. I was able to develop dialogue with some faculty members by turning their question, "What did you think?" back to them. When teachers acknowledged some aspect of the class which they had not felt was successful, I was then able to confirm or disconfirm without being too judgmental.

I faced a similar dilemma in the formal briefings given by departments or teams in each school. Most of these briefings turned out to have been carefully planned. There was some lobbying, most of it good-natured, for pet projects they wanted to develop. In addition to holding my jump reflex in check and not promising to obtain support for a particular program by tomorrow, I also had to resolve the dilemma of how fully I could express my opinions concerning their program. In most cases, I was extremely impressed with what I heard. In a few cases, I had questions. For example, in a school system with a minority enrollment of almost 10 percent, composed largely of students voluntarily bussed from a nearby city, I heard little mention of multicultural education during my briefings in the elementary or secondary schools.

I decided to handle these dilemmas by asking each department what it felt was missing from its programs. I found that the department would raise many of my concerns themselves. In cases where this did not happen, I would summarize briefly what seemed at first glance to be the strengths of the program as well as my concerns, which we might discuss later.

During my school visits, I was particularly conscious of being inspected. The school district was undergoing a period of steeply declining enrollment with heightened anxiety about job security and reductions in force. There was great interest in looking the boss over. Thus, in each school visit I used a meeting with the full faculty as a chance to set forth some of my own views about the superintendent's role in times of decline. Looking back, this was a particularly important aspect of each school visit, one which deserved more attention than I gave it.

I began these meetings by emphasizing some of the difficult issues facing the district in these times of decline: falling enrollments, inflationary pressures, the energy crisis, and growing public criticism of public education. I then made clear that I could not change most of these external factors, and thus I did not see my job as having the power to reverse the decline in enrollments, eliminate budgetary pressures, hold onto jobs in the face of fewer students and fiscal restraint, or persuade a skeptical public that we were better than they thought.

I then went on to describe what I could do, stressing my role in creating confidence about how difficult decisions would be handled during this time of decline. How the district responded to these pressures was something I could control, in part, by developing open communication, by resolving problems fairly, and by making clear in advance the criteria and process by which key decisions would be made. Thus while the faculty might not be pleased with the tough decisions to be made—for example, decisions to reduce the number of jobs or close a school as enrollment declined—I hoped they could have confidence in how these decisions were made.

These comments tended to draw exclamations of surprise. But the distinction between factors I could, and could not, control seemed to make sense to most faculty members. I found it was the theme to which I returned many times during subsequent years.

The school visits seemed to be appreciated very much. Many staff members would stop me in the hall to express their feelings directly; others wrote brief notes or had conversations with their principal which were subsequently reported to me. Running through these comments was a sense of gratitude for a personal approach to leadership, one which took the time to get out of the office and into their schools, to get to know them on a first-name basis, and to risk exposing myself to their scrutiny and skepticism.

Community Visits

The last phase of my formal entry program involved community visits. I had deliberately chosen to become familiar with the community at the end of my entry program for two reasons. First, it seemed important to make a personal statement about the importance of the schools and the professional staff and of my commitment to them by making school visits the first phase of my entry program. My second reason for delaying the community visits was less idealistic and more practical. The community was an affluent residential suburb, a town whose residents were deeply committed to the public schools and involved in them. By putting my community orientation last, I would give myself time to learn about the schools. Thus I would be able to respond to parental concerns on the basis of firsthand observation.

In planning my orientation to the community, I relied heavily on the knowledge and advice of the School Board chairman. She had been involved in town activities for many years and was held in high regard by her fellow citizens. In discussing with her my overall entry design, she had agreed that I could afford to place my community visits last in the sequence of entry activities. At the same time she also had offered to host a cocktail party for my wife and me just before I was due to begin work, thereby giving me the opportunity to have brief initial contact with important community leaders. In hindsight, this offer was important. While every new administrator may not have such a hospitable School Board chairman, some initial contact with key community leaders seems important if the formal orientation to the community may not occur until three or four months later.

I planned my community orientation much as I had planned earlier steps in the entry program. Through interviews with a few key community leaders—the presidents of the PTO and the League of Women Voters, the Town's executive secretary, and the police chief, to give a few examples, as well as the press—I gained a good deal of information about their view of the schools. These interviews also gave me the opportunity to give information about the schools from my own perspective; having spent several days in each building receiving formal briefings from each team or department, I was now more knowledgeable and confident of my conclusions. I was able to challenge any of the community leaders' statements which I felt to be unsupported by evidence and also able to ask their advice about issues which had puzzled me.

Another element of my orientation to the community was a series of "neighborhood coffees" sponsored by the PTO. These coffees occurred in the evening at private homes, and were publicized in advance. Most were well attended; perhaps thirty or forty parents would come to hear a brief summary of my findings about the schools based on the earlier activities in my entry program. This informal talk was followed by questions and answers from residents. While discussion was sharp at some of these coffees, often disagreement emerged between the participants themselves. This allowed me to point out that my job required resolving widely different points of view and establishing a workable consensus acceptable to all.

Finally, apart from attending community events and meetings of community service groups, I ended my orientation to the community by preparing a newsletter which reported my first impressions of the schools.

Conclusion to the Case

As I look back at my entry as superintendent of schools, I must acknowledge that this case describes only that part of my entry which was highly organized and "public," involving me in interaction with others in the system. It omits the private planning steps which preceded events described here,[5] as well as problems I encountered and mistakes I made during those first few months on the job. Entry was not all that occupied me during that busy time, although it was my greatest single task.

The structure and procedures of my entry plan created the conditions which were necessary for me to break my old habit of single-handedly solving problems as they came at me. The plan forced me to slow down when my reflexes said speed up. It enabled me to interact with other people in a reflective, collaborative fashion on the nature and needs of the system. The relationships I began to build then and the good information and trust which followed have enabled me to be effective in my job.

I was pleased to have the School Board, which had initially reacted with skepticism to my entry plan, confirm my positive view of entry by writing in my first-year evaluation:

> Your method of accomplishing your first goal—to get to know the system and the staff thoroughly—was an early indication of your ability to plan, organize, and follow through. Those of us who were concerned that you might be leaving the administration building without a captain became convinced that you know the basics of leadership: get to know your crew before you begin to give orders.

[5] These private planning steps were crucial to the success of my entry plan and omitted here because they are outlined in Selp-Help Exercise: Entering, Number 3, "Designing an Entry Plan and Implementing the Plan," pp. 118–131.

Conclusion to Section Two: Entering

The two entry cases in this section are built on the importance of collecting and testing information about self and setting. "A Bad Beginning as Principal" illustrates what can happen when an administrator thinks he knows what a system wants and needs, and is terribly wrong. In contrast, "A Good Beginning as Superintendent" shows what can happen if an administrator assumes he does *not* know what a system wants or needs, does *not* know how others in the system perceive it or each other, and systematically sets out to collect and validate the information. The purpose of the following exercise materials is to force entering administrators to get clear from the start about their own assumptions, to use the products of this private preparation for public presentations, and to collect and validate information before acting in its absence.

EXERCISES ON ENTERING

Introduction

The exercises on entering will be divided into two categories: self-help exercises for practitioners and exercises for use by instructors in classroom, workshop, or seminar settings. The self-help exercises will be divided into the following categories: Inquiry into How the System Works (done prior to interviewing for the job), Interviewing for the Job, and Designing an Entry Plan and Implementing the Plan.

The instructors' exercises will be a set of simulation or role-play sessions designed to have new administrators present and receive feedback on key parts of their entry activities: Inquiry into How the Community Works, and Testing an Entry Design and Implementation Plan.

Self-Help Exercise: Entering, Number 1

Inquiry into How the System Works

Purpose

To provide a set of questions which will guide initial inquiry into the nature of the community, system, position, and search process as well as the relationships between the four.

Directions

Listed below (see number 3) are questions which you need to answer in order to effectively inquire into the system.

1. *Cautions*

    (a) Do not expect to get answers to all these questions before an interview.

    (b) The worst way to inquire into a system would be to wander around indiscretely asking hard questions about the nature of the community; great discretion is necessary in seeking answers to the questions listed below.

    (c) When you get answers, do not be quick to generalize, judge, and tell people what their problems are.

2. *How to Proceed*

    (a) Get printed matter on the community, system, and position including newspapers and publications by the system.

    (b) Consult with people you know about contacts they have in the community who could discretely, confidentially, help you get to know the place.

    (c) Plan a visit to the community by listing the places and people you might visit.

3. *Questions*

    (a) *About the community, find out:*
    • Who runs it and how, now and before
    • What the ethnic, religious, and economic mix is
    • Who the haves and have-nots are
    • What the community's image of itself is
    • Who owns the news sources and covers the workings of the city government

- What the demographic figures and shifts are
- How the powers-that-be in the community are tied into control of the school system
- How the powers-that-be see the operation of the system
- How the haves and have-nots view the system

(b) *About the system, find out:*
- Who runs it and how, now and before
- How its norms and structures reflect the socioeconomic structures within the town
- Where the staff comes from, the local area or other parts
- How the staff were hired and by whom
- How people in the system are related by blood to families in the community
- What the social-economic-religious background is of the staff
- Who hired the teaching and administrative staff
- If there are any women or minorities in power positions, how they got there
- What immediate, major issues the school system faces
- What major controversies the system has faced over the past five years

(c) *About the job, find out:*
- Why it is open
- What happened to the previous person in the job
- If it is a new position, who created it and why, how
- Who gets directly affected by this new position or by bringing in an outsider
- What constituencies directly relate to the position, how are they organized and led, and what is the history of their use of pressure and power

(d) *About the search process for this job, find out:*
- Who set it up, under what conditions
- Who will be on the interviewing team, representing which role groups
- How the members of the interviewing team were selected
- Who will chair the interviewing committee
- What the function of the interviewing committee is
- How the interviewing committee fits into the larger scheme of the search process

A general thrust of these questions is to emphasize the importance of finding out about the power relations which exist in and between the community, system, and position not only because understanding them is necessary to a successful effort to *manage* but also because understanding them is crucial to any effort at *changing* the status quo.

A second theme underlying these questions is historical inquiry. Successful efforts to manage and change a system follow from understanding the historical context in which the current workings of the system are embedded.

A third theme is purely practical; job applicants should present themselves in an interview as knowledgeable, as "having done their homework" about this community, system, position, and search process. The pursuit of answers to these questions yields information which will help job applicants take the setting into account in forming their responses to questions.

Self-Help Exercise: Entering, Number 2

Interviewing for the Job

Purpose

To guide an applicant in preparing for a successful interview.

Directions

1. Compile lists of questions you might be asked in interviews by:

    (*a*) Listing the questions you most fear being asked.

    (*b*) Listing the constituencies represented on the interviewing committee (e.g., administrators, teachers, citizens, parents, . . .) and contacting friends who are members of these constituencies in other systems; ask these friends what kinds of questions and concerns their constituencies would have of a person in the position you are applying for and list these questions by constituent group.

    (*c*) If you know anyone who recently went before an interviewing committee, ask them what questions were asked and list these questions.

    (*d*) Scanning the table of contents of any educational journal for the past year to help develop categories of questions.

2. Give these lists of questions to a friend or friends and have the friend ask the questions as if the friend were a member of an interviewing committee; audiotape the role playing and listen and discuss your response to each question, giving attention to discrepancies between what you intended to communicate and how you actually came off, as judged by your friend(s) and as judged by you listening to yourself on tape.

3. Use the role play setting you set up in direction number 2 immediately above to test yourself in answering some predictable questions:

    (a) What is your philosophy of education?

    (b) You've never done this job before, what makes you think you are qualified and will be successful?

    (c) What are your strengths and weaknesses as an administrator?

    (d) What was your greatest success, your greatest failure, and what did you learn from each?

    (e) Given (such and such a hypothetical situation), how would you solve the problem? (Practice thinking about "approaches" to getting answers which take the form of a set of sequential steps that engage individuals directly involved in the problem; on the whole, do not try to supply ready-made solutions.)

    (f) What are your special qualifications for this job?

    (g) Take five minutes and tell us about yourself . . .

4. Write out a beginning statement and an ending statement which you will use if the interview committee gives you the opportunity; role-play these, revise them, and then memorize them.

5. Imagine how you feel entering a room full of strangers, all of whom will focus their attention on you, particularly at the beginning of the interview:

    (a) How will you enter the room? Will you shake hands with everyone or just say "hello"?

    (b) What will you do if people on the committee are not introduced, or if they do not identify their roles?

6. In the interview, use the following guidelines in giving answers to questions:

    (a) Make yourself ask questions at the outset which clarify for you the nature of the setting, if you are unclear:
    - Who is the chairman?
    - Who belongs to what constituent group?
    - What will be the format or agenda?
    - How much time will you have?
    - Will there be time built in for you to ask questions and invite dialogue?
    - When and how will you know if you are "out" or "in"?

    (b) Before your interview, design an agenda or format for the interview which you can initiate if you find you are dealing with a disorganized committee.

    (c) Generally, keep your answers concrete rather than abstract and short rather than long.

(d)   After giving a brief answer (no more than a minute in length), stop and check with the question asker to see if you are responding to the question; if so, ask if the person would like you to elaborate. If the question asker indicates that you are not responding to the questions, try to restate what you thought the question was, wait, and allow the person to reframe the question. Do not assume you understand this reframed question; test your understanding. If you're wrong, then ask for help from others.

(e)   Watch out in particular for the broad, abstract, open-ended questions, such as—"What's your philosophy of education?"—do not get suckered into a long-winded, abstract response. Keep your response short, punchy. Stop and give the question asker a moment to consider the answer and reframe the question.

(f)   Do not take questions literally! Make sure you know who on the screening committee is a member of what constituent group, and try to imagine the frame of reference from which the question is coming. If you can imagine the more specific, concrete question behind the general, abstract question, give a short abstract answer, and *then test* your imagining of what the person's concern *might* be. If the person discomfirms, drop it; if the person confirms, address the more specific concern.

(g)   Formulate questions you wish to ask of the committee:
      • How have previous occupants of this job entered it and what would members of this committee expect of a new person during the first months on the job? (Present your approach to entry).
      • Judging from past practice, what is the one thing which the occupant of this job could do to fail with each of the role groups represented on the committee? To succeed?
      • If the new occupant of this job were to accomplish only one thing during the first year, what should it be?

Self-Help Exercise: Entering, Number 3

Designing an Entry Plan and Implementing the Plan

Purpose

To provide a set of charts and materials to guide you in writing a plan, getting it "in place," collecting, organizing, and feeding back information, and building an agenda for future work.

Overview

This exercise is divided into four parts:

1. Designing the Entry Plan
2. Presenting the Entry Plan
3. Scheduling the Entry Activities in Your Calendar
4. Conducting Interviews, Recording, Organizing, and Feeding Back Data

Directions

Designing the Entry Plan

1. To prepare for designing your own entry plan, read the sample entry plan found in Appendix IV-1, pp. 243–254, and read Dan Cheever's outline of his plan on pp. 88–91; your plan should include:
   - A definition of entry
   - A statement of why entry is important
   - A statement of the goals you have for your plan
   - A statement of the activities, involving which people, in a sequence
   - A statement of confidentiality

2. Get a list of all administrators, heads of union groups, and people in the community who impact directly on your position for use in designing the "activities in a sequence" part of your plan.

3. Because structured interviews are an integral part of your entry activities and because you will be asked what questions you want to ask people in these interviews, construct a set of questions now, before presenting your plan. Use as guidelines the sample lists of questions found in Appendix IV-2, pp. 254–255.

Presenting the Entry Plan

4. Practice your verbal presentation of the written plan; force yourself to think through your presentations to your boss and subordinates; practice your presentation out loud, preferably with a friend, before doing it for real.

5. Use Exercise Chart 1 (immediately following these directions) to set up the initial presentation and testing of your entry Plan prior to implementing it; plan to meet with all groups who will be directly involved in your entry activities.

6. Before presenting and testing your plan, do an analysis of your "regular job" responsibilities and tasks. Prepare for this task by reading "Handling the Regular Job," from "A Good Beginning as Superintendent," Chapter 4, pp. 91–94, also read "Mapping and Charting" from Chapter 7, "Supervising a New Assistant Principal," pp. 176–181. Block out particular times during the days, weeks, and early months on the job when you will do your "regular job," keeping in mind the need to keep time available for scheduling entry activities into your calendar.

7. Present and test your entry plan with your boss and other groups directly involved in the plan. Be sure to include in your presentation a way to get responses to your plan and modify the plan to take into account that new information.

Scheduling the Entry Activities

8. To prepare for scheduling the entry activities in your calendar, get a large wall calendar which shows at least a month at a glance. Get all dates of previously scheduled meetings, including school vacations, holidays, meetings—board, PTA, community, central office, etc.— and put them on your wall calendar, showing *ending* as well as beginning times. Plan to schedule your entry activities over a two- to three-month period.

9. Use Exercise Chart 2 to set up your interview and feedback sessions. (This chart is designed for someone who wants to feed back to individuals, not groups; if, like Dan Cheever, you want to do your feedback to groups, then use Exercise Chart 10 to schedule your feedback sessions.)

10. Use Exercise Chart 3 to schedule your department or school visits.

11. Put the dates and times from these planning charts on your calendar.

Informing Others: Interviewees and General Staff

12. Use Exercise Chart 4 as catalyst for constructing your own letter to inform interviewees of interview dates and times; mail these letters *after* presenting the entry Plan to all individuals and groups who will be directly involved in the plan.

13. Use Exercise Chart 5 as a catalyst for constructing your own letter to inform the general staff about your entry Plan.

14. Send Exercise Chart 3, School Visit Schedule, to each school building or department.

Conducting Interviews, Recording, Organizing and Feeding Back Data

15. Record data from interviews on Exercise Chart 6 (for an alternative methodology for recording data from individual interviewees, see p. 100).

16. Record data from school or department visits on Exercise Chart 7.

17. After interviews with a given role group have been completed, collate the information from Exercise Chart 6 on Exercise Chart 8 (for an alternative methodology for organizing this information, see pp. 100–103).

18. Use the information on Exercise Charts 6, 7, and 8 to make a first cut on your priorities for your first year's work; record your work on Exercise Chart 9.

19. Use Exercise Chart 10 to schedule feedback presentations of your priorities *before* beginning to act on them.

Exercise Chart 1   **Key Groups to Present Overview of Entry Plan**

GROUP	DATE FOR TESTING THE ENTRY PLAN
1.	
2.	
3.	
4.	
5.	
6.	

Exercise Chart 2   **Interview Schedule**

PERSONS	DATE	TIME
1.	Initial Interview Feedback Interview	
2.	Initial Interview Feedback Interview	
3.	Initial Interview Feedback Interview	
4.	Initial Interview Feedback Interview	
5.	Initial Interview Feedback Interview	
6.		
7.		
8.		
9.		
10.		
11.		
12.		
13.		

Exercise Chart 2 (Continued)

PERSONS	DATE	TIME
14.		
15.		
16.		
17.		
18.		
19.		
20.		

Exercise Chart 3 **School Visit Schedule**

TO: (Department Head or School Principal, for example)
FROM:
DATE:
Re: Department or School Visits

Sample Content:

> As we discussed when I presented my entry plan to administrators on (date), I plan to visit each (school or department) for (number of days) during the first (number of months) of the school year. Through these visits I hope to learn about the school system as viewed through the eyes of all of you who, indeed, are the system. As well, I want to introduce myself.
>
> As (principal or department head), please work with your staff to schedule my visits on the following dates. If there is a special difficulty scheduling me on these dates, please call right away. Thank you.

Department or School (for example)	*Dates*
Elementary School #1	
Elementary School #2	
Elementary School #3	
Elementary School #4	
Junior High School #1	
Junior High School #2	
Senior High School	

Exercise Chart 4   Sample Letter for Scheduling an Individual Interview

Sample Content for an Assistant Superintendent's Entry

Dear _____.

I would like to schedule an interview with you on _____ from _____ to _____. The purpose of this meeting is to assist me to become better acquainted with you and the school district. As an experienced administrator in the district, there are many areas where you can assist me as a newcomer.

The questions which we will discuss are enclosed. The following ground rules will be observed: Any items discussed which you feel are confidential will be treated in the same manner. I will take notes during the meeting. These notes will be typed and returned to you for your validation and editing as soon as possible. A follow-up conference to discuss these notes will be scheduled for _____.

This letter is the follow-up of my entry-plan presentation at the Administrative Council meeting on _____. If there is any problem with these dates, please call me.

Kindest personal regards.

Exercise Chart 5   **Sample Letter to General Staff Informing Them of Entry Plan**

Sample Content from a Superintendent's Entry

When I was being interviewed by you for the superintendency, you stressed the importance of careful communication at all levels in the school system. In that spirit, I'd like to describe how I am preparing for the job and what I plan to do in the first few months after I arrive.

My first priority is to better understand the school system and those who work in it. To reach this priority, I have begun a series of individual interviews with members of the School Board, the Administrative Council, and the president and past president of the Education Association. These interviews are focusing on such topics as each person's association with the schools, priorities for the future, areas of concern, and examples of how the system makes important decisions. These interviews will be completed in early (month).

When I begin full-time work in the district on (date), I want to learn about the schools and the instructional program by spending time with faculty, students, and support staff in each building. During the first day or two in (month), I will stop by each school simply to meet staff. Following that first visit, I'll return to spend several days in each of the schools. Rather than wander around, I have asked each administrator to plan an orientation to your school or program (elementary, secondary, pupil services, support services, central office). These orientation visits, of a few days' duration, will be designed so we can meet and talk about substantive issues. Especially important, I'd like to see students and visit classes. Administrators have prepared tentative plans, and I have attached a calendar of key activities and dates.

These orientation visits to each school and program area will probably last until sometime in (month). During that time, I will also be administering the school district. The assistant superintendent, principals, and program directors will continue to handle some of the daily operational chores they have picked up during the last year so I can be free to spend time in the schools. I appreciate their willingness to continue helping a little longer.

Transitions are difficult. There is too much work and too little time to meet new colleagues. I'm determined to spend my first few months meeting you and learning about the instructional and other programs. With everyone's help, I think I can do it.

Exercise Chart 6 Data Collection for Individual Responses to Interview Questions:

QUESTIONS	PERSON 1	PERSON 2	PERSON 3	PERSON 4	PERSON 5	PERSON 6
#1						
#2						
#3						
#4						
#5						
#6						

Exercise *Chart 7* Data Collection Chart for Department or School Visits

WHAT'S GOOD AND NEEDS TO REMAIN THE SAME?	WHAT'S ALL RIGHT BUT NEEDS REINFORCING OR SOME IMPROVEMENT?	WHAT NEEDS TO BE IMPROVED?

Exercise Chart 8   Data Collation Chart for Interviews

Questions	AREAS OF CONSENSUS Mentioned by at least ten or more individuals interviewed	AREAS OF DISAGREEMENT Split views of those interviewed	AREAS OF NO AGREEMENT Isolated or infrequently mentioned items
#1			
#2			
#3			
#4			
#5			

Exercise Chart 9 Priorities Chart

PRIORITY	DATA TO SUPPORT SELECTION	TASKS TO BE UNDERTAKEN IN THIS PRIORITY AREA	INDIVIDUALS INVOLVED	TIME LINE AND SEQUENCE OF ACTIVITIES FOR WORK (Who does what with whom, when, where?)
#1				*Time* 1. _____ 2. _____ 3. _____ 4. _____
#2				*Time* 1. _____ 2. _____ 3. _____ 4. _____
#3				*Time* 1. _____ 2. _____ 3. _____ 4. _____
#4				*Time* 1. _____ 2. _____ 3. _____ 4. _____

Exercise Chart 10   **Public Presentation and Testing of Priorities**

FORUM (examples below)	DATE SCHEDULED
1. Board of Education meeting	
2. Administrative Council	
3. Staff meeting in each building	
4. Staff newsletter	
5. Public newspaper	
6. Parent-teacher district association meeting	
7. Teacher Union officials	
8. Supervisory association meeting	

Instructor's Exercise: Entering, Number 1

Inquiry into How the Community Works

Purpose

To introduce applicants for administrative positions to the "ins and outs" of how a community works, forcing them to challenge their own view about the malleability of systems.

Directions

1. Break the class into teams of two or three people.
2. Assign each group a joint task of mapping and charting a set of interrelated search activities which they will conduct in an effort to get answers to the questions listed in Self-Help Exercise Number 1, "Inquiry into How the System Works"; include as a part of the task a requirement that they invent other questions which a job applicant would want to get

answers to and explain why knowing such information would be important to them.

3. Evaluate each group's search design, paying particular attention to the question of whether or not the methods of inquiry will yield the information sought *without* raising people's suspicions, mistrust, even animosity toward strangers prying.

4. When groups report back, evaluate their search designs again and try to generalize on *how* to go about inquiring into the nature of a community effectively; use the results of the groups' searches to develop a better set of questions, to force analysis of what sense they make of the data, and to draw action implications for their entry into new administrative positions.

Instructor's Exercise: Entering, Number 2

Testing an Entry Design and Implementation Plan

Purpose

To give applicants practice in presenting their entry designs and implementation plans.

Directions

1. Assign each member of the class to do the Self-Help Exercise Number 3 on designing an entry plan, p. 119, directions 1 to 5.

2. Ask for volunteers to present their plans to a supervisor (whether a single individual or a group) and to a group of subordinates who will be directly involved in the plan.

3. Have a volunteer take the lead in setting the broad parameters of the community, system, and position.

4. Form two subgroups within the class, made up of persons who will role-play a supervisor and persons who will role-play a group of subordinates. Give each group a task of developing the kinds of questions which each group would predictably have about an entry plan.

5. Run a set of role-play meetings followed by discussion, the first of which has the new administrator present the plan to a boss—an individual or group—the second which has the administrator present the plan to subordinates. The discussions should focus on the following questions:

   (*a*) Was the purpose and definition of entry clear?
   (*b*) Were the steps in a sequence with rationales clear?

(c)   Did the administrator avoid the trap of presenting the plan as a fait accompli, on one hand, or, on the other, as entirely open to question and change?

(d)   Did the administrator make a statement of confidentiality? Did the statement answer questions about "to whom and where" the information goes?

(e)   Did the superior or subordinates come away with a clear picture of the design and intent; did they contribute to improving the design and *feel* as if they had? How would the administrator know if this were true?

(f)   Did the administrator leave the meeting feeling successful? Why? Why not?

6.   Use the data about the system in Chapter 4: "A Good Beginning as Superintendent," pp. 100–103, to stage a data feedback presentation by assigning a class member to present the data to class members who role-play a school board or group of administrators (for example). Give the members of the role-play team typecast roles with preset questions about the nature and credibility of the data, the purpose of the presentation, etc.; run the role play, then focus discussion on:

(a)   Identifying and listing the questions and comment which got the new administrator in trouble

(b)   Generalizing from these problematic situations about the predictable difficulties of getting any group to examine its own behavior, its own part in creating any problem

(c)   Initiating a discussion of the values which lie behind this kind of activity

(d)   Initiating a discussion of the limits of producing organizational inquiry and self-evaluation

(e)   Initiating a discussion of the kinds of skills needed by a new administrator to make data feedback successful

Section Three:

SUPERVISING

INTRODUCTION TO THE SECTION

Effective supervision entails the use of structures and interpersonal skills which are based on a conscious rejection of the reflexive tendency to work alone rather than collaboratively. Very often supervision in educational settings is not collaborative. It is a sink or swim approach. The trouble with this approach is that:

- It is reflexive, not conscious, hence cannot be changed in response to unintended consequences.
- It does not generate information before it's too late, especially if supervisees are not performing to expectation.
- It does not involve supervisees as participants in learning and, as a result, does not improve performance.
- It does not involve supervisors in learning about the efficacy of their supervisory processes or the validity of assumptions about the supervisee's performance or ability to learn.

In the first case, Steve Fisher begins by showing what sink or swim supervision looked like in his own practice when he supervised an assistant in a former job. Then he presents his planned efforts to alter his approach to supervision in his work with a new special education director.

Meredith Jones's case shows a junior high school principal in extended dialogue with a new teacher to whom she gives negative information, thereby breaking her reflex to withhold such information, to leave the supervisee "in the dark" about her status in the eyes of the supervisor, and to leave untested her assumptions about the supervisee's performance and ability to learn. In effect, Meredith's case pictures the quality of collaborative interaction which is the hoped-for outcome of the effective use of the structural and procedural methodologies presented in the other cases in this book.

The final case continues the story begun earlier by Paul Kelleher in Section Two, Hiring. There Paul, a high school principal, told how he hired a new assistant principal. Here, he goes on to present his highly structured collaborative approach not only to supervising his new assistant's entry but to integrating entry activities with an analysis of the new assistant's job responsibilities.

Following the three cases is a set of exercises designed for use by practitioners and by an instructor.

Chapter 5:

Supervising a New Special Education Director

by STEPHEN B. FISHER

I had been in the district a year as Assistant Superintendent of Curriculum and Instruction when we began the process of replacing our Director of Pupil Personnel Services. The person in this position had reported to the Superintendent of Schools. Now, the new Director of Special Services was to report to me. Before I began supervising the new Director, I reflected on a previous experience of supervising a subordinate.

My Form Of Sink Or Swim Supervision: "Laid Back/On His Back"

My journey into the past was not a pleasant one. I recalled an assistant principal whom I had hired in a previous district. The participatory hiring process was a good one, involving faculty members from the various disciplines of the school in developing and asking questions that measured the problem-solving ability of the candidates and their performance in simulated stress situations. Out of that process I hired an energetic assistant principal. Young, bright, talented, with a series of successful jobs behind him, my assistant was excited by his first administrative position. I was sure I'd enjoy working with him as he took charge of the instructional program in that large junior high school.

He lasted only one painful year. What went wrong?

Without knowing it, I "threw him to the faculty," as several of my own faculty members flippantly pointed out. Almost like students with a substitute teacher, the faculty took my new assistant apart. His failure, though, was less the faculty's fault than my own.

My version of sink or swim supervision I call "laid back or on his back." When I was laid back, my behavior followed from two assumptions: maximize freedom and "I am here, if you need me."

Maximize Freedom. I had hired a competent and capable individual to serve as the assistant principal, so I assumed it was my responsibility, as the principal, to maximize his freedom, by leaving him alone to develop his style and solve problems. Even though I knew how the system worked—the shortcuts for decision making, the staff members who needed to be involved in particular tasks—I withheld this information, thinking of myself as helpful for not prejudicing him with my point of view.

"I Am Here, If You Need Me." I assured my new assistant that my "door was open" should he ever need to talk about any difficulties. I gave this assurance totally blind to the obvious implication, "If you can't hack it, come see me." In effect, I set it up so that coming to see me was an admission of failure.

These, then, are the set of assumptions which underlay my being "laid back." It was not long before I was "on his back." The year started, my assistant began to define problems, work with staff members, and, as was predictable, run into difficulties. He had to come to me for help. As soon as he walked in the door and announced that he was having difficulty solving a problem in the building, I jumped from being "laid back" to being "on his back." I'd immediately get out a yellow legal pad and begin to pump him for all the information connected with the problem. Using his information along with my knowledge about the system, I diagnosed and solved the problem for him.

The two assumptions underlying my "on his back" approach were "I'll solve the problem" and rescue the subordinate.

"I'll solve the problem." In my "laid back" approach, my first assumption was to maximize his freedom by saying, in effect, "It's all up to you." In being "on his back", I took back full responsibility for the problem, simply using him as an information source for input into my problem-solving process. When I had a solution, I gave it to him to carry out alone. In effect, I taught him what a good problem solver *I* was.

Rescue the subordinate. By solving problems for him, I was rescuing my assistant from some difficulty. This seemed the responsible thing to do at the time. Now, it is apparent to me that I was robbing him of the opportunity to develop the trust and skill necessary to do what I could do and he could not.

In short, my supervisory style was characterized by jumping back and forth between saying to my assistant: the problems are all yours/the problems are all mine; I trust you totally/I do not trust you.

This pattern of supervision contributed to the failure of my new assistant by keeping him "on a string," as he put it when he left, increasingly "unsure" of himself. On the receiving end, he kept getting terribly mixed messages, at worst, "Go ahead. Stop! Go ahead. Stop!" In the end he felt undermined, abandoned, and used. These were not only legitimate feelings but appropriate to the facts of my either/or supervision. Though I saw myself trying to give my assistant the chance to develop trust and skill, I did just the opposite.

This vignette from my administrative history sobered me as I looked at the prospect of bringing on Nat, our new Director of Special Services. Six years had passed. I did not want to recreate the same scenario with Nat, so I planned three sets of supervisory meetings. The first set was to take place in the spring prior to Nat's assuming his job on July 1. The second set of meetings would occur in the summer prior to the start of school. The third set of meetings was to take place in the fall during September and October.

Supervision Meetings Before Nat Comes On Board

Nat arrived for our first meeting excited, flushed with the joy of having been chosen to fill a new position. We laughed together as we reflected on the massive interview process he had conquered.

Nat's enthusiasm led him to talk immediately about "solving the problems."

"I can hardly wait to get to work on those new resource rooms the interviewing committee kept talking about," he said with relish.

My silent reaction was purely "laid back": "He's new, let him work it out on his own. It's his set of problems; let him solve them. You can always bail him out later."

At the same time, I knew that there were many traps for Nat, should he choose to act immediately on solving problems and should I choose to support him by being "laid back" in my supervision. I had decided in planning for this first meeting to share my perception of these traps and a plan for beginning which could help him avoid them.

"It's great to celebrate, Nat," I began. "I'm enjoying this. At the same time, I want to give you a picture of some of my concerns about your being new to our district. Your're a new administrator in a new job, and my experience tells me there are potential traps for you in being new. You want to solve problems, and you will have to, but before you begin to do just that, I want you to listen to my thoughts about the traps that can come with being new." I then shared with Nat my ideas on the administrators, the staff, his predecessor, the complexity of the system, and the length of time the problems had persisted.

Administrators

"The principals have been here for a minimum of seven years and some for as many as twenty-five. These principals have staff support and parent support developed over long years. They also report directly to my office or to the Superintendent of Schools. You, Nat, on the other hand, are in a staff position relative to principals rather than a line position, and you'll need to discover who goes to what person in the district to get decisions made and in what sequence they do that. The building principals will be quick to understand that in most areas you are a specialist and a resource person to them. If you rush in to 'solve problems,' the principals have access to much more information and decision-making structures. They can easily undercut and sabotage you in your work.

"At a personal level, you might feel that the only way to get things done is to direct people, and the principals are quite used to making their own decisions in running their buildings. You'll need to avoid the trap of directing the principals and will need to find ways to develop your role as a consultant to them in the area of special education."

Staff

"Nat, you're responsible for psychologists, social workers, learning disabilities specialists, and other ancillary staff members who have also been in the district a number of years. These staff members are based directly in the buildings. This means that they report to the building principals for direction on their day-to-day work. Again, you'll need to discover the balance between directing people and serving in a consultant role. The principals have the option to direct these staff people in different ways than you might wish. I'm concerned that you'll be caught in the middle of the trap between staff and building principals."

His Predecessor

"Your predecessor worked in a very different style than you appear to be choosing. For example, he did not go into the schools. When you do, that will be a change. People will question why you are there, so you will have to be clear ahead of time about your intentions and able to clarify the difference in the relationship you expect to have with them."

Complexity of the System

"Even though we are a small district, the interrelationships among staff members, the workings of central office staff, and the budget operation are complex. Our district is like a spider's web. If you touch one far corner of the web, the entire web will vibrate and the staff always feels those reverberations. I hope, Nat, you'll make the time and use your energy to come to know and understand our complex little world before you try to change and direct it. Otherwise, you may make decisions too fast that will shake the web, and it, in turn, could shake you out."

Length of Time the Problems Had Persisted

"The problems you've heard about in your interviews by simulated role-playing activities are not new problems to our district. They have existed over a long period of time. I don't want you to assume that the problems are relatively new and can be solved with simply hard work and effort. Others have worked on these problems before, Nat, and you will need to understand the history of these problems before you can set out to 'solve them.' In light of the history, you will need to analyze your assumptions about how to bring about change in this school district.

I hope that my role as your supervisor will assist you in finding ways to analyze and cross-check your information before you proceed to solve problems."

Nat did not want to hear this lecture. He wanted me to support him in his efforts to enter the job by solving the problems fast. I assured Nat that solving problems and dealing with issues was a major focus of the job, and I wanted him to be successful at it. In the interest of contributing to that success, I wanted him to work with me on a different way of looking at solving problems. My first directive to Nat was to put aside his intent to work on specific problems until the beginning of the school year and begin a planning process for his July/August months in the system. Of course, there were some problems that needed his attention immediately. We reviewed his job description and outlined these specific, routine issues and how he would begin to work on them in the summer.

Nat and I met two weeks later, and we outlined seven activities for him to participate in during his first weeks on the job during the summer. These activities were designed to help avoid the traps I had presented during our first meeting.[1] They constituted his "summer entry plan."

Supervision Meetings During The Summer

During July and August Nat and I met for a series of four planning meetings. By the end of our fourth meeting, we had developed a concrete, specific plan of activities which were to be completed during the first two months of school in September and October; they made up his "fall entry plan."

- A review with me of his meeting scheduled over the summer with his predecessor and his secretary.
- A review with me of the schedule of meetings he intended to hold with each key group that he would be responsible for as Director of Special Services.
- A second series of interviews with the principals (the first series was taking place during the summer) in which Nat would feed back to them the information he had collected from them in the summer. This provided an opportunity for principals to reflect on previous data they had presented and to clarify or change any of it.
- School visitations were planned. This activity included visiting every school in the district for one-half day. Included in that visit would be observations in any special education classes in that building, visits to the regular classroom program, and opportunities to talk with the teachers in each building in the district.
- A memo was to be written and published on the opening day of school indicating Nat's schedule for the first two months. This schedule included the dates he would be visiting each of the schools. He also included a statement inviting the staff to participate with him during his school visitations in forming a list of priorities for his first year's work.
- The development of a list of priorities for his work in the district was to be prepared.
- A plan was devised to make these priorities public. This plan included a presentation to the Board of Education in early November that would review all the activities that Nat had undertaken in his entry program.
- Nat and I agreed to meet weekly for two hours during the first two

[1] See Appendix V-1, "Summer Entry Plan: Seven Activities," pp. 257–258.

months of school, devoting the time to an analysis of the data that he obtained on his planned entry program.

At the conclusion of our four meetings, Nat and I were both pleased with the results. I had been able to avoid my laid back/on his back supervision. Nat was pleased to get my expectations for his performance in clear, concrete form.

Supervision During The School Year

The school year began smoothly, and Nat began to carry out his entry activities in the district. We met weekly to review and analyze the data he was gathering as part of his entry plan. During one of our regularly scheduled weekly meetings, Nat shared with me the information he had gathered from his first meetings with each one of his staff groups. I offer our interaction around this information as an example of the kind and quality of mutual learning which was so different from my you-do-it/I-do-it work with the assistant principal.

"Steve, I've met with several of my key groups for a group interview, and they each want me to meet with them regularly during the school year," Nat said.

"So, your first meetings have gone well, and you feel good about them."

"Yes, I do! I think they like me, and I really feel great that they asked me to continue to meet with them. I want to meet once a month with the psychologists, social workers, speech therapists, special education teachers, learning disability teachers, the Committee on the Handicapped, *and* the consulting psychiatrists."

I thought it would require too much time for Nat to see every group regularly. To simply tell Nat that there would not be enough time would deflate his excitement about wanting to see these groups regularly, and I wasn't quite sure how much time the meetings would actually take.

So I said, "Nat, I'm not sure you'll have the time to do all the work your office requires on a daily basis and see each of these groups regularly throughout the year. I want you to schedule each group in your calendar to get a sense of how much time this will actually take."

I got out the yearly school calendar and asked Nat to "chart out" regular meetings with all his key groups. We did this by listing each group, the day of the week they would meet with him, and the length of time this activity would require. As we began to block out the time for October, November, and December, Nat discovered that most of his time during the working day would be taken up in regularly scheduled meetings with these groups. He was torn. His desire to meet regularly with the staff was strong, and yet, as he looked at the kinds of problems he wanted to solve and the issues he wished to become involved in, the time available to do both was not there.

My silent, reflexive reaction was to jump into the problem-solving situation immediately. How could more time be made available? How could I help Nat accomplish what he wanted? I said to myself, "I am his supervisor and should have an answer." I wanted to get out my yellow legal pad and begin to go through the steps as I had done with the assistant principal years earlier. This thinking did not control me, though; I found another way for us to analyze the problem together.

"Nat, this is a problem that will require some time for us to work out together. Why don't we step back. We don't need to come to a decision immediately."

This comment gave us the perspective necessary to analyze the problem. An additional piece of information emerged as we continued to chart out on a yearly calendar the exact dates and times he would meet with the groups. Not only did it fill his calendar with meetings with each of the groups, it also required that the district provide substitute time for many of the people because they held classroom or building-level responsibilities. For them to meet with him on school time, they would have to miss work with children and/or staff and come to a meeting at central office.

During this period of stepping back and analyzing the situation, Nat and I discovered that some of the groups that he wished to meet with were crucial to the success of his work priorities for the year, while others were not. I asked Nat to review his purposes for meeting with each of the groups and compare them with his list of priorities for the year. As a result of his completing this task, he and I were able to divide the groups into three categories:

1. Those groups that would be scheduled in advance to meet with him throughout the year

2. Those groups that would be scheduled "as needed," for work on a pressing problem

3. Those groups that would not meet during this school year

Once we had sorted through our own stance in relationship to these groups, it became Nat's responsibility to talk with the individuals involved and explain his decision for how they would meet during the school year. He was able to go back to each group and be clear about his priorities and their participation in those priorities.

In a subsequent meeting, Nat commented to me, "I now understand why this entry plan was so important. I'd have scheduled meetings with each one of these groups for the remainder of the year, never realizing that there was no time left to do other work I was hired to do."

At our last planned two-hour review session in the fall, Nat asked me if I would be willing to continue these two-hour weekly sessions for the remainder of the school year. I couldn't have been happier. I scheduled two-hour blocks of time on my weekly calendar to continue the supervision.

In December, the Board of Education began public hearings on closing one of the elementary schools, and my energy was focused on data gathering and public presentations related to the instructional program. As a result, I cancelled many of my scheduled meetings with Nat. From December through April Nat and I met only to deal with those issues that were critical—applications for federal grants, staffing, and budget development.

In May, Nat and I met over lunch to review his entry data so I could verify my information to write this chapter. I was unprepared by Nat's sense of vulnerability in reviewing the year's work. "You know," he said, "I was left alone for the second half of this year. You were busy and so was everyone else with the school closing. I didn't want to disturb you with my concerns. I sure felt abandoned."

I had never considered the impact of my canceling most of the supervisory sessions with him. I was caught up in doing "my work" and concentrated only on that. I had missed those meetings. I was learning as much about my style of supervision as I had thought I was teaching Nat. That lunch ended with me recommitting myself to regularly scheduled meetings with Nat.

Still, I was troubled about finding an appropriate balance between responding to the unexpected, short-term, often urgent demands of my job and persisting in my commitment to prescheduled supervisory meetings of the kind I had had with Nat during the first part of the year. I wish I could say I have resolved this ongoing, unsolvable tension, but I have not! At best, through confrontations of this kind with Nat, I have hardened myself to say "no" to many new "urgent" demands and more often stick to my prior commitments.

During the new set of regularly scheduled meetings, Nat and I began to explore the work for the next school year. As the list kept getting longer and longer, we both realized that the rush of the end of a school year did not provide enough time for good planning. As a result, we agreed to save two full days in July for two purposes—a joint evaluation of Nat's work during his first year, and planning the priorities for the next year.

End-of-the-Year Evaluation and Follow-Up

I spent several hours planning our first session in July, because I knew that some of the information I wanted to share would be "negative." I wanted Nat to get my negative information about his work in as specific, concrete a form as possible so that our chances for dialogue would be enhanced.

STEVE: "Nat, you've had a very successful first year. The Superintendent has commented on at least two occasions how much he has appreciated your work. In particular he said your planning for the special education programs for next year was well done.

"I've admired the way you've learned the intricacies of federal funding.

"You've had your share of difficulties with the Committee on the Handicapped, but then, so has every other district in this area. The committee has run smoothly on the whole, and has worked well with your office. They used to pull end-runs all the time—bypassing the Special Services Office straight for the Superintendent. That isn't happening now.

"Finally, I'm surprised and delighted with the apparent ease with which you've begun to make the transition into administration.

"There are two areas in which I have concerns. The first is in your relationship to the staff in the buildings. I have very little data to back up my concern in this area. Two staff members have commented to me that they don't see you in the buildings very often and, as a result, don't feel they know you well. That isn't much to base a concern on, but I wanted you to know I'd be looking at this area next year. My second concern is a very broad one, and I want to test some of my assumptions about it with you. As we have talked in the past two months about planning priorities for next year, I had a sense that you were unclear as to what "involving the staff" looks like in operation, so I've developed mistrust of you in that area."

I had hoped to give some specific, concrete examples but Nat spoke immediately.

NAT: "That's tough, Steve. I do know how to set up meetings and involve people and resent your assuming that I might not. Maybe you just don't understand how I view administration. I think of the administrator as an architect designing the structure. The staff, then, does the work."

STEVE: "My concern, Nat, lies in how that 'structure' gets developed. What involvement, if any, does the staff have in helping to shape the plan?"

NAT: "I guess you call a meeting about it. Tell the staff there is a problem and ask them to suggest solutions." Nat said this tentatively, and then continued. "But where does my role as a leader fit with this? I should know which way we're going or I'm not a very good leader."

Nat's attempt to articulate his views of good leadership deepened my concern about how he involved his staff in decision making. As Nat continued talking, he spoke of a current set of problems he planned to discuss with the Committee on the Handicapped. I suggested that we plan together how he would go about involving the Committee in work on their particular problems. I told him that I assumed there was a crucial relationship between effectively involving staff in problem solving and the clarity of thought which a leader brought to organizing the staff's participations.

Nat and I began to outline the problems. The list was long. Each problem was role-played. I was the committee and Nat would present the problem to me. I'd respond with questions such as, "What kind of solution do you see?" "What are the legal implications?" "Policy implications?" "Why do you think that's a problem?" "We gave you a list of concerns; why have you chosen to work on this problem?" Each of these questions was designed to help Nat clarify how, why, and in what direction *he* wanted to take each problem area. The role playing took an entire day.

Nat took his notes from the role plays and divided the general issues into ten specific concerns. The committee was then scheduled to meet for three afternoons, a total of nine hours. Nat took each of the ten concerns and developed a one-page outline for each concern to give to the committee to aid their involvement in reaching solutions. Each page began with a statement of "need," outlining the reasons the issue was to be examined. Second on the page was a statement of a final objective to be achieved. Solutions had to meet the criteria established in the objective. Boundaries for decision making were stated. Finally, at the bottom of the page, subcategories of the issue to be examined were included, if needed, and a time line for completion was listed.

When Nat had his set of one-page outlines finished, we began a new phase of role-play preparations. I was the committee again, and he addressed me as if he were actually starting off the meeting and introducing these outlines. We developed a disciplined format for presentation of the outlines aimed at allowing the committee members to review each outline with Nat, raise questions, supply new information, suggest revisions, and witness his modification of the outline or decision to keep it intact. The goal here was to have Nat systematically "involve" the committee in shaping the definition of problems and the process for engaging them.

This planning activity was difficult for Nat. It took more time than the actual meetings. But the clarity with which he conducted those meetings was excellent. Everyone knew exactly where Nat stood on each issue, and, as a consequence, was able to be involved effectively. These same ten items had been floating around the district for four years causing irritation and concern. In three half-days they began to be addressed.

The pay-off was twofold. First, Nat did effectively involve the committee in working on problems. Second, and more important, he saw the ineffectiveness of his past practice in "involving" others and discovered in his gut the necessity of forcing *himself* to be clear as a necessary prerequisite of effectively involving others in task work.

Conclusion: Summarizing My New Approach to Supervision

My approach to supervising Nat contrasted with my previous laid back/on his back style of supervising my assistant principal:

Structure

My meetings with Nat were scheduled and planned well in advance. These meetings were defined from the beginning as dealing with issues around whole problems and not specific problem solving on individual portions of the problem. The meetings were reflective and analytic, rather than specifically problem solving. This regular meeting structure with Nat allowed me to fulfill my hope of dealing with the person, in addition to the specific tasks of the job.

Getting Good Data

My work with Nat was designed to put to use my knowledge of the organization rather than withhold it. I designed a structure for Nat's entrance into the school district which allowed him to get information before he had to make any decisions and act on key issues. This entry program allowed him to get information pertaining to the relationship between parts of the school district and the whole district. Specifically, he looked at the relationship of building principals to central office and the predictable authority issues centering around the Director of Special Services.

Collaborative Inquiry or Making Sense of Data Together

My regular series of meetings with Nat were designed for mutual sense-making of the data he had collected. I brought my knowledge about the district to bear within the context of his examination of the data. This was particularly seen in the vignette of charting out the number of meetings he would hold with the staff during the year and in our analysis of how he involved staff members in decision making. Instead of jumping in to rescue Nat by taking problems from him, solving them, and giving back solutions, I provided methodologies for joint analysis, planning, and skill practice.

The powerful implication of my new approach to supervision for Nat's growth as a leader came out in a comment he made recently. His attitude and view of leadership has been shifting. He began the job thinking, "I have answers, solutions, and the world sees me as competent. When I don't have

answers, I see myself as incompetent and feel vulnerable, anxious." As Nat
and I reviewed how we had worked together, he commented on the way in
which we had analyzed the data and searched together for answers to problems. He had found it superb. "I used to see someone who had answers and
solutions as someone who 'makes magic.' It's now a joint effort and that is
terrific."

Chapter 6:

Supervision: The Giving and Receiving of Negative Information about School Performance

---

by MEREDITH HOWE JONES

How to Read This Chapter

"Supervising a New Special Education Director" emphasized the importance of setting up the structure of regular meetings and entry activities for a new supervisee. Only snap-shots of dialogue were presented. In this chapter, a reader will find an extended dialogue. The case pictures the kinds of collaborative interaction which good structure allows. In other words, the purpose of using the structural and procedural methodologies presented throughout this book is to achieve the kind of human, collaborative inquiry presented here. In an effort to highlight this interaction, some of the structural components (such as the evaluation instrument itself) have been removed.

Introduction

Sally was a new teacher with one year's experience in another setting. I met with her in July to go over the faculty handbook and to set forth my expectations for teaching performance and my approach to giving negative information about performance. Normally, I try to give both my positive and negative impressions right from the beginning because of my dual role as supervisor and evaluator. As Sally's evaluator I had only seven months (September to March) to decide whether or not to rehire her. As her supervisor, I wanted her to have the information that was critical of her performance in time for her to use it to improve her performance before I had to make my rehiring decision. This seven-month time constraint upon the evaluation/supervision process is a typical problem in schools during times of decline.[1] Because Sally's case is used to illustrate the role of negative information in this process, it is important to note that the case presents an imbalance of attention to the negative; it does not emphasize the amount of positive information that was actually shared.

My Initial Assumptions About Sally Get Disconfirmed

With the start of school, Sally's room remained quiet, under control, and apparently productive. It came as a welcome relief to feel that Sally was getting off to a good start.

Other initial information about Sally was also consistently positive. Three weeks after school began, we had a fall open house for parents. Several parents spoke to me about "that wonderful new teacher," how their children loved her, what interesting things she did with students. A teacher also mentioned to me how great Sally was with kids. I happily told Sally the good things I heard.

The information that her room was under control, that Sally was great with kids, and that she produced creative lessons led me to feel that not only were there no control problems but Sally had "no problems" generally. I therefore postponed a classroom observation.

At the time, this belief that Sally had "no problems" was a comfortable one for me because I had too many other burdens, like observing and meeting weekly with a long-tenured teacher who was having difficulties, and working on school reorganization as a result of declining enrollments. Often the forces of other priorities, such as these, influence how tenaciously I hold on to my assumptions.

One day a teacher across the hall from Sally—a successful and respected teacher—commented to me that he wondered about Sally's teaching. Sally didn't seem to be teaching the required curriculum or setting high enough standards for student work. The teacher's tone said, "Why aren't you doing anything about these problems?"

---

[1] See "Leadership and Learning in a Time of Decline," Chap. 3, pp. 10–14, in Jentz and Wofford, *Leadership and Learning: Personal Change in a Professional Setting*, McGraw-Hill, New York, 1979.

I was distressed; I didn't want there to be a problem. I had made the assumption that there were "no problems." Now a teacher was threatening that assumption. I responded to that threat by recalling a conversation I had had with Sally early in the year where she said she could not relate to this same teacher across the hall: the teacher was set in his ways, and Sally couldn't discuss curriculum ideas with him.

Now I was faced with conflicting information and didn't know how to make sense of it. Perhaps the teacher across the hall was responding to something other than Sally's teaching performance? Was there a personality clash? Was he negative about Sally because Sally was young and popular with students and parents? On the basis of these speculations, I didn't initially take any action designed to test my assumption about Sally's performance against the new information.

Several weeks later, I passed some students outside my office who were talking about what a "neat" teacher Sally was. I overheard one student say, "and the work isn't that hard." I probably wouldn't have given that comment a second thought if it hadn't reminded me of the remarks made by the teacher across the hall from Sally. I decided to visit Sally's classroom in order to get concrete data about Sally's performance.

My observation, which also included a review of student notebooks and folders, revealed there were "problems"! Sally was accepting final products that were messy, had many mechanical errors, and were inadequately done generally. Although some assignments were creative and imaginative, students were given a large proportion of fill-in-the-blank sheets and workbook exercises. The class was well-organized, students responded well to Sally's directives, but Sally lacked clarity of goals and was not adequately following the required curriculum. She did have a wonderful relationship with students; she used humor and spoke their lingo. In short, her room was well-run, but she was not holding students to high enough expectations on written work, meeting the demands of the curriculum, or providing adequately balanced instruction.

Essentially, the bits and pieces of indirect information collected from others had been confirmed by my direct observations, which I recorded using the school system's formal evaluation instrument. My next task was to plan how I wanted to convey both the specific information and my assumptions about her performance to Sally in the observation postconference.

The apparently simple task of how to start the conference required me to again look at yet another set of assumptions, this time about Sally's ability to learn. These assumptions would form the basis of what I would see as the most effective way to conduct the conference.

I asked myself what I already knew about Sally. I knew little. Still, from our contact to date I did hold some assumptions about her ability to learn. I saw some aspects of her as scary. She was quiet, almost withdrawn. When alone, she often looked angry. She always had a rationale for why something should be the way *she* saw it. I assumed she was quite defensive.

With these thoughts in mind, I decided to give her hard observational data about her performance rather than start by trying to share the discrepancies I saw or the effect they had on me of creating ambivalence. I have found a person who is defensive may see the sharing of ambivalence not as an invitation to discussion but as an invitation to see me as weak. Then the supervisee writes me off as a poor supervisor, even a poor leader, because I am not "right, sure, in control."

First Post-observation Conference

By accident I was passing Sally's room a few minutes before our scheduled meeting in my office, and I saw her sitting at her desk, staring down at a book. Putting my head in the door, I said that I'd see her in a few minutes. She didn't seem to hear me. As I stepped into the room, she looked up, taken aback, and immediately began to speak: ". . . of all the days you should have come to my class"; the day was atypical; the kids behaved differently than usual; "I'm so annoyed with them," she complained.

As I took a seat across from Sally, my silent reaction was, "Hey, wait a minute. I have data here from student folders that has nothing to do with what day I observed. Who are you trying to fool?" I wanted to "shoot her down" with the data I had collected, to disconfirm the case I imagined she was trying to build against the validity of anything I was going to say.

With experience I have learned to listen to my own private reactions as I try to make sense out of another's spoken words. In this situation I recognized the part of me that wanted to respond reflexively—to "shoot Sally down," to confirm my already held assumption that she was too defensive to learn. At the same time, I listened to another part of me, a voice of inquiry, which asked, "What's going on here? Is she sincere, or is she putting me on?" This voice told me I'd get nowhere by confronting her with observation data in an attempt to "prove her wrong." At the same time, I couldn't get reliable answers to my questions by asking directly, "Are you defensive?" or "Are you sincere?" I tried putting into words what I thought Sally was saying.[2]

"So, you're really frustrated and discouraged because on the day I came

---

[2] See Chap. 6, "Paul's Case," pp. 37–60, in Jentz and Wofford, *Leadership and Learning: Personal Change in a Professional Setting*, McGraw-Hill, New York, 1979.

the kids behaved differently than they usually do," I queried sympathet-
ically.

"Yes. Usually my exchanges with them are more relaxed. The class was
not the kind of class I usually have. They were so apathetic and unrespon-
sive," she said, with contained anger.

"And you're really upset this has happened," I inquired.

"Yeah! I was so mad I told the kids that I was really annoyed and disappointed in how apathetic they were."

Through this exchange I was able to trust that Sally's anger, discourage-
ment, and frustration were genuine. I was puzzled by her repeated references
to the "behavior" of the kids, her relationship to them, and their apathy. I
had not been critical in these areas. Were these the things she saw as
different during my visit?

If so, we weren't in conflict; my concerns were about her instructional
methods and her expectations for student academic performance.

To explore further, I said: "It sounds to me as if you think there is a big
discrepancy between the quality of your relationship and the exchanges with
kids in the classroom when I'm not there as compared with when I am there.
That you and the students are more relaxed, that they are more enthusiastic
and involved when the principal isn't in the room."

"That's right! . . . you're right", she said.

Sally confirmed my imagining of what an "atypical day" looked like to her.
I continued, testing my sense of the meaning this atypical day might have for
her at this time. "And you're afraid you are going to get a bad evaluation
because the class wasn't the way it usually is."

In response to this statement Sally didn't answer directly, but her actions
were confirming. My acknowledgment of her fears seemed to allow her to
look at them, thereby freeing her to go further. She launched into a long
monologue about the strength of her relationship with kids. As she continued
to talk, she began to make comments like, "I may not always get papers
corrected on time," and "I'm still having a hard time trying to learn the
curriculum, but . . ." As she continued to talk, I began to hear what sounded
to me like a monologue about her strengths and weaknesses in general. In
response to this monologue, I improvised, again abandoning my intent to
share the observational data early in the conference.

My improvised response began, "You seem to be thinking about what you
do well and what you think you do less well. How about listing for me what
you perceive to be your strengths and weaknesses?"

This request was based upon the premise that if she could hear, and
know that I also heard as legitimate, the way she looked at her own compe-
tence, then she would not have to hold on to her view so tightly—she would

not have to defend it. As long as she was busy defending, she could not listen to any information from me without distorting it.

This was a risky request, not only because it is difficult to speak about our weaknesses out loud—especially to the boss—but also because in this case the job future for new teachers was bleak. Declining enrollment meant the chances of getting tenure three years hence was slim.

Yet, she responded and I took notes. Part way through she stopped, stiffened in her chair, looked at me, and said: "Why am I telling you these things? You're not supposed to tell the principal these things."

"That's one way to look at it. You can stop if you like. I'm asking you to do this to help me get a better sense of the discrepancy between what I saw of your teaching and your perceptions of how you teach when I'm not there. I imagine, however, this presents a real dilemma for you. You know, as I do, that because of declining enrollments, your position may be eliminated in a year or two. It seems to me that you are probably wondering how open you dare be about problems you may be facing in adjusting to a new school. You are probably thinking you should appear invulnerable and flawless because otherwise I will give you a bad evaluation and not hire you back even if there is an opening."

Sally paused at this point. Then she said, "No, I'll continue. You have a way that makes people want to tell you things."

Again, by speaking out loud what I imagined she was thinking and feeling, it seemed I was able to free her to go further.

Sally finished her list. I outlined back to her what I had jotted down. She made a few changes, but otherwise agreed that the notes were accurate.

I continued: "How do you see these strengths and weaknesses as being different on the day that I visited?"

As Sally and I explored this question, she realized that she was concerned about her informal exchanges with kids, that she had seen herself as acting stiffer than on a "typical day," that my presence had made her feel less relaxed. But she finally indicated that the material and format of the class itself had been typical.

This was a different stance from the one Sally had taken when we began our conference, a stance which classified the day as *totally* atypical. Had I stuck to my original plans or reflexively responded in a defensive way to her initial complaints, the chances are she would never have been able to hear me. Now I felt she would be more ready and available to hear what I had to say about my observation.

We went up to my office where I shared with Sally the observational data and the assumptions I was now making about her performance. For example, together we looked at selected final drafts of student papers and I pointed out the discrepancies between what she was accepting from students—

crossed-out words, misspellings, sentence fragments, incorrect grammar—
and my expectations for student papers.

She responded: "But I have really been concentrating on the level of
sophistication of thought in the papers. To me that's just as important."

"I agree."

"I've tried to give written assignments that are creative and thought provoking."

"And you have. For instance, the assignment for this paper on the bicen-
tennial was an excellent one. At the same time, you also have to set high
standards for the mechanical part of writing."

"Yes, I guess some of these are pretty sloppy. It shouldn't be hard for me
to get on that."

We also discussed other information and assumptions—both positive and
negative—about Sally's level of performance: ability to meet individual
needs, relationship with kids, and discussion skills. At the end of the conference with Sally I outlined specific steps for improvement and developed a
time line for working on the steps.

My hope in this conference had been to foster mutual inquiry and toward
that end I tried to be as clear as possible about my expectations for performance, about my assumptions about Sally's level of performance relative to
those expectations, and about the observational information which served as
the basis of those assumptions.

I came away from the conference having changed my original assumption
of "defensive and closed to learning." I now held a new tentative assumption:
Sally was willing to work on the issues raised; she was open to learning.

The next step in the evaluation process is to give the teacher a written
summary of the material we discussed.

Two days after sending Sally my memo, by chance, in conversation with
two different teachers, each mentioned that Sally had been complaining to
them as they sat with a group of other teachers about how I had unfairly and
inaccurately judged her teaching. Both teachers felt comfortable about my
wish to speak with Sally. I stopped into her room, and without mentioning
the teachers' names, said I was upset that she was so disconcerted with our
conference and, in addition, that she was speaking negatively about my
evaluation of her to others without seeing me about her complaints first. I
acknowledged that it is difficult to confront one's boss, particularly when
new; still in the interest of keeping our communication open, it was important she try to share her concerns with me.

Sally responded to all this quite lightly, saying that she had been upset
after our conference, more so than she knew at the time; it had been a way to
blow off steam, but perhaps she had "sounded off" inappropriately. It was
history, as far as she was concerned now. That was that.

Second Post-observation Conference

My ambivalence about Sally was renewed at my next classroom observation. She had made positive changes in her expectations for student written work, but the remainder of the steps outlined had not been addressed. Her actual classroom teaching did not show much progress. There was a discrepancy between the improvement I had hoped for and that which had actually taken place. Before meeting with her I tried to get clear about why I was disappointed and what I was actually feeling. In the process, I discovered a new factor: I was feeling internal pressure because the time would be approaching when I must make a rehiring decision. Although it was still early in the year, I now knew declining enrollments were going to eliminate Sally's position as it presently existed, but that I could reassign her to another position if I felt she really wanted to grow and learn. Other data also continued to feed my ambivalence. I kept getting comments from parents about what a nice addition she was to the school.

As I sat down to prepare for the postconference, I realized I must share with Sally my ambivalence about her level of performance—the discrepancy between what I had hoped for and what I actually observed, and my renewed ambivalence about her openness to learning as a result of the discrepancy between the number of steps I had outlined and the number she had actually completed. It would be very easy—and less time consuming—to write her off as not caring, to assume that her level of performance would remain low, and to see her as closed to learning. Those assumptions were the reflexive ones. If I responded reflexively, I would decide not to rehire her. And so we met again.

"Sally, I am confused and disappointed. Although I have seen clear progress in your expectations for student work, I am aware that you have not followed through on all the steps for improvement outlined on your prior evaluation. On the basis of our previous conference I thought that you were going to work on the other steps we outlined—observing a colleague, tape-recording a discussion—yet you have not taken those steps."

Faced with this statement, she made a few attempts to explain why she had not completed the steps as outlined. She had been sick. A teacher she was to observe had been too busy.

"Sally, I don't see those as valid reasons. You were only sick for three days. You have had plenty of time to visit him."

Sally looked at the floor. "You're right. I don't know why I haven't followed through."

I felt helpless. She wouldn't go further. I began wondering if I should rehire Sally. I decided to bring forward that concern so that Sally would be clear where I stood.

"As you know, Sally, I am here to work with you to help you become the best teacher possible. At the same time, you know that I have to make rehiring decisions about next year. At this point we both know your job will be done away with. However, I might be able to hire you in another position if I felt you were committed to improving. But, at the moment, I'm doubtful about the extent of your commitment."

I had hoped that bringing forward my concerns would allow us to talk further, though I realized that I risked coming across as cruel and heartless.

Sally was silent. "I can see that," she said, and stopped. She seemed closed off. I checked, "It seems to me you don't want to talk right now." "Yeah," she replied.

I continued, "Perhaps later we can make some sense out of all this, but right now I'm wondering if you want to proceed with the evaluation? Should we make another appointment instead?"

She chose for us to continue, so I did. Yet, I could see she was distressed. I felt sad. As I proceeded she verbalized agreement with the criticisms, but as hard as I tried to engage her in discussion about the evaluation, I could see she remained withdrawn and did not want to talk. Time constraints forced me to end the conference.

As soon as she left I said to myself, "I've had it! I'm not going to rehire that kid! It's too risky. She's not open to learning after all. She's too defensive!" At the same time I still felt sad; I liked Sally and knew she had real strengths.

With distance from the conference, I began to feel a general sense of discomfort about my reflexive thoughts. I began to realize I remained ambivalent. Something wasn't right! I realized I was solidifying an assumption that she was closed to learning. I was planning to act on the basis of those assumptions and not rehire. If I made that decision, I would proceed to behave in ways that would make the decision clear—more evaluations and/or a conversation with Sally to tell her of my decision. I realized my assumption about her inability to learn was based on her reaction to the written summary of my first observation and on data from one conference, while I still had information from the other encounters that was more positive. I came to the conclusion I needed to try again to check out my assumptions and to explore what assumptions lay behind *her* actions. It would be unfair to give up.

I tried to imagine what impact the evaluation might have had upon Sally to affect her in the way it did—making her appear closed to learning. First I had told her I was disappointed in her progress and was feeling ambivalent about rehiring her. Second, I had proceeded to give her an evaluation which contained negative information, although I had attempted to reinforce the positive. I speculated about what impact this information might have had on her. Anger at me, disappointment with herself, feeling picked on, unfairly treated? Perhaps those were feelings getting in the way of our ability to communicate and resulting in my assumption that Sally was not open for learning. If she was making assumptions that I was picking on her or that I was unfair, then she might feel helpless, hopeless, and therefore unable to take any action. No action would look like "closed to learning."

Follow-up Meeting to Second Post-observation Conference

In planning for this meeting, I decided to start by sharing my imaginings of how she might be feeling in response to our last conference and see where it went from there.

"Sally, I've been thinking a lot about you since my last evaluation. As a matter of fact you have probably noticed that I haven't yet given you a written version. I have been imagining that you have probably been feeling pretty angry at me about that evaluation."

"Yes, I have."

I was puzzled. She didn't say anything more, just looked at the floor. I tried again. "I've also been thinking that you have probably felt picked on and unfairly treated."

"Yeah, I have."

I waited for what seemed like a long time and then . . .

"You don't say anything good about me! Classroom management used to be one of my problems. Do you realize I have learned to manage those kids! Do you know what an accomplishment that is! Those kids behave! All you have said are negative things about me. No matter how hard I work, it's never good enough."

She went on about her past experience in another school system, how grim some of it was, and how she had really worked on the management issue.

"So you really feel dumped on?"

"Yes."

I was excited. I had finally made real contact with Sally. She was bringing forward the assumptions through which she was viewing my evaluation. Until she looked at those assumptions and felt them as legitimate, she would be unable to give them up—to make a different set of assumptions. She would remain trapped in them.

To explore further, I asked, "I'd like you to do something for me. Would you list out loud for me all the negative things I have said about you?"

She did.

"Now I want you to list all the positive things I have said about you."

She did, but more slowly than the negative list. She had trouble remembering what they were but finally recalled twice as many positive statements as negative. We wrote each list down and looked at them. She was taken aback. "But," she stammered, then stopped.

I filled in: "It doesn't feel like I've said anything nice. Right?"

"Yes."

What happened at this point was confirming of my theory about the importance of trying to imagine the world from her point of view as a necessary step toward breaking a conflict and allowing a mutual change. Sally began to talk! She talked about her previous experience where she had learned a curriculum only to come to this new school and everything she had learned before was useless in this setting. She talked about the number of books she had to read to keep up, how the curriculum was so different in that the specifics were not spelled out. I tried to listen for the meaning of what she was saying rather than to the extensive content she was relating to me. It sounded to me as if she was saying she was overwhelmed, so I tested my thoughts.

"It sounds to me like you are feeling confused and overwhelmed?"

"That's right! I do feel that way. At the last conference I thought you were unfair, that I could never be good enough. I think you expect me to learn everything overnight. Do you realize how I feel every time I walk around this school? I think you expect me to be as good as all these other teachers, to have subgroups all the time, creative lessons, meeting every child's needs and providing creative and well-organized lessons."

"So, I'm the cause of your having no room to operate?" I asked.

"That's right," she said, but with little conviction.

We sat for a few silent moments.

"Yes, I do expect these things from you over time," I said. "And perhaps I have expected too much from you too fast. At the same time, I think there are other forces contributing to your feelings of being overwhelmed." It was my hope that if she could feel heard, she would be ready to hear my different view.

"Remember in July I shared with you my perspective on supervision? I want to review that perspective with you in the context of the supervision I have tried to provide for you this year. There are at least two stances a principal can take in relationship to a new teacher. The traditional approach has often been to protect you, by serving as a supporter and problem solver—like the time I handled that difficult parent. I could have protected you, too, by not meeting with you. Then you would not have had to face the pain of my negative observations and consequent assumptions about your performance and learning.

"This behavior is grounded in a definition of ourselves as caring people: A caring person is seen as one who avoids hurting others. A corollary says: Growth cannot take place through hurt but only through protection by withholding negative information. This view of a caring person argues for the sharing of positive information only. From this perspective, to share negative information is heartless, especially in the case of a new teacher who is often seen as needing a 'chance to get started.' The hitch is that at the same time the principal is supposedly protecting the new teacher, the principal must make judgments about whether or not you are up to standard in level of performance and ability to learn.

"I look at supervision differently. I believe if I don't share with you my observations and assumptions, even if some of the information is potentially hurtful, you can only guess at how I view your performance. You are kept in the dark when I don't give you the information you need in order to change and succeed. Also, I am in the dark because I would not be testing my assumptions by getting new information that would confirm or disconfirm them. Neither you nor I would have the opportunity to look at those assumptions together in the interest of questioning them or using them to help you improve your performance. For example, just now I came in here thinking you were closed to learning. By testing that thought with you I found it was wrong. Actually, you are overwhelmed. You don't know which way to turn. If I had not found this out, I might have hung on to that assumption and already decided not to rehire you.

"But there is a risk in sharing negative information. Often when one is told both positive and negative things about oneself, only the negative is heard, as we just saw when you made these lists of what you had heard me say that was positive and negative about you. It feels like one's whole person is condemned, that you are wrong/bad/no good. Such feelings can be overwhelming and immobilizing."

"Yeah, you know I've felt that way. It's hard, though . . . to hear . . ."

"Yes, it is hard."

We sat in silence for a moment.

Sally broke the silence. "What you said makes sense, though. I'd rather know where you stand. If you don't confront me, you're protecting me from being hurt or angry at you, but you're also increasing my chances of failing." She stopped. Then she continued, "Now I understand why teachers around here say you really care. I never understood how they could see you that way, because I didn't."

After a long pause, Sally continued, apparently beginning a new topic but actually thinking from a new perspective about why she had not visited the other teacher.

"You know, one of the reasons I didn't visit the other teacher is because," she paused, "Well . . . when you see someone else who's able to do all those things . . . like when I walk around the school and see how good the teachers are . . ."

"You mean, seeing the discrepancy between your hopes for your own teaching and what other teachers are able to do also contributes to your being overwhelmed?"

"It makes me feel even more overwhelmed—their ability to subgroup and meet individual kids' needs, their knowledge of resources, all that stuff. . . ." Again she paused, continuing with a reference back to my talk about supervision: "What you said about hearing only the negative . . . I guess I want to be perfect."

At this point it seemed to me that Sally was becoming clear that there were several forces responsible for her feeling overwhelmed: my pressure on her, her view of the discrepancy between her skill level and that of other teachers around her, and her own need to be perfect.

As we talked further about each of these forces, we again looked at the list of steps for improvement. We did some revision and ended up with three priorities Sally was to tackle for the remainder of the year.

By our next conference, Sally had completed two steps—audiotaping a classroom discussion and reading a series of literature books. The third step—observing a colleague—was in process. Sally expressed dismay at the poor quality of her recorded classroom discussion, so we talked about how she might change her approach. At this conference I informed Sally I would be rehiring her for next year because her performance had improved and she had demonstrated an ability to learn. We would continue to work together to set priorities for improvement.

Conclusion

July rolled around again. To my surprise I received two parent phone calls about Sally. In the first case, Sally had twice not followed through on the parent's request for a conference. In the second, the parent was concerned that some of her daughter's papers had not been corrected and returned.

Another hot July, and I sat thinking about Sally, only this time there was a year's learning behind us. The problems the parents had raised were not new to Sally or to me. I was sure when I shared the calls with her in the fall she would be open to looking at the issues again.

September came. Sally was anxious to share with me the work she had done over the summer—attending a writing institute for teachers and outlining plans for a very creative unit she wanted to try where students would be grouped in a variety of ways. At our first conference, Sally was pleased with her unit plans but was struggling with the amount of work required to implement them—gathering a wide variety of materials, matching materials with kids' abilities and needs, correcting the papers and projects afterwards.

On the other hand, she had "loved" designing it and looked forward to trying what she called her "experiment."

During our discussion I told her the content of the two July phone calls. She groaned, "Demands, demands. I never thought teaching required attention to so many different demands. I admit I didn't call that parent. I didn't think anyone would notice, and I didn't get some papers back toward the end of the year. I realize both are "no, nos"! But, you know, I was thinking over the summer, do you realize the number of people I have to respond to— parents, you, each kid, other teachers—not to mention all the number of details—planning, correcting papers, curriculum, it's never ending!"

It was this comment, coupled with my observations of Sally's teaching and her struggles implementing her "experiment," that led us in a direction neither of us expected at the time. Sally left teaching.

Her decision evolved slowly. We discovered that Sally was very conflict-ed about teaching. She loved the kids and having what she called "fun with them," and she was crazy about thinking up creative and exciting lessons. But she "hated" and could not seem to come to grips with the other parts of teaching—attention to details like correcting papers, calling parents, or-ganizing the classroom in ways aimed at individualizing instruction. With time we found that because of these things, she didn't really like teaching. In December she acted from this information and decided she would leave at the end of the year in order to pursue graduate work in another area.

Sally's decision to leave left me with bittersweet feelings. I hated to see her leave because of the time and effort I had put into her learning and, most importantly, because of the loss to the students of her fine qualities as a teacher. At the same time, I knew her decision was right for the school and for her over the long run. Apart from her decision to leave, I was pleased with my ability to create conditions for mutual learning and growth through my own ability to (1) set clear expectations for performance, (2) identify discrepancies between expectations and performance, (3) present my obser-vations in a context of expectations on the one hand and the assumptions I held on the other, (4) stay open to disconfirming data, even actively seek it by making my assumptions known instead of withholding them, and, perhaps most importantly, (5) empathize with Sally, to imagine out loud my sense of what she might be saying and the assumptions which might give rise to her point of view.[3]

---

[3]   See "Lew's Case," Chap. 12, pp. 123–170, in Jentz and Wofford, *Leadership and Learn-ing: Personal Change in a Professional Setting,* McGraw-Hill, New York, 1979, for another illustration of these skills.

Chapter 7:

Supervising a New Assistant Principal

by PAUL KELLEHER

How To Read This Chapter

In the chapter that follows, Paul Kelleher walks the reader through a series of structural activities designed to integrate the entry activities for a new supervisee with an analysis of the new person's job responsibilities. This chapter leans more in the direction of being technical and detailed than in the direction of storytelling. We recommend this chapter highly to those readers who actually want to learn how to go about *doing* these activities in contrast to *reading* about them.

Introduction

When the hiring process ended, which was described in an earlier case, I faced the challenge of helping my new assistant, Phil, make a successful entry into his job. I hoped in beginning the process of supervising Phil's entry to extend the effort of role clarification, which I had begun in the hiring process. I wanted to bring specific clarity about everyday, concrete job expectations and responsibilities to Phil and to others in the organization as he began his new job.

Time was critical. The hiring process ended with Phil's official appointment at the end of the second to last week of summer. Teachers would return to school on the day after Labor Day. Phil and I had just one week before the onslaught of teachers, students, and parents to do all our complex planning.

Although I already planned daily meeting time for supervision with Phil after the start of the school year, I knew that the ongoing daily responsibilities for each of would creep into the time set aside. We did of course meet regularly after the start of the year. But much of the entry work Phil and I did occurred in a series of meetings in the last week of August.

In deciding to cram these planning activities into so short a period of time, I knew I took a risk. Phil might feel overwhelmed by my attempt to do complex, technical, and probably unfamiliar work with him in so short a time. Yet, in weighing that risk, I also knew from my own experience the dangers of an unplanned entry. What tipped the balance for me in favor of the activities described here was the fact that we had hired, in Phil, an experienced, proven administrator. He had held administrative positions at both the junior high and elementary school level in a district which was forced to release him because of drastic budget reductions. His proven success, then, confirmed my decision to undertake the following supervisory action.

I have divided this chapter into five different sets of entry activities in which Phil and I engaged. Considerable overlap in time occurred, of course, as Phil began these different activities. But what follows is a list of the five sets of activities and the dates when most of the work occurred between Phil and me in planning the activities.

1. Clarifying Norms—last week of August

2. Mapping and Charting tasks—last week of August

3. Building Bridges to Key People in the Organization—September 1–15

4. Making Sense and No-Sense—October 1–15

5. Expanding Responsibilities: The Administrative Calendar—October 30–November 15

This time sequence limited Phil's entry activity to the first quarter of the year. I do not know when planned entry activities should end—three months, six months, one year? But I do know that the structures the supervisor sets up for a new administrator's entry become less and less necessary. As well, I know that the critical sets of activities described in Phil's first two and a half months of work set a norm of activity for Phil that influenced his actions far beyond the first few months on the job.

Clarifying Norms

Just as different geographic regions have different topographical characteristics, different schools have sharply dissimilar territorial characteristics. Many of these differences can be easily observed and quickly "mapped" by an observer entering the school for the first time. They are explicitly written as policy statements, rules, procedures, job descriptions, statistics on student performance, or community profiles. Other characteristics of the "territory" of a school, which may sharply distinguish that school from another one, are much trickier and more difficult for a "mapmaker" to discern. They are the implicit rules governing the behavior in interactions between people in the school which we call *norms*.

The most important qualities of norms are that they are both implicit and powerful. Teachers new to a school do not learn faculty norms by reading the teacher handbook. Instead, they learn them by observing more experienced teachers in the faculty cafeteria, faculty lounge, meetings, and all other settings in which norms govern behavior. Consistent with the implicit nature of norms, learning them often occurs tacitly. Even after we have become successful in integrating new norms into our behavior, we have difficulty articulating what those norms are. Yet we know they exist.

We also know how powerful they are when we observe someone who unwittingly breaks a norm. A good example is the eager rookie teacher who extravagantly praises the administration's help and support in front of a group of old cronies gathered in the teachers' room. Norms no longer stay tacit when they are violated. This new teacher quickly hears that such comments are not appropriate to faculty-room conversation. Word quickly spreads of the transgression, and the teacher learns, perhaps painfully, that the norm in most schools is that the faculty room is a place for teachers to blow off steam, to ventilate their hostility and frustration, particularly toward the administration.

In learning the norms of his new school territory, my new assistant principal, Phil, had important advantages that this eager, new teacher did not have, for Phil was an experienced school person. He had worked in a large high school before, though as a social studies teacher. He had previous administrative experience as a principal in both elementary and junior high schools. Finally, he came to this job from a school district similar to our own in socioeconomic conditions, values and aspirations of parents, and attitudes of students and staff.

As I thought about how to help Phil learn the norms of his new school, I realized how important these advantages were. Already, in our interview conversations, for example, he had begun to test the degree of similarity between the norms of his old situation and the norms of this one. Though we had not yet talked explicitly about norms in the way I am discussing them, he had made comparisons between the attitudes of the PTA people on his interview committee and the PTA in his old district. By his questions and comments, he showed himself to be one who, at least implicitly, made an important distinction. He knew that some norms are universal. Like the norm about faculty-room conversation, they seem to apply in almost all school situations. Others are specific to situations and must be ferreted out by the perceptive newcomer.

My Assumptions about Learning Norms

In the week before the beginning of school, I had daily meetings with Phil to begin planning his entry into the school. As I pondered how to help Phil learn the norms of his new school, I took into account his social science background in developing an anthropological metaphor to clarify my own assumptions about how he should go about learning the norms. In our first discussion, I offered Phil this list of assumptions I was making:

As an entering administrator, Phil should be like an anthropologist. Like the anthropologist who tries to determine the myths, lore, and traditions of a foreign culture, Phil would need to learn the social and political norms of the school, its traditions, its procedures, and the historical context in which all these phenomena reside. Phil's need to learn about the "culture" of the school is even more imperative than the anthropologist's since he must quickly become an actor in the new setting.

Phil might decide to break the norms that exist by attempting to change the culture of the school in some way, but that decision ought to be conscious and deliberate and made only after careful consideration of the consequences. In these terms, it would be costly for him to initiate some activity and then discover, to his surprise, that he did not accurately predict its consequences. His actions might have violated someone's sensibilities, intruded on someone's turf, or elicited some other painful response to perceived change. However well-intended, if Phil took significant action in ignorance of the norms of the school, he might find surprising consequences. These consequences might also set up a pattern of resistance to his attempts at change that would have lasting impact.

As Phil entered his new job, he had an opportunity, which he would never have again, to signal to his colleagues as well as to students and parents how he viewed the responsibilities of his position. With my help, he could initiate activities that communicated clearly to others his expectations before their expectations forced him into a reactive mode in which he was not in control of how his position became defined. The "honeymoon" period, a phenomenon which all administrators new to a setting have experienced, offered Phil a unique chance to establish control of his job before it overwhelmed him. In those early days, people would simply listen more carefully, and they would pick up signals that would help both him and them define role expectations.

Taking advantage of this "honeymoon" time, Phil could step forward in his early interactions with others in the organization and legitimately claim the right to take the time to learn about the place before he set about to "fix it" or "solve it." These early learning activities, thus, could help him to define himself as a learner as well as a performer. He could make clear that he valued providing himself as well as others with opportunities to learn. He could begin the process of becoming a leader who creates the conditions for learning.

Phil responded well to this catalogue of assumptions. One of his qualities that made him my choice for the job was his intelligence, and my analytic approach to the practice of the assistant principalship appealed to him. In addition, my anthropological metaphor interested him because of his prior administrative experience. He had experienced the differences in norms that distinguish one school from another, and he knew the importance of knowing those distinctions.

Categories of Norms

In this first meeting, I reinforced the testing Phil had already begun about the degree of similarity between norms in his new school and norms in his old. I encouraged more questioning and testing, and we began to talk in concrete terms about the norms of our school as I answered his questions and responded to his observations. In this meeting and subsequent ones, we developed various categories of norms existing in the school.

NORMS DEFINING ROLES

Phil understood that the responsibilities of various roles in the organization are not all defined by job description. Implicit norms govern some important definitions of role. An essential responsibility in our school, for example, nowhere defined in the rules, policies and procedures, is curriculum development. A norm of the school—understood by faculty, administration, parents, and students—is that teachers have autonomy in curriculum issues. This norm is specific to our situation and not universal. In other schools, by contrast, administration—principals, curriculum directors—may have much more control of cirriculum development.

NORMS DEFINING INFORMATION FLOW UP AND DOWN THE HIERARCHY

Another important set of norms influence how people serving in different roles in the organization interact with each other: who talks to whom; who is consulted when decisions get made, and how does that consultation occur? Again, the norms of our school in this case are quite specific to the situation. In other schools, such questions are answered in rigorously hierarchical terms. Like the Cabots who talk only to the Lodges, and the Lodges who talk only to God, teachers talk only to chairmen, chairmen talk only to principals, and principals talk only to the central office. Organizational interactions do not skip levels in the organizational chart (for example, a teacher talking to the School Board members) without suitable deference to the prerogatives of the roles passed over (the sensibilities of the principal involved, for example).

Our school and school district are markedly different, being small and highly participatory for everyone. Within the norms of the organization, the structure is less a hierarchy and more a network. Everyone talks to everyone. Everyone assumes the right to information. This norm means that in decision making, anyone who has anything to gain or to lose from a decision must be consulted before that decision is made.

NORMS DEFINING INTERACTIONS BETWEEN PEOPLE

Another set of norms governs how people behave with others in both one-to-one and group situations. Norms in our school tend to be the same universal norms of interactions that apply not only in other schools but in most other organizations. A partial list of these universal norms includes:

- Say you believe in collaboration but make sure you do not lose anything in the process.
- Don't risk vulnerability: be right. And prove rationally that you are.
- Don't allow a "show of feeling"—be logical.
- Withhold negative information you have about someone else's performance.
- Don't take personal responsibility for your actions; attribute responsibility for organizational problems to others.

Neither this list of categories nor the examples within them is complete. They merely illustrate part of the complex structure of norms which these early conversations with my new assistant helped to unearth. We not only engaged in the difficult task of trying to make explicit what is normally tacit, but we also attempted to clarify the relationships between different norms.

We discovered both consistencies and discrepancies between norms through this analysis.

The consistencies were the most obvious and the most simple. For example, the norms of our school define an active role for the PTA. Parents expect to be informed, consulted, involved in all major decisions in the school. This practice is consistent with the norm described above—everyone talking to everyone.

The contradictions are more complex and more difficult to handle, since they often create "either/or" binds for administrators, in which no matter which alternative they choose, they often lose. For example, one powerful norm which the school community holds for the school administrator is that of being a strong leader, willing and able to act forcefully and to make important decisions. But another norm among the faculty is that teachers should govern in much of school decision making. Powerful individual teachers and coalitions of teachers try to determine the policy direction. No important decision can be effectively made, then, without faculty consensus. The bind for administrators is that by acting forcefully as the "strong leader," they risk charges of being autocratic and dictatorial. If the administrators always consult the faculty, defer to its wishes, and wait for consensus, decisions will be delayed or not made at all, and they risk being judged weak and ineffective.

This double bind illustrates the importance of these conversations with my new assistant about the complex relationships between the norms of our school. I knew that these traps existed for him. I also knew that discussion and analysis of "either/or" binds had often helped me to free myself from their hold and to find alternate strategies for action. I hoped that by this process of unearthing norms in the school and relationships between them, I would help Phil not only to learn about them but also to discover appropriate ways to handle them. With this kind of dialogue, I hoped to model for him ways to struggle with, to identify, and to find appropriate responses to double binds which the norms created. This kind of discussion was a regular refrain in our conversations through much of the first year.

Developing the Historical Interview: The Last Week of August

Talking with a supervisor can help the new administrator clarify the norms of the new environment. But how else can these norms be learned? Learning them as quickly as possible is obviously essential. New administrators do not want to make the kind of mistake that the new naïve teacher does. Even more than a new teacher, they cannot afford such errors in judgment. The school community's tolerance of these errors is much narrower for new administrators than for new teachers. People expect considered leadership, not naïve blundering from the new person. Administrators do not want to be caught by surprise, discovering that in acting unawares of a norm which might have been learned, their efforts are thwarted.

In our conversation about norms, I had made clear to Phil my rationale for wanting to plan carefully his entry into the school, but I was not sure I had convinced him. After all, he was an experienced administrator. From the recommendations I had received in the hiring process, I knew that his superiors believed he had successfully entered two other schools.

In our meeting the day after our conversation about norms, I tested my concern. Phil's comments affirming the legitimacy of this effort reassured me. He said that he had had entry experience before, but it had come in much smaller schools and not at the high school level. In addition, as he reflected on his past practice, he described problems with faculty in his last school, and he wondered whether or not the kind of planned entry we were attempting would have helped to avoid some of those problems.

With this confirmation, I launched into the next step in the entry process. Phil had academic training as an historian and had been a teacher of history prior to entering administration. In order to relate his entry to his past experience, I discussed with him the possibility of conducting historical interviews, as activities which would enable him to carry out his task of learning about his new culture. As a social scientist, he would talk with people in the organization about the history and structure of his role as it related to them. Obviously, he could profitably initiate these interviews with practically everyone in the organization. I gave him a list of key people with whom he would have to interact in the early weeks of his job. We decided that he would conduct these historical interviews with them.

Phil liked the historical interview idea. In the rest of this discussion, we tried to set up a structure for these interviews. We decided that each historical interview should:

Be highly structured and purposeful. In initiating them with interviewees, Phil would clearly set the purpose around issues of his job. For example, in interviewing secretaries with whom he would work on budget processes, he would be clear that the focus of the conversation would be on budget procedures that he needed to learn. This structure and purpose was necessary so that interviewees would understand why this unusual activity was taking place and not feel that Phil was prying into their business trying to unearth problems.

Take an historical perspective. One of the purposes of the interview would be to discover evolution of practices and procedures. Phil would try to elicit from interviewees as much detail of the history of the task as possible, particularly focusing on when, how, and why procedures for accomplishing a task had changed. This historical view, thus, would set a context for considering whether and how to make future changes.

Make the interview one of mutual participation. In our discussion, I emphasized to Phil that though he would take the stance of a learner in these interviews, he also needed to communicate that he was not just an observer. He was learning to be a participant in the organization, and the first step in that participation would be an active role in the interview. In this way, Phil's role in entering his new setting would diverge from the role of the anthropologist, who can content himself with observing and recording. Since Phil would become an actor in this situation, he needed to incorporate that expectation into his personal stance in the interview. Even if he did not view himself as an actor, interviewees would. They expected him to be a powerful participant in the organization. One danger, then, was that if he merely asked questions, observed, and recorded, interviewees would feel more and more anxious. They would feel he was withholding negative judgment, even if he were not.

As Phil and I discussed, one way to reduce that anxiety and to take the stance of being both a learner and an actor in the situation was for Phil to give feedback to interviewees on how he made sense of what he was hearing. Thus, he needed to exercise all his skills in listening, paraphrasing what he heard and confirming those understandings with people. His goal would be to have interviewees leave the interview thinking that the "new man" knows "how we see things and feel about them."

Let people know where he stood on issues discussed. The critical way Phil assumed the stance of both learner and actor in the interview was to "put himself on the map."[1] When what he heard about how things are done made sense to him, his task would be relatively easy. He would reconstruct what he heard, check its validity, and indicate his positive feeling. However, when what he heard seemed problematic, his response would be more difficult. He did not want interviewees to leave feeling that they had not been heard and that his intention was to impose his own judgment on their past experience. Nor did he want them to leave feeling that they did not know where they stood with him on the issues discussed.

I then described some techniques for working with this bind:

1. Claim and acknowledge negative feelings in the situation by saying, "I feel uncomfortable about _____."

[1] For a discussion of the skill of "putting yourself on the map," see Chap. 12, "Lew's Case," pp. 132–133 in Jentz and Wofford, *Leadership and Learning: Personal Change in a Professional Setting*, McGraw-Hill, New York, 1979.

2. Clearly relate the negative feeling to the specifics that are of concern.
    Interviewees would be anxious for Phil's approval. Any negative infor-
    mation would tend to be distorted. People would hear his negative
    feelings about a small part of a process as criticism of the whole. Thus, he
    must use his skills to explicitly and carefully distinguish the specifics that
    were of concern from those that made sense.

3. Relate his negative feelings to his past experience by saying, "My past
    experience and judgment cause me these concerns. As I come to under-
    stand this organization better, my feelings may change."

Work with groups as well as individuals.   If Phil chose a group format for
interviews, he would need to be clear at the outset that the purpose of the
interview was not to solve problems, not to resolve differences. He would
acknowledge that different perspectives would emerge from individuals in
the course of the conversation. The task would not be to resolve those
differences, but to identify and understand them. In setting up these group
meetings Phil would be sure to allow enough time—at least an hour—so that
he would have adequate time to elicit different information from different
individuals. Finally, Phil and I agreed that if he used the group format, he
would ask the person who had been in the school the longest to take the lead
in providing the historical context.

Be set up in advance.   Interviewees need to recognize this was a formal
conversation with a clear structure and set of purposes which was part of a
larger set of interviews designed to bring the new person into the school.
Otherwise the interviewee would tend to be mistrustful, questioning why
they were being singled out and what the new assistant intended.[2]

These sets of activities were designed to help Phil map the new territory
with respect to its norms so that he could perform his tasks more efficiently
and sensitively. He needed simultaneously, however, to begin to establish
himself with respect to tasks. We adopted a mapping approach to tasks as
well.

Mapping and Charting Tasks

Though a job description is a map of the positional territory a new incum-
bent must fill, it only sketches the broad boundaries. The job description
tells new administrators essential information about what is within and what
is outside the limits of their position. But new administrators who are going

---

[2]   For another discussion of how to interview, see Chap. 4, "A Good Beginning as Superintendent," pp. 97–99.

to explore "foreign territory" need a much more detailed map of the responsibilities if they are to be successful.

We were fast approaching the opening of school and the hurly-burly of activities which would immerse both Phil and me. He was now officially hired and in his office, learning from his secretary the myriad details of office management and routine. Teachers were stopping in to meet him and size him up. From my office, I could hear his hearty laugh as he engaged in the informal "getting acquainted" conversations essential to any new administrator presenting himself to a school community. Before the new school year closed down around both of us, I scheduled two more meetings with him on the days prior to teachers' return to school. In these meetings, I hoped to take his job description and, with his help, develop it into a much more detailed map of what he would be doing in the early months of the job. Prior to these meetings, I had prepared a list of specific tasks that I thought would occupy Phil for the first two months of this job. I had also prepared blank forms on which we could list the tasks, the time frame in which they had to be completed, and the sequence of steps involved in completing them.

I began the meeting by explaining that together we would use the blank forms to develop a map of tasks for the first two months. These maps would be made up of deadlines and sequences of steps to accomplish each task. During these two meetings, we used the two forms I had made up in advance. One (the "Overview" chart) forced us to view the interrelationship between tasks, steps, and deadlines. An early draft of this chart, which focused only on a few steps and deadlines in Phil's entry, is shown in Chart 7-1.

The second chart (Chart 7-2, "Sequence of Steps Chart") allowed us to record the detail of each step leading to the accomplishment of a particular entry task. Two examples follow. The letters of the alphabet on the time line beside each task on Chart 7-1 correspond with the steps on Chart 7-2. The generic tasks retain their original number, thus budget is number 1 and competency testing is number 4.

At the end of the second meeting, when we had completed the mapping and charting for the first two months, I asked Phil to do a last but important step in this activity. I asked him to translate our work into his personal calendar. Unless he took the initiative to block out time for each step in the different sequences we had developed, his calendar would quickly fill up in the early days of the school year with the demands of others in the school community who wanted his time. The arena of time is one in which the conflict would be fought between these specific expectations that I had developed for him and the expectations of other people.

This mapping and charting activity was one of the most important in which Phil and I engaged in planning his entry. Why? First, through the preparation I had done for these two meetings and then through the dialogue in

Chart 7-1 Overview

	AUG. 27	SEPT. 4	SEPT. 10	SEPT. 17	SEPT. 24	OCT. 1	OCT. 8	OCT. 15	OCT. 22	OCT. 29
1. Budget	ABC						*			*
2. Teacher absence		A						*E		
3. Student enrollment		A*	*	*						
4. Competency testing		A	BCD	*E						
5. Learning Resource Center			A	B						
6. Open house			A						*	*
7. Standing Committee										

Symbols:

A, B, C, etc. = steps in a task to be delineated on next chart.
  * = deadlines.

Chart 7-2   **Sequence of Steps**

	TASK TITLE: BUDGET (1)	
Date	*Sequence of Steps*	
(To be filled in with dates as we schedule)	A.	Interview accounts clerk
	B.	Meet school district finance officer
	C.	Read budget guidelines and procedures

	TASK TITLE: COMPETENCY TESTING (4)	
Date	*Sequence of Steps*	
(To be filled in with dates as we schedule)	A.	Read regents' handbook on competency testing
	B.	Interview director of guidance
	C.	Interview testing secretary
	D.	Interview principal
	E.	Make a decision about October testing date

them, I had brought concrete clarity to my general expectations of what he was to do in his early days on the job. When we concluded, I felt confident that, unlike my experience with my previous assistant, I had developed and then communicated clearly my specific expectations for his performance. This process of refining the general expectations of the job description into the concrete terms of day-to-day experience was one that I hoped would continue.

A second reason for the importance of this mapping and charting activity was that it began the sorting out and separating of my role from my assistant's role. This separation happened unavoidably as we mapped specific steps to accomplish each task.

A third consequence of the mapping and charting activity was that it helped in the development of my new assistant's understanding of how the major parts of his job fit into the whole administrative structure. We were able to clarify the overlap between parts of a particular task for which he had responsibility and parts for which administrative bodies had responsibility. For example, the Learning Resource Center staff, which was Phil's direct responsibility, had major responsibilities for our competency testing program, for which he was also responsible. The listing of the steps in mapping and charting helped to clarify how these "fit" together.

A last, and important, consequence of the mapping and charting was that it began a delegation process I hoped would serve as a model for our continuing work together. Mapping and charting not only told Phil what he should do but gave him specific directions on how to do it. Through this process, Phil and I avoided "either/or" binds in our work together that could have trapped us. One of these "either/or" binds would have led me to *either* give Phil "his head" and assume that he knew how to do a task I delegated *or*, if he did not finish it, do it for him. Mapping and charting helped us to avoid that trap by making explicit that delegating responsibility can mean not only describing what has to be done but also how it should be done.

Through this delegation process, Phil and I avoided a second "either/or" bind. Delegation is ordinarily one-way communication. Either I told Phil what to do, or he reported back that a task was accomplished or not accomplished at the deadline. Mapping and charting was a procedure which forced both of us to put in front of one another our best pictures of steps leading to deadlines for completing work, *before* we acted. By exposing our best scenario in an established format, we opened it to question, analysis, and revision. We forced one another toward clarity while producing a product (the "Sequence of Steps" chart, chart 7-2) which allowed us to monitor our progress.

In effect, mapping and charting established methods for delegation of work which allowed Phil and me to break the either/or pattern of most delegatory interaction. The steps in that pattern were:

Setting the task.   Through memos and meetings I communicated to Phil specific tasks I wanted him to accomplish and wanted him to question and present new data which could result in redefinition of tasks.

Review of steps.   As in the mapping and charting activity, we met together to outline a series of steps to accomplish a task and the sequence in which the steps were to be done.

Setting of time lines.   Without our agreeing on a clear time frame, tasks could drag on indefinitely and interminably.

Ongoing review.   This step, too, was essential to mutual participation in the delegation process. We both used these reviews as checkpoints. I could be assured that Phil was doing what I wanted him to do, and I could also offer him interim feedback on how he was doing it. He, in turn, could ask me questions about both the what and the how of my charted task work. In the process of this exchange, we both could take into account unpredicted events that would force us to alter the steps in a process.

Accountability. As I have indicated before, one of the unique features of this delegation process was that it asked Phil to be accountable not only for what was done, but for how it was done. This process, again, worked both ways. Since we both knew ahead of time how one another planned to proceed, we could each hold the other accountable.

Through the steps of this delegation process, then, I could define my authority as principal in operational terms for my assistant. Through the process, Phil knew that he was not an independent actor in how he defined his roles and responsibilities in the school. Thus, I avoided the problem which I created with my previous assistant in which my own lack of direction and confusion about direction enabled him to carve an independent role for himself as assistant principal. Yet, the mutual exchange of the delegation process gave my new assistant opportunities to respond to the direction and structure which I set forth for him, to present problems with them, and to participate in helping to change them.

Building Bridges To Key People In The Organization

Information is power for administrators. Almost always, we have to act on incomplete information. We never know, for example, what precisely happens in that moment of conflict between teacher and student. We listen to the different versions and make a decision based on our best guess about what happened. More and better quality information increases our chances of making effective decisions. But just as the quantity and quality of information we get is important, so is the quantity and quality of information we give. Particularly in moments of crisis, we must have networks of people in the organization through which we disseminate information so that those we lead can make sense of what we are doing.

Opening these two-way bridges of communication was essential for my new assistant principal in his early weeks. As quickly as possible, Phil needed to tap into the "grapevine," that network of informal sharing that characterizes any organization. Good data would be necessary to his accurate interpretation of events and effective decision making. In addition, these two-way bridges were essential to helping the school organization understand my new assistant's role. In order to enhance his effectiveness, the organization needed good data—specifically, a clear and accurate sense of the new role definition of this assistant principal.

"Bridge building" must be done through both formal and informal structures. Members of the Interview Committee, of course, were key resources in helping Phil become part of the informal network of school communication. They were the people in the organization who had the most and the best information about the new structure of his role, as well as the changes in my assumptions about it. At the end of our screening process, each felt some commitment to Phil. Obviously, some felt this more than others. But, in our last meeting, most committee members acknowledged and claimed their responsibility to try to make our new assistant principal's entry successful. Some members of the committee took up that responsibility with a special zeal. Through invitations to dinner and other social contacts, they tried not only to make him feel welcome but also to introduce him to others in the organization.

Screening committees make the process of selecting new administrators more complicated than it once was. Yet, when the committees work well, they can prove a tremendous advantage to the administrators' entry. Before beginning, new administrators have a group of key people who know them and the new role well. Even more important, to prove the wisdom of their selection, the committee members want new administrators to be successful. Helping to "build bridges," particularly to the school "grapevine," is an important way that some members of our screening committee tried to ensure this success.

As a supervisor, finally, I was the key person in helping my new assistant to "build bridges," particularly within the formal organizational structure. The authority for changing the structure of his role rested with me. The responsibility for communicating that changed structure and its new set of responsibilities, therefore, also rested with me.

One dilemma I faced in publicly describing changes in my subordinate's role was that, on the one hand, I needed to compare my new assistant's role with that of his predecessor. On the other, I did not want to reinforce the inevitable tendency of people in the organization to compare the two people. In responding to this dilemma, what I tried to do in the activities I shall describe was to depersonalize the discussion as much as possible. I did not share my internal struggle over my previous assistant's role. Instead, I shared the consequences of that struggle—its effect on my personal stance about the assistant principalship and the organizational changes that resulted, namely, the development of the approaches described here.

In order to promote the clarity in communication necessary, I included my assistant principal from the beginning of the school year in regular meetings with the following groups with whom he would have direct working contact:

Building administration.   With my prior assistant, I had scheduled no regular meetings between myself and my two assistant principals. Because of this lack of regular contact and discussion of role relationships, problems had developed between us. I have discussed some of these problems as they occurred between me and Glen, my former assistant principal. They also occurred, to a lesser extent, between the two assistant principals. For example, in the area of management of the school, some confusion existed over which tasks belonged to one assistant and which to the other. I hoped, in setting up a weekly meeting of the three of us, to involve my returning assistant principal in the process of bringing concrete clarity to the responsibilities of my new assistant.

These meetings also served as an arena in which I could carry out with both my assistants the delegation process described earlier.

Department chairmen.   The most important people in the school with whom my new assistant would have regular contact were the department chairmen. Confusion in responsibilities between myself and my previous assistant occurred most acutely in our working contacts with this group of administrators. For example, my lack of clarity about the limits of his budgetary responsibilities allowed my previous assistant to move from the mechanical task of overseeing the processing of purchase orders by chairmen to the policy task of making decisions about what should be purchased. The department chairmen were equal partners in this confusion. Because, again, of my lack of clarity, they did not understand who, among their superordinates, was responsible for what.

During the first of my regular, weekly meetings with the group of department chairmen, I introduced my new assistant, explained that he would meet with us each week, and tried to make clear some of the changes in job responsibilities that would affect them. For example, I explained that Phil's budget responsibilities did not extend to making decisions about what would be purchased. The chairmen would have to get that approval from me. The other major area of reclarification that I described in this first meeting was my new assistant principal's schedule responsibilities. I told the chairmen that Phil had direct responsibility for student scheduling—all the processes that attended on student selection of courses. However, I held direct responsibility for teacher scheduling—a set of decisions about which courses to teach and which teachers would teach them.

Lively discussion followed my presentation of my new assistant's job responsibilities. Department chairmen asked many questions. Clearly, they had great concern about the job responsibilities of their supervisors. Questions from some suggested that they simply wanted to get the new arrange-

ment right. I devoted considerable time, then, in reiterating the changes as
clearly as I could and confirming whether or not these changes had been
heard correctly. Questions from other chairmen, though, indicated that
though they understood the nature of the change in my assistant's role, they
were puzzled as to why it had occurred. In the facial expressions and the
tones of voice of the people asking these questions, I thought I heard other
questions that the chairmen were not asking directly: Was I dissatisfied with
my previous assistant? Was I trying to reduce the status of my assistant
principal in order to enhance my own power? In the politics of our school,
some chairmen, I knew, viewed a strong assistant principal as a way to keep a
check on a strong principal. The clear limits I was introducing into the
organizational relationships, then, closed down opportunities to exploit the
confusion between my role and that of my assistant by asking him to make
decisions.

I tried to answer these stated and unstated concerns by clearly and unam-
bivalently saying that dissatisfaction with my previous assistant was not the
way to make sense of these changes. He was a talented administrator who
had done an exceptional job for the school. The problem I was describing in
our organizational relationships was really mine. I was responsible for what I
now viewed as vagueness and confusion in role responsibilities. And I had
the authority and responsibility to clarify that confusion. Since I believed the
organization would run more efficiently and more effectively with greater
clarity, I was, therefore, making these changes. I was, it is true, putting
limits around my assistant's role. But I was also putting limits around my
own. Even though he would report to me on issues of students' scheduling,
for example, the organizational structure I was imposing also meant that I
would not directly interfere in an issue of a student's scheduling between, for
example, department chairmen and my new assistant. Finally, this clearer
statement of job responsibilities was intended to help department chairmen
since they would know more clearly which of us to go to about what issues.

At the conclusion of this meeting, I reminded everyone that Phil would be
attending these weekly sessions and that an ongoing review of how these
organizational changes were working would occur.

Guidance counselors.   The other key group with whom Phil would interact was the group of guidance counselors. In the first of our regular meetings
in the year, I, again, introduced him to the counselors and tried to define the
extent of his responsibility for scheduling and the extent to which that responsibility remained with me. The scheduling issue here was more complex
than with the department chairmen. At the beginning of the school year, we
were refining the schedule that we had developed in the previous year.

Because of the incredible wealth of detailed information I had from the process in the previous spring, and that Phil did not have, I explained to the counselors that I would keep control of the student scheduling throughout the early weeks of the year. However, later in the fall when we began the student scheduling for the next year, my new assistant would have the direct administrative responsibility for working with the counselors.

Throughout the fall, then, in our meetings with the counselors, my new assistant was in a position in relation to me that did not occur in any other public arena. He was an apprentice, learning the set of complexities involved in supervising the student scheduling process for a school of 1,700. This apprenticeship role was one that he accepted willingly. Though he was an experienced administrator, he had not worked on a high school schedule before. He acknowledged to me that he felt some anxiety about the range of tasks involved. Working alongside me as an "apprentice" would enable him to learn the tasks without having to take full responsibility immediately.

I think these "bridge-building" activities, overall, went well. In retrospect, though, I wish that my assistant and I had thought through more carefully his role in these initial meetings. Quite rightly, I had taken the responsibility for explaining the changes in role. In planning the meetings, however, I had only thought about what I would say and do. I had not thought about, nor had I talked with Phil about, what he would say and do. As a result, in both the department chairmen's meeting and the counselors' meeting, there was some awkward fumbling between us. Since some people would view this new assistant as having reduced status, I was anxious that he be able to exercise some legitimate authority even in these meetings. He was, of course, even more anxious among a group of strangers, one of whom was his boss and the others were those he would supervise. In the working agenda of both meetings, there were places for Phil to take an active role in the meetings that would have signaled his new job responsibilities, relieved our anxieties, and reduced the awkward fumbling that occurred when I tried to involve him in the meetings spontaneously.

Making Sense And No Sense

"Custodians know before I do!" Among some principals I know, this statement is a recurring joke, a humorous way to deal with the anxiety we all feel about "getting caught" without information we readily need to make sense of events, to make decisions. Most of us, as administrators, have a voice inside that shrieks at us when we "get caught" in this way. It yells, "You should know!" Without the information we need to make sense of discrepancies we experience, we feel surprised, we feel vulnerable, we may even feel ashamed. Thus, we tend to hide these moments rather than explore the discrepancies and find how to make sense of them.

In our meetings prior to the beginning of school, I had encouraged Phil to bring to our regular meetings any situations in which he was having difficulty "making sense." I told him that I felt it was important that we discuss discrepancies between expectations we had set and his experience of the reality of the school. I expected he would get discrepant information as he heard from various constituencies in the school what they expected of him. Some of those expectations had to be different from mine. Rather than hiding the puzzlement and pain of these discrepancies or unilaterally redefining his job in terms of those expectations, I wanted him to feel comfortable bringing discrepancies to me and exploring them.

In the early days of the year we met together frequently and at length. Generally, these meetings occurred late in the afternoon when everyone else had gone home and we had time to survey the wreckage of the day or to celebrate its triumphs.

In these early meetings, Phil did share an example of a situation in which he, and then, I were not able to "make sense." Within a few weeks of the start of school, he told me one afternoon that he simply did not have enough to do. He was on schedule in terms of accomplishing the tasks we had charted; he was making his way in meeting people around the school. But he found himself sitting in his office at times with nothing to do.

I was caught off-balance by this startling information. Given the length of the list of tasks I had prepared, I never expected that he would feel underworked! After all the work we had both put into planning and organizing his entry into the school, I thought he would be immersed in his maps and charts at least until November. I simply did not know how to make sense of this information at first. I thought that perhaps he was uncomfortable with the learning activities that were such a large part of his entry activities and that he needed more reassurance that I really meant it when I had said that learning was more important to me than doing in these early activities he was undertaking. I told him, then, that I felt he was doing what he should be and accomplishing exactly what was necessary at this point in his entry into the job.

As I thought about his feeling of being underworked and tried to observe this phenomenon in succeeding days, though, I began to make sense of it in at least two new ways. Our offices are adjacent, so I was able to observe Phil. First, I noticed that he seemed to spend much time in his office alone, working at his desk. This behavior contrasted sharply with that of his predecessor who was often, even usually, out of his office during the school day. I remembered a comment that one of the central office administrators made to me during the entry phase of my previous assistant. This administrator had sarcastically asked me if my assistant at that time was doing any work since he seemed to spend so much time walking through the halls greeting people. I remembered that at the time I did not pay attention to this warning. I justified my assistant's actions as simply "making himself visible," an activity which most of us assume is important for all school administrators.

I now considered, however, that my former assistant's absence from his office during the day was a consequence of his attempts to make himself into the ombudsman for the school. I did not, of course, formulate that conception of his role until much later, until I had consciously realized how his definition of his job was in conflict with my own. I now realized why I had underestimated the time Phil had available. Since he was not acting as an ombudsman for students and teachers in the halls, he could do work for me!

This perspective on Phil's sense of being underworked was one way that I came to understand his working alone in his office. The other perspective was that people simply were not bringing problems to him. He certainly was available in his office, yet people were not going in to him with the usual list of routine complaints that a school organization spawns from day to day. People did not yet know him well enough to trust that he could or would get things done. They did not yet know if they could rely on him to resolve their problems. In these early weeks of school, he was an unknown quantity. Since he had not yet established his legitimacy, people preferred to bring their problems to me or to the other assistant principal. Since many of these complaints involved issues of schedule, and since I had kept control of the schedule temporarily, their choice was appropriate. I could not very well refer them back to my new assistant who simply did not have the backlog of necessary information to help. But I had again underestimated the time my new assistant would have available since he would not be asked to deal with these small problems.

Shortly after making these discoveries, I shared them with Phil. With great delight I began to give him more tasks to do. I received almost immediate confirmation that he could handle more work through his responsiveness to these new tasks. In the previous school year, for example, I had done a survey of faculty to gather data on the specific amount of time teachers give each week to various activities of teaching. Analyzing and interpreting results from this survey could be important to my attempts to persuade the community how demanding a job teaching is, how important it was to try to keep the present staffing levels in spite of budgetary problems. Within a week of delegating this task to my new assistant, he had a chart of results on my desk.

This example, and there were others, showed Phil's understanding of the importance of exploring discrepancies between the expectations we had set and his experience of the reality of the school. I felt pleased that he had demonstrated his capacity for testing and inquiring in this way. In addition I felt pleased that I had created the conditions in which he felt he could bring forward examples of "no sense," rather than simply hiding them. He understood that only through examining the "no sense" could we adjust his job description and our entry plan to fit the new situations he was encountering.

Expanding Responsibilities: The Administrative Calendar

At the end of October, the initial phase of Phil's entry ended. The tasks which I had mapped and charted with him prior to the opening of school were now nearly completed. Without exception, he had accomplished them well. I now faced a decision about how to proceed. Because of the success and ease with which he accomplished not only the initial tasks but the subsequent ones I had given him, another detailed round of mapping and charting tasks and activities seemed unnecessary. On the other hand, I wanted to continue the delegation process which we had begun with the mapping work and which I felt was working well, helping me to provide clarity in my expectations for Phil.

To resolve this dilemma, I turned to a concept that I and my department chairmen had first heard about from our consultant. He had told us about an administrative calendar, which is fundamentally different from the usual school or school system calendar. In purpose, the calendars with which we are all familiar are static. They simply attempt to set dates, deadlines. The administrative calendar, in contrast, attempts not only to set on a time line *what* will be done—dates and deadlines by which tasks must be accomplished—but also to describe *who* will do the tasks, *how* they will be done, and *what* the sequence of steps will be. The administrative calendar, then, is a process calendar. As such, it can help an organization to inquire into its own structure. Through building the calendar, the organization thinks through how people in different roles and responsibilities interrelate.

I now saw the concept of this administrative or process calendar as a way to extend—at a more general, organizational level involving more people—the mapping and charting work I had done with Phil in the narrower, more specific scope of his work in the first two months. Within the structure of the administrative calendar, I could continue the work of clarifying my expectations for my assistant and holding him accountable. In addition, if the structure of the calendar extended to clarifying the intricate and interlocking responsibilities of various administrative roles in the organization, then this work would certainly help the organization to learn and improve.

I proposed the possibility of an administrative calendar to Phil, explaining it as an extension of our mapping and charting activities to the larger group of administrators. After some discussion, he saw that if we could develop a detailed and explicit process calendar, he would know what I expected of him for the rest of the year as well as what the other administrators expected of him.

We began the process by reintroducing the concept of the administrative calendar at a meeting of the department chairmen. The chairmen had understood the rationale for the calendar from our consultant's description earlier. They readily saw the advantages that its clarity could provide us. We then outlined the steps for planning the calendar to the chairmen:

1. Identification—by the chairmen—of the administrative tasks which require a clear differentiation of interlocking role responsibilities.

2. Detailed and specific development—by the chairmen—of the steps involved in how each task is accomplished.

3. Identification—by the chairmen—of who in the organization is responsible for each step.

4. Identification of deadlines—by Phil and me—on which tasks had to be completed in order for the organization to successfully do its work.

5. Discussion and modification by the group of department chairmen, Phil, and me of these tasks and steps. That discussion would focus on questions of completeness—Is every necessary step listed?—and on questions of sequence—Are the steps in the appropriate order?

6. Placement of the various tasks and steps into an integrated sequence on a time line—by Phil and me—with tentative dates and deadlines.

7. Discussion of questions about whether sequences of steps for different administrative tasks interlocked properly; whether dates and deadlines could be adjusted to spread work out more evenly over the year; whether the administrative calendar we had fleshed out was possible, given the limits on everyone's time and energy; and if not, where we could cut either tasks or steps.

8. Final publication of the calendar to members of the group by my assistant.

After setting forth this plan for building the calendar, we asked members of the group to write a memo to my assistant within a week, accomplishing the tasks set forth in steps 1 through 3 above. After Phil and I had compiled that material, and added the deadlines called for in step 4, we would have the discussion described in step 5, and then proceed through to step 7.

Our discussion with the guidance counselors, the other administrative

group whom we would involve in the administrative calendar, was more
lengthy. They had never heard of an administrative calendar, and we had to
walk them slowly through the rationale for the process calendar, contrasting
it with the usual static school calendar.

Some counselors immediately saw the benefit of the clarity the calendar
could bring to questions of who does what and when in the organization.
They also perceived that the calendar would give more, vital information to
every member of the organization about *how* various tasks were done and by
whom. They expressed considerable interest, for example, in knowing how
chairmen accomplished the tasks involved in setting teachers' schedules,
because those tasks interlocked with their work in student scheduling.

In the meeting with counselors, we outlined the same steps that we had
set forth for department chairmen for building the calendar. Again, we asked
them within a week to write a memo addressing steps 1 through 3.

Over the next few weeks, the entire administration worked its way
through the series of steps described above for building the calendar.
Slowly, through the processes of gathering data from the various people
involved and presenting it back to them, we constructed the skeleton of
steps, sequences, ownership, and deadlines which clarified the administrative tasks of the organization.

Two products resulted from this work: a set of Time Line and Activity
charts and a Monthly Process Calendar. An example of the first product is
shown in Chart 7-3 for the task of evaluating teachers. The second product,
not included here, the Monthly Process Calendar, shows the deadline dates
and activity steps for key administrative processes.

In my discussions with Phil about our use of the administrative calendar as
a tool in our relationship, he described three major consequences that he felt
resulted from this work. First, building the calendar worked as an extension
of the mapping and charting activities. The calendar gave him a road map he
could follow for the rest of the year. Second, the formal process of building
the calendar became another way that he interacted with other administrators and learned the history of administrative tasks and procedures in the
organization. He felt that the knowledge of that history helped him to make
fewer mistakes as he moved through the work of the year. Finally, he found
the calendar particularly helpful to him in planning his time and in assessing
what other tasks he could take on in addition to the ones on the calendar.

Conclusion

Clarifying the importance of norms and probing their historical
significance, mapping and charting tasks, building bridges to key people,

Chart 7-3   **Evaluation of Teachers Time Line and Activity Sequence**

	NONTENURED TEACHERS
10/31	Deadline for first observation/write-up of nontenured teachers by department chairman
12/21	Deadline for first observation/write-up of nontenured teachers by building administration
2/28	Deadline for final observation of nontenured teachers by department chairman and building administration
3/7	Drafts of progress reports on nontenured teachers by department chairman sent to principal
3/28	Teachers notified on recommendation for hiring/tenure by principal

	TENURED TEACHERS
10/1	Goal-setting conferences completed
5/2	Observations/write-ups and conferences completed
5/9	Chairman's PAP drafts sent to principal
6/20	Principal's final reports written and distributed

making sense and no-sense, and expanding responsibilities through an administrative calendar—these were the mechanisms which Phil and I used to attempt to make rational and systematic what I had learned through my experience could often be inappropriately intuitive and chaotic.

These techniques, as I have indicated throughout, enabled me to guide the development of Phil's job so that his responsibilities could complement my own. These entry activities also helped Phil to learn as quickly and thoroughly as possible what my expectations were and to take control of the job early in his term before it got control of him through the conflicting expectations of the various constituencies he served. Finally, these entry techniques helped us to communicate clearly and efficiently to the rest of the organization what Phil's job responsibilities were. As a result of this planned set of activities, both Phil and I felt that his entry into our school was efficient, satisfying, and effective.

Conclusion to Section Three: Supervising

All three cases demonstrate different techniques for avoiding the reflexive patterns of supervision which isolate both the supervisor and the supervisee. The techniques are based on an administrator's conscious recognition of the adverse effects of previous supervisory practices and a deliberate effort to change. In the case "Supervising a New Special Education Director," the techniques include regular rather than ad hoc meetings and assigned entry activities rather than none at all. The case "Supervision: The Giving and Receiving of Negative Information about Performance" shows a supervisor sharing and analyzing negative information rather than withholding it until it is too late for the supervisee to use it in changing behavior. The sharing of negative feedback permits the supervisor to test and change her assumptions and involves the supervisee as a participant rather than leaving them both isolated in their confusions.

In the case "Supervising a New Assistant Principal" we see three additional techniques for breaking supervisory patterns which leave the supervisee alone. Rather than leaving the new person alone to interpret abstract statements of job responsibility, the principal uses mapping and charting to make them concrete and time-bounded. Rather than leaving the new person alone to interpret her or his new role to the organization, the principal builds bridges to key people. And rather than leaving the supervisee alone to intuit or ferret out the vagaries of complex organizational process, the principal initiates the use of calendar planning to coordinate and focus diagnosis and definition.

The materials section which follows is designed to help readers break reflexive patterns of supervision and develop new, more collaborative supervisory methods.

EXERCISES ON SUPERVISING

Introduction

The exercises here fall into two categories: self-help exercises for practitioners and group exercises for use by instructors in classrooms, workshops, and seminars. Of the three self-help exercises, two invite readers to discover or confirm that they withhold data from others. This recognition of withholding precedes any conscious attempt to develop new interpersonal skill in giving and receiving negative information about performance to new supervisees early enough in their entry to facilitate efforts to change and succeed. It is beyond the scope of this book to do more than introduce a reader to the skills of giving and receiving negative information, but we provide references for pursuing in-depth work.[1] The third of the self-help exercises focuses on how to structure and present a set of task responsibilities, including entry activities to a new supervisee.

There are two instructor's exercises: one, a set of role-playing exercises which focuses on the giving and receiving of negative information, and, the

---

[1] See Jentz and Wofford, *Leadership and Learning: Personal Change in a Professional Setting*, McGraw-Hill, New York, 1979; also Robert Bolton, *People Skills*, Prentice-Hall, Englewood Cliffs, N.J., 1979.

other, a role-playing exercise which focuses on structuring the work of a new supervisee.

Self-Help Exercise: Supervising, Number 1

Analyzing A Difficult Interaction

Purpose

To discover or confirm that individuals do withhold information about other people's performance.

To set the stage for inquiry into the hows and whys of giving and receiving negative information about performance early enough during new supervisees' entry so that they have time to use it before others in the organization, including the supervisor, form a negative "set" toward the supervisees' performance.

Directions

1. Please identify a challenging interaction with one individual which you have already experienced, preferably with a new supervisee.
2. Write a paragraph about the purpose of the interaction, the setting, the people involved, and your hopes for its outcome.
3. Divide the page lengthwise in half. Along the right side record the dialogue as you remember it (or taped it), labeling the actors' dialogue as you would in a play.
4. Along the left-hand side, record your internal dialogue, the private thoughts and feelings as they occurred relative to the dialogue and other interpersonal events.[2] (See the accompanying example, "The Case of the Message Undelivered," of how to carry out directions 1 to 4.)
5. Circle the instance in your case of the greatest discrepancy between what you said and what you thought and felt.
6. State in one sentence the content of the information you were withholding.
7. State in one sentence (or one word) the feeling you were withholding.
8. Finish this sentence: "If I had conveyed the information I was with-

[2] We learned this methodology from Argyris and Schön, *Theory in Action*, Jossey-Bass, San Francisco, 1974.

holding, the other person would have ———————————————————
———————————————————————————————————.”

9.   Finish this sentence: "If the other person had ———————————
     ———————————————, I would be afraid the other person would.
     ————————————————————————————————————.”

THE CASE OF THE MESSAGE UNDELIVERED

Setting.   A director is concerned about the deteriorating performance of a teacher. During the past four months this teacher's absenteeism and tardiness have risen sharply, and her interactions with the children have become increasingly lackadaisical. The director calls the teacher in, intending to inform her that unless she improves her performance, she will have to fire her. After skirting the issue by talking about the children, the director finally gets to the point.

Director's Thoughts

Well, here we go! I can't beat around the bush any longer. But maybe I shouldn't make this too devastating. I should cushion the blow a bit and then gradually lay it all out.

I sure have. The teachers are really fed up with having to cover for you and about your bad attitude. But I don't want this to sound like a conspiracy, like no one cares about you.

Dialogue

DIRECTOR: I've been meaning to talk to you about your work. For the past two years you've been a valuable member of the staff, and I've really enjoyed working with you. But lately I've noticed your enthusiasm seems to be waning.

TEACHER: I have been having some problems with my marriage, but I've tried not to let this affect my work here. Have you been getting complaints about me?

DIRECTOR: I didn't say that, but I have noticed you've been calling in sick a lot lately.

TEACHER: Yes, I guess I have. But some mornings when I get into fights with my husband, I don't think I'd be in the right mood to be with children. Don't you agree?

Oh, boy! I was afraid it was something like that! The children really do suffer when they don't know who their teacher will be from one day to the next. But with those problems, probably the last thing you need is for me to dump on you, too.

Oh, yes, yes, yes! Your performance has been perfectly dismal. But maybe if I just give you a pat on the back and a bit of encouragement, you will shape up. Then if things don't improve, I can talk turkey with you later.

DIRECTOR: Well, you're probably right. But on the other hand, when you do come in, you don't seem to get as excited about working with the kids as you used to.

TEACHER: Are you trying to tell me I'm not doing my job?

DIRECTOR: Oh, no, no, no! I mean, you seem to care very much for the kids and to plan some good activities for them. But there's still much room for improvement. Maybe we could send you to some workshops to get you fired up again. All right?

When we analyze these kinds of cases what we find is that most people withhold information as an act of unilateral protection of the other person. Such a stance of protecting others usually results from a wish to protect one's self from feeling or thinking in certain ways or being perceived by others as different from the ways we like to be seen. If you find you are intrigued by the content presented here, we suggest you examine two books: Argyris and Schön, *Theory in Action,* Jossey-Bass, San Francisco, 1974, and Jentz and Wofford, *Leadership and Learning: Personal Change in a Professional Setting,* McGraw-Hill, New York, 1979.

Self-Help Exercise: Supervising, Number 2

Analysis of Patterns of Withholding Information: Preparation for Sharing Withheld Information

Purpose

To analyze your patterns of withholding information from a supervisee, either a current or a past one.

To prepare yourself to face a new supervisee with withheld information about the supervisee's performance so that you create conditions for mutual learning.

Overview

This exercise is based on a distinction between two categories of information which most supervisors implicitly used in organizing their observations and judgments about a supervisee. Those two categories are information about the performance of the supervisee and information about the supervisee's ability to learn through interaction with the supervisor.

The exercise is divided into the following four parts:

  I.   Analyzing Information about the Supervisee's Performance
  II. Analyzing Information about the Supervisee's Ability to Learn
 III. Reviewing Background Information
 IV. Constructing Your Plan

I. ANALYZING INFORMATION ABOUT THE SUPERVISEE'S PERFORMANCE

A. Rank the person's overall performance compared with either your expectations or past performances by other supervisees:

TOP 25%	TOP HALF	BOTTOM HALF	BOTTOM 25%

B. Briefly describe concretely one or more key incidents or concerns which form the basis of your opinion of this person's overall performance. Then, in the box attached to the information in the right-hand column, estimate for each incident or concern the percentage of information which falls into each of the categories (each incident should add up to 100%):

1.

	Written and shared
	Written but withheld
	First-hand observations and shared
	First-hand observations but withheld
	Reported from trusted others and shared
	Reported from trusted others but withheld
	Rumor, hearsay
	Overall, personal impression and shared
	Overall, personal impression but withheld

100%

2.

Written and shared	
Written but withheld	
First-hand observations and shared	
First-hand observations but withheld	
Reported from trusted others and shared	
Reported from trusted others but withheld	
Rumor, hearsay	
Overall, personal impression and shared	
Overall, personal impression but withheld	

100%

3.

Written and shared	
Written but withheld	
First-hand observations and shared	
First-hand observations but withheld	
Reported from trusted others and shared	
Reported from trusted others but withheld	
Rumor, hearsay	
Overall, personal impression and shared	
Overall, personal impression but withheld	

100%

II. ANALYZING INFORMATION ABOUT THE SUPERVISEE'S ABILITY TO LEARN

A. Briefly describe this person's interpersonal behavior which might affect—positively or negatively—her or his capacity to learn through interaction with you. Then, in the column on the right, check whether you have tested directly your assumptions about each personal characteristic listed below (for example, if you see a person jumping at you to argue every point, and missing the whole message, you could test your perception by saying, "Over the three months of our working together, I repeatedly see you jump at me to argue points and thereby miss the major messages I'm trying to send. This frustrates and angers me because I'm left feeling mistrust of your capacity to listen in other settings, as well . . .").

	TESTED	NOT TESTED
1.		
2.				
3.				

B. Briefly describe key attempts (if any) you have made to help this person act on your concerns. Describe, also, whether this approach worked or did not work, and why (see Chapter 6 for examples of attempts made by the supervisor).

1. _____

_____

_____

_____

2. _____

_____

_____

3. _____

_____

_____

C. On the basis of your attempts to help the supervisee (listed above), answer each question listed below by writing *Yes*, *No*, or *Maybe* in each box. After answering each question, ask yourself whether or not you have withheld or shared the information in each category with the supervisee. Circle your answer to each question *if* you think you have explicitly shared the information. An example of explicitly sharing the information with a supervisee about your conclusion that the supervisor cannot learn in a particular area would be: "I know you have committed yourself to changing and have tried, diligently." (Here you would list concretely the efforts made by the person.) "But you haven't gotten results. For whatever the reasons, you seem not to have the capacity to change in this way. Do you see yourself this way?"

IS THE OTHER PERSON					DO I		
Aware of my concerns about her/him?	Interested in working on them?	Committed to changing?	Capable of change?	Recognize the right problem?	Have interest in working on it?	Have the commitment to pursue it?	Have the competence to make a difference?

III. REVIEWING BACKGROUND INFORMATION

A. List information from the personnel file which might influence your success in working with this person. (For example, check recommendations from prior jobs or education for clues to understanding current difficulties.) Check whether each item has been explicitly discussed previously or left tacit.

	TALKED ABOUT RECENTLY	NOT TALKED ABOUT RECENTLY
1.		
2.		
3.		

B. List other information from your own knowledge of this person which might influence your success in giving and receiving negative information with this person. Check whether each item has been explicitly talked about or left tacit, unspoken.

TALKED ABOUT

NOT TALKED ABOUT

1. _____

_____

_____

2. _____

_____

IV. CONSTRUCTING YOUR PLAN

1. Set up the conference in advance, not on the spur of the moment (do not piggyback this kind of conference on some other event).

2. State the unusual content of the conference: sharing withheld data rather than working on day-to-day problems, for example.

3. Set up at least two, perhaps a series of meetings.

4. State that you have information in two categories of learning and performance which you want to share.

5. Claim personal responsibility for the problem as *yours* (you withheld the data), perhaps saying why you withheld data and then describing what has happened which changed your mind from thinking that withholding was a good idea to a bad idea.

6. Set out your agenda for presenting and discussing this information.

7. Give your current assumptions ("bottom line," tentative conclusions which follow from the information you plan to present) in both categories of learning and performance.

8. Review the data which has led you to your current assumptions; as you present the data, be concrete where possible and attach to this data the feelings evoked in you by the data, as well as the consequences to you (not the other person).

9. After the supervisee responds, force yourself to repeat back what the supervisee said, in feeling as well as content, *before* you move on (examples of this skill abound in Chapter 6).

10. Seek mutual recognition of problems; jointly analyze, seek understanding; plan steps for improvement; set steps in a time frame with follow-up meetings scheduled in advance.

11. Close the meeting by using a continuum of some kind to illustrate how much of the supervisee's total performance you have focused on in this meeting; for example: "I am pleased with 80 percent of your performance; today I focused on only and exclusively the 20 percent which concerns me." Briefly review those categories of performance where you are pleased with the supervisee's performance.

12. Role-play and discuss with a trusted colleague your outlined plan before attempting it in practice.

Self-Help Exercise: Supervising, Number 3

Mapping a Supervisee's Task Responsibilities and Entry Activities

Purpose

To guide a supervisor in a joint effort with the new supervisee to create a graphic picture of the supervisor's expectations for the supervisee's entry activities and task responsibilities.

Directions

The steps listed below set forth a series of private planning activities which you test with your new supervisee and then modify. Because of this two-step process, some repetition occurs in the steps.

PRIVATE PLANNING

1. Rewrite your job description for the new supervisee, using the model presented in Chapter 2, "Hiring a New Assistant," pp. 43–45, (see as well Appendix III-1, pp. 239–241); force yourself to subdivide each major responsibility into two subcategories which define decision-making power: "Direct Responsibility," "Assistance to (title of supervisor)"; then state concretely the subtasks which fall within each of these two decision-making categories.

2. Using this new job description, do some preliminary mapping and charting (see "Mapping and Charting Tasks," pp. 176–181):

    (a) Develop a "Sequence of Steps Chart" for each subtask (see pp. 177–179);
    (b) Develop an "Overview Chart" (see pp. 177–179).

3. Do some preliminary planning of your new supervisee's entry interviews; identify the person or persons with whom the supervisee will have to work on each subtask.

4. Review your new job description, "Sequence of Steps Chart" and "Overview Chart." Decide which tasks and/or which steps and time lines in accomplishing the tasks can be changed if your new supervisee has new information or a better idea.

5. Before meeting with your new supervisee, assign the reading of Chapter 7, "Supervising a New Assistant Principal," pp. 167–191 of this book.

PRESENTATION AND TESTING OF YOUR PRIVATE PLANNING

1. In your initial meeting with your new supervisee, to begin developing an entry plan:

   (a) Set up regular supervisory sessions to run throughout the year; set the dates in each of your calendars.

   (b) Define your expectations for entry and the dates of the entry period; set an end point for entry.

   (c) Present an overview of the content (developed during "Private Planning") which you plan to present in future meetings with your supervisee.

   (d) Set up your performance evaluation process and schedule dates for your evaluation sessions.

2. In subsequent sessions:

   (a) Present your revised job description and your preliminary charts; differentiate between those tasks which are nonnegotiable and those on which you invite modification in response to new information or argument; engage your new supervisee in additional mapping and charting.

   (b) Review with the supervisee "Clarifying Norms," pp. 169–176; set up with her or him a schedule of interviews, feedback sessions, and visits to key departments or schools.

   (c) Build bridges to other parts of the organization for your new supervisee, through both formal and informal channels (see "Building Bridges to Key People in the Organization," pp. 181–185).

   (d) Expect and require the supervisee to present and analyze data with you that the supervisor has collected about the whats and hows of the organization.

   (e) Encourage your new supervisee to bring situations of "no-sense" to your supervisory session for discussion (see "Making Sense and No-Sense," pp. 185–188).

   (f) When you reach the end of entry activities, review the effectiveness of the effort, perhaps with members of the screening committee; plan additional activities if needed (see "Expanding Responsibilities: The Administrative Calendar," pp. 188–190).

Instructor's Exercise: Supervising, Number 1

Exploring the Gaps between the Intended and the Spoken Word

Purpose

To test the degree and quality of discrepancy between the intended and the spoken word.

Setting

Any interaction between supervisor and supervisee where the supervisor must give and get negative information about performance.

Directions

1. Create as a role play a supervisory situation in which one person will be the supervisee and another the supervisor; have the class agree on the context and the basic details of the supervisory situation.

2. Ask the supervisee to leave the room and ask the supervisor to explain concretely to the class what (s)he hopes to accomplish in the upcoming session and what (s)he intends to say to the supervisee to accomplish the objectives (tape-record this presentation about intentions, and tape-record the role play); as well, ask the supervisor how (s)he will "test" what the supervisee's understanding of the interaction is all about.

3. Ask the supervisor to leave the room.

4. Ask the class to observe the interaction and specifically to watch for the congruence or discrepancy between what the person playing the supervisor *actually* says to the supervisee and what (s)he indicated ahead of time (s)he *intended* to say. Have them note what was shared and what withheld; as well, have them note whether or not and how the supervisor tested to find out if (s)he knows what the supervisee's experience of the interaction is; if the supervisor did test for the information, have them note how the supervisor worded the test. Give them the form shown in Chart III-1 to use in completing these tasks.

5. Ask the supervisor and supervisee to return and allow the session to go forward.

6. After the role play is complete, ask all persons in the class including the two persons who role-played to use their notes (charts) to write, for a maximum of five minutes, an evaluation of the supervisor's effective-

ness in sharing negative information and testing what the other person heard.

7. Ask supervisor number 1 (S_1) to leave the room. Select a new supervisor (S_2) and ask her or him to read what (s)he wrote. Ask her or him to state to the class what (s)he intends to say to S_1 about S_1's performance in matching what was actually said to what S_1 had intended to say.

8. Ask the class to fill out the preobservational side of the charts (asking S_2's intentions).

9. Ask S_1 to return and S_2 to offer S_1 feedback.

10. Repeat this pattern for a third time asking for a new supervisor (S_3) who will in the absence of S_2 state what (s)he felt was inadequate about S_2's performance with S_1.

DIAGRAM

Supervisor 1 ⟶ Supervisee
Supervisor 2 ⟶ Supervisor 1
Supervisor 3 ⟶ Supervisor 2

11. Focus discussion of the three role plays on identifying the gaps which existed between each supervisor's intended and spoken words.

12. Assign *Theory in Action* and *Leadership and Learning: Personal Change in a Professional Setting* for further analysis of the patterns and consequences of withholding data and for help in developing the skill to share rather than withhold data.

Instructor's Exercise: Supervising, Number 2

Testing Task Responsibilities and Entry Design

Purpose

To allow a supervisor to test the quality of her or his task responsibilities and entry design for a new supervisee in class before presenting it to the supervisee.

To produce new information for the supervisor which will lead to revision of the design.

Directions

1. Assign each class member to do the "Self-Help Exercise: Supervising, Number 3" for a new supervisee.

Chart III-1   Observing Attempts to Give and Receive Negative Information

PREOBSERVATIONAL	OBSERVATIONAL	
Intended	*Shared*	*Withheld*
Hoped to Accomplish:		

Intended to say: _____

TESTED:

UNTESTED:

2. Divide the class into small groups of three; divide each group of three into a supervisor, supervisee, and an observer; assign each supervisor the task of presenting her or his supervisor design for task responsibilities and entry at a simulated first formal session with the supervisee; the supervisor's presentation, an outline, should take no more than ten minutes and be followed by feedback from the supervisee, then the observer; repeat the procedure with the individuals switching roles; assign each class member to revise her or his entry design by the next class period.

3. Ask the same group of three class members to take turns presenting their revised designs a second time; after each presentation the feedback should focus on whether or not, and how, improvements have been made.

Conclusion

This book began with the assertion of a paradox: to create the kind of organizational climate in which people feel they can contribute and produce requires the use of that which is often thrown out in the effort to create such a climate—structure. The word "structure" is used in a generic sense to include four elements: (1) a stance toward collaboration which assumes the importance of testing one's assumptions about oneself and others and of carefully organizing people instead of expecting collaboration to emerge unplanned; (2) a set of methodologies by which to make operational the stance toward testing assumptions and organizing people; (3) a resulting plan, tested with and understood by those it involves, which defines who will do what in relation to whom, when, where, and why, and (4) an assertive management of the plan which takes charge of it, revising it, if necessary, utilizing all the previous steps to ensure that the revisions are tested and understood.

STANCE

If an administrator is to confront successfully the paradox about collaboration, the stance which we think is necessary can be illustrated through a series of statements which assert what not to do:

215

Don't believe that you know your own mind;

Don't believe that you know others' minds;

Don't believe that you can enter a system knowing the direction it needs;

Don't believe that you can afford to play it by ear, without a plan, and avoid being eaten up by the system;

Don't believe that structures must be used by administrators only to seek unilateral control; they can also be used to integrate collaborative inquiry and action.

METHODOLOGIES

The methodologies necessary to translate this stance, or set of attitudes, into action include the following, here asserted as a series of "Do's":

Engage in systematic introspection and public planning. Your reflexes will doubtless lead you to behavior that will be different from the way you think you behave. Utilize a methodology which forces you to examine your assumptions. One methodology pictured in this book is to analyze a discrete event for the assumptions which guided behavior. Another methodology is called mapping and charting or planning. It entails creating a time line, establishing deadlines and projected outcomes, then laying out the sequence of activities to arrive at and follow up on deadlines.

By taking the product of this private introspection, namely a plan, and presenting it to others, you can twice force yourself to test your assumptions before you act, first by finding out what is really entailed in your initial thinking and second by presenting your elaborated plan to others and inviting feedback.

Engage in systematic data collection and feedback. The methodology represented in almost every case in this book is data collection and feedback using interviews with individuals and group meetings. By analyzing and feeding back the information collected, you both validate the information and take people into account by imaginatively entering their view of the organizational world.

THE PLAN

A plan defines who will do what, in relation to whom, when, where, and why. Before being acted on, it is tested and revised in response to new information from those upon whom its implementation depends. Plans can organize work at a systemic level—how a system will be organized over six months to examine itself; at a group level—how a committee will be organized to conduct an activity; at a level of one-to-one interaction—how an individual goes about giving and receiving negative information. In all cases, a plan's purpose is to shape collaborative inquiry and decision making.

TAKING CHARGE OF THE PLAN

Once completed, the plan must be assertively managed. It will not run itself. Nor is it to be seen as cast in concrete. It will need active implementation, scrutiny for emerging problems, revisions which are fully tested and understood, and reassertion of the plan's importance as the best shared picture of a vehicle to guide collective action.

The paradox implicit in the phrase, "structured collaborative inquiry," is best confronted at a time of beginnings and by individuals who know: (1) how to go about getting to know themselves in the context of the new community/organization; and (2) how to go about getting the community/organization to examine itself, so that the future management and direction of the organization emerge from a mutual inquiry into current practice. Such an inquiry is a rejection of the reflexive way in which individuals and organizations begin a relationship. It is a rational attempt to enhance both the new person's and the organization's ability to learn and perform.

Afterword

by DALE G. LAKE

I knew before I received the manuscript for this book that the authors had high hopes for communicating with practitioners. For the most part they are, themselves, practicing administrators with a desire to share their experiences with their counterparts. It would be hard to imagine a practitioner who could not use this book (even under extreme time pressures) to design and implement a screening process, a start-up process, or a new supervision task. The writing achieves a uniform clarity and a level of detail which makes it truly useful.

What came as a complete surprise—indeed a shock, was that this book is a social psychology of the entry process! In the course of reading this book, I came to understand it as a book about theory as well as a book filled with helpful designs for practitioners. Even more importantly, it is a book filled with theory as practiced, not just as espoused (to use the distinction provided by Argyris and Schön, 1974). Much has already been said about its usefulness for practitioners, I want to say a few words about its potential for teaching.

Social psychologists, sociologists, and organization theorists have written volumes on the concept of norms. But, it is always very difficult to help the beginning student grasp how pervasive norms are in organizational life and how important they are. In this book we are presented not only with several

219

examples of important norms, but more importantly, with examples of how the failure to diagnose and accommodate to such norms ultimately led to the loss of a job and a sense of failure. In addition to showing graphically what organizational norms are and their import, the book shows how to *diagnose* the nature, norms, and needs of an organization. Persons trained to be change agents and organization-development specialists soon learn that their very survival depends on their ability to diagnose organizations. However, the authors of this book make just as strong a case that the line manager (i.e., superintendent, principal, and director) needs the ability to diagnose organizational conditions if he or she is to survive. I couldn't agree more!

Another conceptual issue which has raised all sorts of difficulty for social scientists is that of participative decision making. Historically, in discussing participation, theorists have written about dysfunctional polarities, such as authoritarian versus participative leadership; hidden versus open decisions. In this book, such polarities are easily integrated by pointing out, time and again, how structuring participation makes it possible for large groups of people to be involved without anyone giving away the right of management to make decisions. This is illustrated beautifully in the screening process developed for the superintendent search.

Currently, a great deal of research is being devoted to cognitive models in such areas as moral development, learning styles, and management styles. The authors of this book do a considerable amount of teaching about such cognitive models without ever using the word *model* or *cognitive*. The authors speak of learning to reflect on one's assumptions before "dumping" angry feelings on a new administrator; they also speak of "imagining" how the new teacher felt about the last evaluation and sharing such imaginings. Finally, they speak of "listening to my own private reactions while trying to make sense out of what is being said to me." In teaching about cognitive models, it is commonplace to refer to mental habits that evolve into a particular learning or management style. Such styles can become rigid, and in order to make them more flexible cognitive theorists teach precisely the same processes these authors do; namely, diagnose your own reactions, test your own assumptions, take the role of the receiver, share your reflections as well as your requests. Thus it becomes possible in reading this book to learn very basic skills for modifying cognitive style without being aware that this is what is happening. A marvelous tribute to the authors.

I would call a reader's attention to one last concept, equally difficult to teach in the abstract and yet cleverly managed in this book. The concept is feedback. Once again, volumes exist on this concept. And once again these authors make it a routine tool of the manager, whether the manager is collecting and feeding back information to an entire community, feeding back negative data to a finalist applicant for a new job, or feeding back data to administrative groups or a school committee, to name only a few examples.

Using an example of feedback not yet mentioned, I can make some generalizations on how to make feedback useful. In the case about giving and receiving negative information, the principal carefully analyzed and organized her information, imagined what its impact would be on the teacher, was direct in her presentation of negative findings, tested to see how the information was received and made sense of by the teacher, suggested helpful remedial activities, and, followed up to see that they were implemented. Moreover, the principal made feedback a two-way process by both giving good information to the teacher *and* inviting it from the teacher in order to change her own performance as a supervisor. Such activities represent an excellent general prescription for the use of feedback.

Finally, I was impressed with this book because it is a book about planning. In the chapters on screening, developing an entry plan, and supervising, we see excellent examples of operational planning. No matter how well courses on planning are taught, many practitioners leave such courses with the lingering, uneasy feeling that people on the "firing line" never have time for all that priority setting, charting, and writing. This book should help reduce such feelings. Further, with the details provided, it should help practitioners plan. There are abundant examples of people under pressure taking time to determine what they want to accomplish, by when, and with whom.

The authors want practitioners to use this book. I see a different purpose. I hope it will be used by teachers of administration, management, and organizational theory and practice. Used with the students who will be our future leaders, this book will do much to close the gaping distance between theory and practice.

Appendix I

Biographies of the Writers

Daniel S. Cheever, Jr.

Daniel S. Cheever, Jr., is Superintendent of Schools in Weston, Massachusetts. Previously, he held the position of Superintendent of Schools in Lincoln, Massachusetts. His work has focused on the management of declining enrollment, curriculum development and evaluation, long-range planning, energy conservation, and school closing.

Prior to becoming Superintendent, Dan served as Director of Project Development at Education Development Center (EDC) in Newton, Massachusetts. He also has been a classroom teacher and department chairman in schools in Massachusetts, North Carolina, and Pennsylvania. He is the author of several articles and case-studies and serves as a trustee of Milton Academy and Wheelock College.

A graduate of Harvard College, Dan also earned the master's and doctorate degrees from the Harvard Graduate School of Education.

Stephen B. Fisher

Stephen B. Fisher received his Ed.D. in Curriculum and Supervision from Teachers College, Columbia University. His undergraduate work was completed at Franklin College of Indiana and graduate work in elementary and secondary curriculum was completed at Xavier University and the University of Cincinnati.

He has worked as a classroom teacher at elementary, junior high, and high school levels. He has served as a building principal in Morristown, New Jersey, and Scarsdale, New York, and is presently Assistant Superintendent for Curriculum and Instruction in the Bedford Central Schools, Westchester County, New York.

Steve has been active in many professional organizations. He is a member of the Association for Supervision and Curriculum Development and has frequently served as a convention presenter. He serves on the executive board of the New York State Commissioners Advisory Committee on the Gifted and Talented. In addition, Steve is a member of Phi Delta Kappa, the American Association of School Administrators, and the School Administrators Association of New York State.

He has coauthored articles with Barry Jentz and Daniel Cheever that have appeared in *The National Elementary Principal*, *Educational Leadership*, and *The Executive Educator*.

Barry C. Jentz

Barry Jentz holds his B.A. from Kenyon College and an M.A.T. from Harvard Graduate School of Education. Beginning in 1966, he focused his attention on questions of personal and organizational learning, first through four years of training under the auspices of NTL, the National Training Laboratories, which made him a Professional Member in 1969, and second, through starting the Murray Road School in Newton, Mass. He left the Murray Road School in 1969 to pursue a career as a private organizational consultant.

From 1969 through the present, Barry has consulted with administrators, managers, and teachers on organizational issues in universities, school systems, corporations, professional firms, and government agencies. In 1973 he joined three other administrator-consultants in starting the Leadership and Learning Cooperative: An In-Service Program for School Leaders (LLC). Started with grants from the Carnegie Corporation of New York, LLC provided the framework for sustained consulting work with school administrators and for a rigorous study of how administrators can learn to lead. This study resulted in the book *Leadership and Learning: Personal Change in a Professional Setting*, coauthored with his colleague, Joan Wofford (McGraw-Hill, 1979).

Meredith Howe Jones

Although a zoologist by training, Meredith Howe Jones has been a junior high school principal for ten years. She is presently on leave from the principalship of the Joseph Brooks School in Lincoln, Massachusetts, in order to pursue her doctoral degree in Administration, Planning, and Social Policy at Harvard University Graduate School of Education. Her interest has focused on developing creative management techniques during a time of declining resources. She has successfully maintained staff morale and developed innovative school programs in the face of declining enrollment and rising cost. Meredith has presented numerous workshops on the principalship, middle school organization, and communication and conflict within schools.

Paul Kelleher

Currently, Paul Kelleher is Superintendent of Schools in Bedford, New York, though at the time of writing this book he was principal of Scarsdale High School, Scarsdale, New York. Previously, he was a junior high school assistant principal, and then a middle school principal in Massachusetts communities.

Paul graduated from Harvard College and holds a Master of Arts teaching degree from the Harvard Graduate School of Education. He began his career in education as a teacher of English at Newton High School, Newton, Massachusetts, and has had experience in writing book reviews and in teaching English curricular methods to beginning high school teachers.

Paul is a long-term participant in the programs of the Leadership & Learning, Inc.

Dale G. Lake

Dale Lake received his doctorate in education from Teachers College, Columbia University, in 1967. He is a certified psychologist and member of the American Psychological Association and the International Association of Applied Social Scientists. He has done extensive research in the field of applied behavioral science with the National Science Foundation, the National Institute of Education, and the Institute of Health Team Development. He has also studied the effects of planned change within school systems under grants from the United States Office of Education and the New

York State Education Department. He has consulted with educational and scientific associations, public school systems, federal agencies, and private organizations.

Dale has published research articles on concepts of planned organizational change, program evaluation, and staff development. In addition he has published two books: *Perceiving and Behaving* (Teachers College Press, 1970) and *Measuring Human Behavior: Assessment of Social Functioning* (Teachers College Press, 1972), with M. B. Miles and R. Earle.

William R. Torbert

Currently the Associate Dean responsible for the Graduate School of Management at Boston College, Bill Torbert took both his B.A. in Political Science and Economics and his Ph.D. in Administrative Sciences at Yale University, in 1965 and 1971, respectively. His administrative roles have included Associate Director, Yale Summer High School, 1965–66; Director, Yale Upward Bound, 1966–68; and President, The Theatre of Inquiry, Inc., since 1977. He has consulted to businesses and educational institutions.

He has also served as Assistant Professor, Southern Methodist University School of Business, 1970–72; Associate Professor, Harvard Graduate School of Education, 1972–76; and Associate Professor, Boston College School of Management, since 1978. In addition to articles and reviews, he has published three research books: *Being for the Most Part Puppets: Interactions among Men's Labor, Leisure, and Politics* (Schenkman, 1972); *Learning from Experience: Toward Consciousness* (Columbia University, 1973), and *Creating a Community of Inquiry: Conflict, Collaboration, Transformation* (Wiley, 1976). He is currently working on a book entitled *Creating an Improbable Future*.

Torbert is a member of the Academy of Management and of the Society for Values in Higher Education

Joan W. Wofford

Joan Wofford, who holds her B.A. from Bryn Mawr College and her M.A.T. from Yale University, has taught high school English and trained teachers in both suburban and urban schools. She was a teacher at Newton High School in Massachusetts and Cardozo High School in Washington, D.C., and a Master Teacher in the Yale University teacher training program and in the Cardozo Project in Urban Teaching, of which she was also a creator and manager.

Since 1967 Joan has pursued her interests in institutional innovation, organizational theory, and interpersonal learning, first as a staff member of OSTI, the Organization for Social and Technical Innovation, in Cambridge, Massachusetts, of which she became chief executive officer in 1973, and then as a partner in Leadership and Learning, Inc., in Lincoln, Massachusetts.

She teaches educational administration and organizational theory courses at Lesley College Graduate School in Cambridge, Massachusetts, and at Wheelock College Graduate School in Boston. She has also been for the past eight years an elected member of a local school board, serving twice as chairman of that body. Together with Barry Jentz, she coauthored the book *Leadership and Learning: Personal Change in a Professional Setting* (McGraw-Hill, 1979).

Appendix II

A Superintendent Search Process

Appendix II-1   Consultant's "Package"

CALENDAR OF SIGNIFICANT EVENTS

Feb. 17	Ads appear
Feb. 27–29	Constituent input collected
Feb. 29	Application forms mailed
Mar. 12	Consultant paper delivered
Mar. 20	School Board agrees on evaluation criteria
Mar. 21	Applications close
Apr. 1	Applicants reduced to 20 to 30
Apr. 14	Applicants reduced to 8 to 10
Apr. 14–25	Applicants interviewed and reduced to 6 to 8
Apr. 28–May 9	Interview semifinalists
May 15	Subcommittee reviews semifinalists
May 22	School Board selects three finalists
May 30–June 4	Interviews with finalists
June 5	School Board votes
June 13	Sign contract

MEMBERSHIP, TASKS, AND TIMETABLE FOR
THE ENTIRE SCHOOL BOARD

MEMBERSHIP:	All
MEETINGS:	February 7 Appoint subcommittees
	March 20 Agree to evaluation criteria
	May 15 and/or Determine finalists based
	May 22 on subcommittee evaluations
	June 5 Make decision
TIME FRAME:	February–July

- Receive regular reports from subcommittees
- Agree on evaluation criteria
- Determine finalists based on interview committee recommendations
- Interview finalists
- Make final decision

CHAIRMAN:	Handles media; makes final offer

Sample Subcommittee Chart

MEMBERSHIP, TASKS, AND TIMETABLE FOR
RECRUITMENT SUBCOMMITTEE

MEMBERSHIP:	(Names listed here with chairman designated)
MEETINGS:	First meeting, Saturday, February 9, 9:30–11:00 A.M.
	Second meeting, Thursday, February 28
	Third meeting, Thursday and Friday, April 3 and 4
TIME FRAME:	February 7 to April 14
CHAIRMAN:	Final authority in consultation with consultant

Tasks: To review and decide upon:

I.
- Format and substance of advertisements
- Placement of advertisements
- Number of advertisements

February 9
- Universities and other institutional placement offices
- Networks to be contacted
- General form of recruitment circular

II.
- Review application format, form, and substance of recruitment circular

II.
- Review résumés of 20 to 30 applicants who have been screened by consultant
- Reduce number of applicants to 8 to 10

April 1 to 14
- Develop statement on each candidate's strengths and weaknesses
- Develop evaluation format

CONSULTANT'S FUNCTIONS

1. Develop search plan and time line
2. Interview constituents
3. Place advertisements
4. Develop system description and brochure
5. Circularize schools of education, associations, individuals
6. Contact knowledgeable people
7. Read and screen all applications
8. Check references
9. Cut list to 20 to 30 candidates worth interviewing
10. Write assessments of candidates' strengths and weaknesses
11. Interview likely prospects
12. Develop evaluation format
13. Suggest procedures for interviews
14. Inform candidates of dates and place
15. Help committee process results of interviews
16. Work with committees
17. Develop regular progress reports for the School Board
18. Complete consultation once three finalists are presented to School Board

Appendix II-2   Consultant's First Progress Report

April 9

MEMO TO: Members of the School Board
FROM: Joan Wofford
RE: Status of Recruitment/Screening Process

The Recruitment Subcommittee completed its efforts with a seven-hour marathon of reading applicant dossiers. The recruitment/screening process has produced the following results:

> 165 original applications
> 67 completed applications
> 28 applications, read and reviewed by the Subcommittee
> 12 applications selected by the Subcommittee for further exploration and ranked in order of Committee preference

I think I speak for the Committee (but I know I speak for myself) in saying that the final applications look strong and exciting.

Between now and April 25, I will check the references of the top candidates and interview most of them, producing by April 25 six semifinalists for interviews in the district.

Appendix II-3 Questionnaire on Superintendent's Role

Constituency (circle one): Teacher   Administrator   Parent
                           School   Board Member   Citizen
Please circle the school/town you are associated with (schools/towns listed here):

PRIORITY CHECKLIST ON SUPERINTENDENT'S ROLE

At this stage in your thinking about a new superintendent, what view do you hold of the central function of the next superintendent? (Check one.)

1. Is the major function of the next superintendent to consolidate gains made in the past, develop procedures, and produce   _____
stability?

or

to provide an educational vision which will allow the schools to move forward in new directions but which will also create   _____
instability?

> NOTE: The qualities of individuals who would perform one function are very different from the qualities required by the second task. I therefore see the above as posing a choice.

2. Please rank in priority order (with 1 as most important and 8 as least) the following administrative functions:

- Curricular leadership   _____
- Financial management   _____
- Personnel administration   _____
- Buildings and grounds supervision   _____
- Construction project management   _____
- Trouble shooting capacity (to move into troubled school and help straighten it out)   _____

- Resource center for principals and teachers with knowledge of how to meet schools' diverse needs   ___
- Informing and responding to School Board members   ___
- Other (please specify and rank)   ___

    ___

    ___

3. Please rank the following skills in priority order with 1 as most important and 8 as least (see chart in Appendix II-4)
   - Human relations skills   ___
   - Grantsmanship skills (obtaining state and federal grants)   ___
   - Negotiating skills   ___
   - Budgeting skills   ___
   - Writing skills   ___
   - Speaking skills   ___
   - Public presentation skills   ___
   - Group management skills   ___
   - Other (specify and rank)   ___

    ___

    ___

Appendix II-4   Three Charts Summarizing Questionnaire Results

TEACHER RESPONSES (92)

Question 3 (in Appendix II-3): Please rank the following skills in priority order with 1 as most important and 8 as least important.

	1	2	3	4	5	6	7	8
Human relations	67	17	3	1	2	0	1	0
Grantsmanship	1	7	11	10	19	11	10	19
Negotiating	3	10	14	20	6	12	9	16
Budgeting	3	8	15	11	21	12	13	5
Writing	1	2	2	11	7	18	24	25
Speaking	1	4	16	14	14	19	14	11
Public presentation	7	10	21	18	10	10	4	9
Group management	19	41	9	8	5	1	3	2

Appendix II-4 (continued) Three Charts Summarizing Questionnaire Results

SCHOOL BOARD RESPONSES (13)

Question 3: Please rank the following skills in priority order with 1 as most important and 8 as least important:

	1	2	3	4	5	6	7	8
Human relations	9	2	1	0	0	0	0	0
Grantsmanship	0	1	0	0	1	3	0	6
Negotiating	0	0	2	3	1	4	2	1
Budgeting	0	1	1	3	3	2	2	0
Writing	0	1	0	1	4	0	4	3
Speaking	1	0	1	3	1	1	3	2
Public presentation	0	3	6	1	0	1	0	1
Group management	5	6	1	0	1	0	0	0

Appendix II-4 (continued) Three Charts Summarizing Questionnaire Results

HIGH SCHOOL STUDENT RESPONSES (21)

Question 3: Please rank the following skills in priority order with 1 as most important and 8 as least important:

	1	2	3	4	5	6	7	8
Human relations	15	2	0	2	0	0	2	0
Grantsmanship	0	1	4	5	4	3	2	2
Negotiating	0	10	1	3	1	2	4	0
Budgeting	3	0	4	3	6	2	1	2
Writing	0	2	0	0	2	5	4	8
Speaking	2	1	1	1	4	2	7	3
Public presentation	0	2	5	3	2	6	0	3
Group management	1	4	5	4	2	1	1	3

Appendix II-5   Questions for Semifinalist Interviews

(How the candidates think about education)

1. What issues do you see us as educators wrestling with nationally in the coming years?

(What the candidates value in their previous experience)

2. What are the three most important changes you have made as an educator in the institutions or communities in which you've served?

(How the candidates reflect on previous experience)

3. Describe an unpopular decision you have recently made.
    *   How did you reach the decision?
    *   How did you announce it?
    *   How did you know it was unpopular?
    *   How did you respond to its unpopularity?
    *   How do you find yourself thinking about it now?

(How the candidates think about organizations and leadership)

4. Assuming that you have been superintendent here for five years and are now moving on, how would you judge your success?

(How the candidates think they would handle the district's organizational structure)

5. Given the fact that informing and responding to School Board members is an essential part of the Superintendent's role and that there are eighteen School Board members spread across seven different overlapping School Boards, what mechanisms would you hope to develop for effective communication?

    If you develop a core support group, how do you deal with the feelings of those not in that support group?

6. Everyone on a local School Board eventually serves for a year on the Regional School Board. A member of one of the local school boards who is not currently on the Regional School Board calls you as Superintendent to complain about a teacher at the High School and to repeat to you what you had said confidentially about that teacher to a member of the Regional High School Board. How do you respond? Would you respond differently if the local Board member has a child at the High School?

7. In the field of Special Needs it would be more cost effective and beneficial to develop specialized programs for children with low-incidence special needs within each school. Yet repeated discussion among Special

Needs teachers and administrators do not lead to action. How would you view this situation? What would you do?

8. A principal institutes an innovative math program for the eighth grade level. Many parents support the program and call School Board members to tell them so. You, as Superintendent, do not think it will adequately prepare the students for ninth grade math and your reservations are ignored by the principal. What would you do?

Appendix II-6   Public Rating Sheet on Semifinalist Candidates

Please fill out and turn in before you leave. The results will be collated tonight.
Indicate whether primary interest is as a:

| Teacher | _____ | Parent | _____ |
| Administrator | _____ | Citizen | _____ |

Name of Candidate: _____

Each of the candidates appearing for semifinal interviews has been carefully screened and is known to be a highly competent, skilled, and admired leader in other educational settings. The ultimate question for the School Board is which of the candidates' competencies, strengths, and personality best match the needs of our schools.

You are asked, on the basis of what you have observed tonight (and without knowing of the candidates' experience, or how other people judge him) to share your impressions of the candidates.

With 1 as outstanding, 2 as good, and 3 as adequate, please circle the number which best expresses your judgment of each of the candidates' qualities:

- Intellectual capacity   1   2   3
- Thoughtful response to difficult questions   1   2   3
- Personality   1   2   3
- Skills in managing groups, assessing people,
  handling conflict   1   2   3
- Skills in handling money, managing programs,
  working with state agencies   1   2   3
- A vision of education   1   2   3
- A theory of organizations and leadership   1   2   3
- Flexibility   1   2   3
- Capacity to listen   1   2   3

- Appropriateness and quality of previous
  experience   1   2   3
- Overall assessment   1   2   3

Additional Comments

Appendix II-7   News Release and Summary of Semifinalist Ratings

NEWS RELEASE
May 16

The Interview Team, consisting of six School Board members, two teachers, and one administrator, recommends three candidates as finalists for the school superintendency. These recommendations are based on five hours of deliberations in which the following data were considered:

- Confidential dossiers
- Telephone reference checks conducted by Joan Wofford
- Written evaluations by each candidate of a difficult subordinate in their own systems
- Written observations by each candidate of the schools and of their visit here
- Collations of 175 interview evaluation sheets

The attached sheet displays the collations of 175 interview evaluation sheets of the five semifinalists. The candidates are not identified by name in order to protect their rights. We request that you honor their rights and reputations, particularly the unsuccessful ones in their search for other jobs. We give you this information so that you can see that your views were tallied and your participation important in our decision making. It should be emphasized that all five candidates received exceedingly good scores. The three candidates who received the best scores were recommended by the Interview Team to be the three finalists.

Summary of Semi-Finalist Ratings

	CANDIDATE A	CANDIDATE B	CANDIDATE C	CANDIDATE D	CANDIDATE E
Interview team	(8) 1.41	(9) 1.67	(9) 1.21	(9) 2.07	(8) 1.50
Teachers	(6) 1.80	(2) 1.0	(2) 2.0	(10) 1.50	(7) 1.42
Guidance	(2) 1.10	(1) 1.8		(1) 1.90	
School Board	(3) 1.20	(2) 1.05	(2) 1.20	(3) 1.28	(2) 1.36
Parents/citizens	12 1.50	(20) 1.87	(10) 1.20	(15) 1.10	(14) 1.80
Administrators	(3) 1.70	(4) 1.95	(2) 1.68	(7) 1.40	(2) 1.45
Average Score	(34) 1.50	(38) 1.74	(25) 1.31	(45) 1.46	(33) 1.60

NOTE: The numbers in parentheses represent the number of persons in each constituency who evaluated each candidate. Since all candidates were rated on a scale of 1 to 3, with 1 as excellent and 3 as average, a score nearer 1.0 is better than a score nearer 2.0.

Appendix II-8   Additional Criteria Implicit in Questions Asked During Finalist Interviews

	FINALISTS		
JUNE 5	A	B	C
	___	___	___

- Skill in supervising individual principals
- Capacity to provide structures to enhance local, regional, and School Board functioning and decision making (avoid bouncing from crisis to crisis)
- Capacity to put limits on an "impossible" job
- Skill at conflict resolution
- Disciplined management of information (particularly secondhand information about individuals)
- Defensiveness in face of criticism
- Capacity to set forth shared vision of education
- Skill with detail work (day-to-day paperwork)

Appendix III

Hiring a New Assistant

Appendix III-1   Job Description: Assistant Principal for Instruction

Budget

- Direct responsibility for supervising the accounts clerk in managing budget expenditures.
- Assistance to the Principal in developing budget allocations.

Schedule

- Direct responsibility for supervising the deans in student scheduling—from the beginning of course conferencing in January to the final print of student schedules in late August.
- Assistance to the Principal in developing the structure of the master schedule and setting up the process for decision making about courses, sections, and teachers.

Evaluation

- Direct responsibility for the observation and evaluation of performance of nontenured, substitute, and part-time teachers.

- Assistance to the Principal in writing final reports on these staff members and in making decisions about rehiring.

Program

- Direct responsibility for supervising the:
  - Career Internship Program
  - Learning Resource Center Program
- Assistance to the Principal in supervising curriculum and in the development of new programs.

Daily Operation of School

- Direct responsibility for:
  - Enrollment procedures and record keeping
  - Teacher absence procedures and record keeping
  - Grade reporting procedures
  - Open House evenings
- Assistance to the Principal for operation in:
  - General supervision of the building
  - Monitoring student attendance
  - Advisory and supporting student activities

Testing

- Direct responsibility for:
  - Administering and keeping accurate records of the Basic Competency and Regents Competency Testing Programs
  - Preparing school final exam schedules as well as proctoring schedule

Committees

- Chairman, Awards Assembly Committee
- Member, Principal's Cabinet
- School Administrative Representative, Districtwide Committee on the Handicapped, and School Administrative Representative, Building Study Team
- Administrative member, School Senate
- Administrative member, Faculty Advisory Committee
- Administrative member, Title IX Committee

Appendix III-2 Possible Interview Questions

1. The candidates about their and her or his performance:
   - What characteristics do you have that make you suitable for this position?
   - What personal and professional strengths would you bring to this position?
   - How would you assess your weaknesses?
   - Describe a situation in which your work was criticized. How did you respond?
   - Describe a situation in which you made an error of judgment. How did you handle your mistake?
   - Why do you think you want this job?

2. The candidates about this position:
   - How do you envision this job?
   - What do you imagine are the major conflicts, dilemmas of this position?
   - The responsibilities of this position may require you to work twelve or more hours per day, including many evenings and parts of weekends. The demands of the job would take away time and energy from your family and personal life. How would you and your family handle this problem?

3. The candidates about the High School—hypothetical problems:
   - A student and his parent complain to you about a final grade in a course. You investigate and decide that the grade is unfair. The teacher is angry at the student and has reacted in a harsh and arbitrary manner. What would you do?
   - You discover that a teacher regularly dismisses her or his class before the bell at the end of a period. Other teachers complain that this disrupts their classes. How would you handle the situation? In general, how would you deal with teachers who are not living up to their responsibilities?
   - The enrollment in the courses in a particular department is declining. Parents and students complain that the teachers are boring and the subject is uninteresting. You become convinced that the curriculum and teaching methods need revitalization. How would you go about effecting a change?
   - It is clear to you that a tenured teacher is in trouble. Many students ask to be transferred from the class, claiming that the teacher is not effective. Many parents have also complained that the teacher is ineffective. The specific complaints strike a pattern—the teacher

assigns little homework, makes few demands of the students, spends much of class time discussing irrelevant topics. How would you begin to deal with this problem?

- Ninth graders face the transition from small, closely supervised eighth grade experiences to the large, freer atmosphere of the high school. Both staff and parents indicate that ninth graders sometimes "get lost," feel the school is impersonal, develop bad habits in the use of their free time. What improvements would you suggest for helping ninth graders become better assimilated into the high school?

4. The candidates about their philosophies:
   - A number of recent educational theorists—including Fantini, Illich, Silberman, Jencks, Coleman—have taken strikingly different positions about the future of public schools. Discuss some of their recent theories and indicate your attitude toward them.
   - At least three recent national commissions studying secondary education in the country have recommended far-reaching changes in how we organize instruction. What new programs would you like to see developed at the High School?
   - At present we organize curriculum for freshmen and seniors in the same way. They both study discreet fragments of subject matter— English, math, etc.—in separate, equal compartments of time— e.g., four 50-minute periods per week. How would you reorganize how we present knowledge to students to take into account the developmental differences between ninth and twelfth graders?
   - In the pressure and competition for college that characterizes life in an academic high school experience, the fine and applied arts can be devalued by both parents, teachers, and students. How would you work to develop a healthier attitude toward the arts?

5. The candidates about the people with whom they work:
   - How would you describe your "style" in working with others?
   - How would you involve the parent body in the life of the school?
   - How would you involve teachers in decision making?
   - How would you involve students?
   - What kinds of decisions should be shared with these other groups? Which should be reserved for you?

Appendix IV

A Good Beginning as Superintendent

A NEW SUPERINTENDENT'S ENTRY PLAN

This entry plan was tested with the School Board and the system's administrators and revised in response to new information. The plan has six parts:

1. School Board
2. Central office
3. Principals
4. Teacher associations and other employee organizations
5. School visits and staff contact
6. Community contact

MEMO TO: Members of the Board of Education and the Administrative Council

    FROM: (New Superintendent's Name)

      RE: Getting Started

    DATE:

In my various interviews for the (Town) Superintendency, many people stressed the "diversity" of the (Town) community and emphasized the importance of the new Superintendent learning about this "diversity" in order to be successful. The plan which follows attempts to acknowledge the critical priorities for me of: meeting the many diverse individuals and groups which comprise the school system and community; learning what they care about, take pride in, aspire to, worry about; and discovering how (they) have worked together to maintain and improve education in (Town). To accomplish these priorities, I have planned: a set of interviews to collect information; a set of reporting sessions to feed it back to interviewees and to test its validity; and a set of school visits and community contacts. Most of these activities will occur over my first three months on the job. I believe they will enable me to learn quickly and efficiently about (Town) and to take that learning into account in my decision making.

GENERAL GOALS

1. To get to know the school district and its people as fully as possible in a brief period of time, outside the daily context of crisis and problem solving;

2. To examine key issues in the school system's past, in order to make sense of how such issues are handled and to identify the norms which affect how the organization may function in the future;

3. To identify the tasks which need to be done and to rank them in order of priority;

4. To establish how these tasks should be accomplished.

Specific Objectives

1. To examine the groundrules and procedures which have governed how the Board of Education has conducted business in the past;

2. To develop with the Board a set of groundrules and procedures which will govern how we operate in the future;*

3. To determine the issues on which the Board believes we should concentrate in the next year and then to ask the Board to rank these in priority order;

4. To develop charts of the predictable tasks on which the Central Office and the Board will work in the next year. The chart will not only list *what* has to be done but also describe *how* it is to be done.

---

* See Questionnaire on School Board Procedures & Groundrules.

Activities

PHASE I (7/20–8/31)

1. A questionnaire on Board procedures and groundrules*   (7/22)
2. A two hour interview with each Board member   (7/27–8/14)
3. Two meetings with the past Board President
   re: developing charts of predictable tasks   (7/27–8/14)
4. One meeting with the new Board President
   re: the role of the Chairperson.   (7/27–8/15)
5. Collation, interpretation, organization of information
   from interviews and questionnaire for presentation   (8/14–8/28)
6. Full-day Board Workshop for: presentation of data,
   validation of it, commitments to action   (8/29)

PHASE II (9/1–11/30)

1. Weekly meetings with Board President
   re: implementation of plans
2. Follow-up session on all-day workshop: presentation
   of results in written form   (9/23)
3. Budget workshop–review of chart of budget development: who does what, when, how, in relation to
   whom   (11/15)

PHASE III (12/1–6/30)

1. Continued weekly meetings with Board President
2. Progress Review Workshop: review results of August
   workshop and progress to date   (1/15)
3. End-of-Year Review   (5/15) •

Interview Questions:

1. Please give me a brief autobiographical sketch of yourself.

2. When did you first join the Board? What are your general impressions
   of the schools? Have your perceptions changed since you joined the
   Board?

3. What are the strengths and the weaknesses of the Administrative staff?
   of the teaching staff?

4. What are the key issues which you think the system must face? Why is

each important? Which issues need immediate attention? Can you rank these issues in priority order?

5. What network of people in the schools or the community try to influence school issues? What do the members of each network share in common? Neighborhood? Blood relationship? Jobs? Concern for issues?

6. Describe a moment when the school system was in great conflict. How did the conflict arise? What people played roles in it, and how did they react under pressure? How was the stress resolved? How should it have been handled and resolved?

7. Describe a very difficult decision you had to make. What was the issue? Why was it important? How did you reach a decision? What did others think? What would you do differently now?

8. What do you most want to preserve in the (Town) schools?

9. What leadership has the Superintendent provided to the schools in the past? What do you wish he would provide in the future?

10. As you think about how the Board operates as a group, what frustrates you?

Specific Objectives

1. To determine the issues which the Central Office staff face in their work next year:

2. To determine the norms, procedures, and processes which govern how each of the tasks of the Central Office is accomplished;

3. To develop workplans for the predictable tasks which Central Office staff will undertake next year. The workplan will describe not only what has to be done but how—the steps in the process, the time-frame, the role responsibility;*

4. To clarify the role responsibilities of each member of the Central Office.

Activities

PHASE I (7/30–9/30)

1. Briefing sessions for me conducted by appropriate Central Office members on the following topics: staffing Board agenda, curriculum development, special education,

---

* See Work Plan Format.

budget development, transportation, food service,
maintenance, puchasing, finance   (7/27–8/14)
2. Coffee and cake with secretaries, introduction to other
   Central Office staff, head custodian, other custodians
   and maintenance people   (7/28–7/31)
3. Development of workplan by Central Office staff for
   each predictable task   (8/17–9/4)
4. Meeting of Central Office staff to review all workplans   (9/14–9/18)
5. Interviews (1½ hour) with each member of the Central
   Office staff, including my secretary   (8/17–8/28)
6. Collation, interpretation, organization of data from interviews   (8/31–9/11)
7. Series of meetings (4–6) with Central Office individuals
   and/or groups to: present data, test it, and reaffirm
   and/or change role responsibility   (9/14–9/30)
8. Series of meetings (4–6) with (outgoing Superintendent)
   to review past history of the organization   (7/27–8/31)

PHASE II (9/1–6/30)

Weekly meetings of Central Office staff to: review progress on workplan;
monitor effectiveness of role responsibility decisions.

BRIEFING FORMAT

1. Please tell me as succinctly as possible the status of this area of responsibility. What has been accomplished in preparation for the next
   school year? What remains to be done? What needs attention next
   year?

2. Please tell me as *specifically* as possible *how* tasks are accomplished in
   this area of responsibility. What are steps in each process?*

Interview Questions

1. Please give me a brief autobiographical sketch of yourself.

2. Which Central Office tasks are your responsibility alone? Which tasks do
   you share with others on the Central Office staff? How does the overlapping of responsibilities occur? Are there areas where role responsibility
   is unclear?

3. What is the key issue for your own work in the school system? Why is it
   important? Does it need immediate attention?

* See Work Plan Format.

4. What is the school system's key issue—it might be different from your own—in the next few months? What should I know about this issue? When should it be resolved?

5. What network of people in the schools or the community try to influence school issues? What do the members of each network share in common? Neighborhood? Blood relationship? Jobs? Concern for issues?

6. Describe a moment when the school system was in great conflict. How did the conflict arise? What people played roles in it, and how did they react under pressure? How was the stress resolved? How should it have been handled and resolved?

7. Describe a very difficult decision you had to make. What was the issue? Why was it important? How did you reach a decision? What did others think? What would you do differently now?

8. What do you most want to preserve in the (Town) schools?

9. What leadership has the Superintendent provided to the schools in the past? What do you wish he would provide in the future?

Specific Objectives

1. To determine what the key issues are at the building level;

2. To clarify the role responsibilities of Building Principals and how they coordinate with Central Office administration.

Activities

PHASE I (8/17–9/30)

1. Interview (1½ hour) with each Principal	(8/17–8/28)
2. Collation, interpretation, organization of information from interview for presentation	(8/31–9/11)
3. Two meetings with Principals and (Assistant Superintendent): a) to present data, test it; b) to reaffirm and/or change role responsibilities and to decide on action-steps with regard to issues to be addressed	(9/14–9/25)
4. Meeting with (Assistant Superintendent) to discuss follow-up to feedback sessions with elementary and middle school Principals	(9/28–9/30)
5. Series of meetings with (High School Principal) to discuss issues at the high school to be addressed during the year and to develop workplans for responding to them	(9/21–9/30)

PHASE II (10/1–6/30)

1. Weekly meetings with (Assistant Superintendent) to review progress of elementary and middle school Principals in accomplishing agreed upon tasks

2. Weekly meetings with (High School Principal) to review progress in accomplishing agreed upon tasks

Interview Questions (see Interview Questions—Central Office)

Teachers Association and Other Employee Organizations

Activities

1. Interviews with members of the (Unions) Leadership   (9/8–9/25)
2. Collation, interpretation, organization of data   (9/28–10/9)
3. Meeting with Executive Committees to present data, test it, and decide on its implication   (10/12–10/16)

Interview Questions

1. Please give me a brief autobiographical sketch of yourself.

2. When did you first come to the school system? What have been your responsibilities in it? What are your general impressions of the school system?

3. What are the key issues which the system must face? What are teachers' concerns? Why is each important? Which issues need immediate attention? Can you rank these issues in priority order?

4. Describe the history of Union-Administration-School Board relationships in (Town). What conflicts have arisen in your experience? How have they been resolved?

5. What has been the nature of your contact with the Superintendent? How would you like to see it changed? How should it remain the same?

6. What in the new contract is important for me to know? What issues are unresolved?

7. What has administrative leadership provided to the district in the past? What do you wish it would provide in the future?

8. To what extent has the formal grievance procedure in the contract been used in the past? Why? Or why not?

School Visits and Staff Contact

Activities

1.	Letter to staff	(8/15)
2.	Opening Address to Faculty	(9/8)
3.	Follow-up letter re: entry plan	(9/14)
4.	School visits:	(9/21–11/25)

    (*a*) one school per week
    (*b*) two half-days in each school
    (*c*) visits scheduled and organized by the Principals

5.	Regular, short informal school visits throughout year	(11/25–6/30)
6.	Attendance at one Faculty Meeting in each school	(9/8–6/30)
7.	Attendance at plays, concerts, sports events, etc. throughout the year.	

Community Contact

Activities

A. PARENT GROUPS

1.	Attendance at one PTO meeting in each school	Sept.–Dec.
2.	Monthly meeting with PTO District group	Sept.–June
3.	Attendance at PTO Sponsored Functions in each school	Sept.–June

B. TOWNS' OFFICIALS

1. Meet:
—Mayors of each town
—Board Members of each town
—Police Chiefs
—Fire Chiefs

C. COMMUNITY ORGANIZATIONS

Recreation
Churchs
Athletic Associations
Rotary Clubs
Kiwanis Clubs

D. STUDENTS

1.	Attendance at High School G.O. Meeting	Sept.–Dec.

E. PRIVATE SCHOOLS

1. meet administration of:
    (School 1)
    (School 2)
    (School 3)

F. OTHER INDIVIDUALS OR ORGANIZATIONS SHOULD CONTACT AND INTERVIEW?

1. ?

2. ?

3. ?

WORK PLAN/FORMAT

TASK:

_____
_____
_____

Date

Steps:

1. _____
2. _____
3. _____
4. _____
5. _____
6. _____
7. _____
8. _____
9. _____
10. _____
11. _____
12. _____

Outcome: _____

_____

_____

Questionnaire on
School Board Procedures
and Ground Rules

Agenda Setting and Timing

1. In general, how do agendas for board meetings get set? How do you as a board member get an item of concern to you on the agenda for a particular meeting?

2. Rate the items on the agenda, on a scale of 1–5 with 1 as highest, etc., with respect to their being:

	Yes		Sometimes		No
	1	2	3	4	5

    the appropriate ones

    too many

    too few

3. Generally, how far in advance of a meeting do you receive the board packet? In what ways are the background materials you receive adequate or inadequate in preparing you for board discussion?

Board Efficiency

4. On a scale of 1–5, with 1 as high and 5 as low, how efficient do you think the board is in:

following up on issues raised in discussion	1	2	3	4	5
the length of meetings	1	2	3	4	5

the frequency of meetings   1   2   3   4   5

apportioning its time among agenda
items   1   2   3   4   5

Board Confidentiality

5. On a scale of 1–5, with 1 as high and 5 as low, how successful has the
    board been in maintaining the confidentiality of discussions in execu-
    tive session?

                                   1   2   3   4   5

    Comments:

Role of Chairman

6. Rate the importance of each of the following tasks in the chairman's role:

inform members on issues prior to meetings 1   2   3   4   5

meeting and conferring regularly with
Superintendent   1   2   3   4   5

handling public relations   1   2   3   4   5

running the meetings   1   2   3   4   5

explaining the background of an issue 1   2   3   4   5

clarifying the issue   1   2   3   4   5

insuring that everyone gets heard 1   2   3   4   5

summarizing discussion   1   2   3   4   5

closing off discussion   1   2   3   4   5

handling the public   1   2   3   4   5

Board Communication with the School System

7. Are you as a board member aware of established procedures for ob-
    taining or exchanging information with:

    the Superintendent ....Yes   No

    the Central Office........................Yes   No

  the Building Administrator . . . . .Yes   No

  Staff . . . . .Yes   No

  If you answer "Yes", please explain.

8. You hear from your child (or neighbor) that a school bus had an accident on the way home. What do you do? Whom do you call?

9. At a cocktail party, you are informed by an angry parent that a fourth grade teacher publicly embarrasses children by talking about their failures in front of the whole class. Whom do you call?

10. You feel that you need information on the reading test scores on Middle School kids going to the High School. What do you do? Whom do you call?

Appendix IV-2 Interview Questions for Entry

INTERVIEW QUESTIONS FOR ENTRY BY A NEW ASSISTANT SUPERINTENDENT FOR CURRICULUM AND INSTRUCTION

  Below is a set of questions asked by a new assistant superintendent during his entry. He inquires into the nature of the community and students and keeps the whole set of questions rigorously focused on the function of his job. This was particularly important in his situation because his job and role were brand new in the system. His entry was explicitly an act of defining his role:

1. Could you provide me with the history of the district? When did you come here? What's it like to work here? What's the makeup of this community? What's important to the people who live in this community?

2. What are the students like in this community?

3. Could you review for me the curriculum in this community?

4. How do you see curriculum decisions made in this district in the past? How are these decisions made in your buildings? What format for decision making would you recommend?

5. What curriculum problems need attention in this district?

6. What do you expect this new position of the Assistant Superintendent for Instruction to do?

7. What are you most proud of in the schools of this community?

INTERVIEW QUESTIONS FOR ENTRY BY A NEW MIDDLE SCHOOL PRINCIPAL

1. Please give me a brief autobiographical sketch of yourself, including information that as Middle School Principal, I should know or would find useful about you. (When did you first come here? Why? What have your responsibilites been? What's it like to work here?)

2. As a new principal, what should I know about the makeup of the community and about community expectations? What's important to the people who live here?

3. What are the students like here?

4. What is the key issue for your own work in the system (or in your school)?

5. What are your overall impressions of the Middle School—its strengths and weaknesses?

6. What is the key issue that the Middle School faces in the near futue? What should I know about this issue? How should it be resolved?

7. How are important decisions made relative to the Middle School? Who is involved? How effective is the process? Should it be changed?

8. Describe a major issue or conflict that the Middle School faced while you were in the system. How did it arise? Who played key roles and how did they react under pressure? How was it resolved?

9. Describe a difficult decision you had to make that related to or affected the Middle School. What was the issue? Why was it important? How did you reach a decision? What did others think?

10. What are you proudest of relative to the system/your school? What is your own proudest accomplishment while working here?

Appendix V

Supervising a New Special Education Director

Appendix V-1 Summer Entry Plan: Seven Activities

We outlined seven activities for Nat to participate in during his first weeks on the job during the summer. These activities were designed to help avoid the traps I had presented during our first meeting.

1. *Schedule a meeting with his predecessor.* This meeting was designed to review the history of the position, his predecessor's point of view on the position, and a list of any unfinished business which would need Nat's attention.

2. *Schedule a meeting with his secretary.* Nat was to explore the activities his secretary had been involved in and the areas for which she held responsibility.

3. *Planning and organizing a series of interviews with the Committee on the Handicapped.* Nat was responsible for the work of this committee which carries out Public Law 94-142. He was to schedule a meeting with the chairman of that committee to determine its history, decide which meetings during the summer work of the Committee on the Handicapped he would participate in, and clarify his role in those meetings. He was to review this with me prior to implementation.

4. *Participation in summer administrative workshop.* I directed Nat to participate with the administrative group of the district in a summer administrative workshop. This workshop was to focus on supervision skills. I hoped this activity would allow him to meet the principals and central office staff in a more relaxed, informal summer activity.

5. *Develop a schedule of meetings with his staff.* I asked Nat to think about the ways in which he would meet with his staff. I asked that he develop a set of questions to ask each group as he began to meet with them. In this way his first meeting with staff could be held as a group interview.

6. *Develop and schedule interviews with the principals.* I asked him to schedule individual meetings with each of the principals and to conduct a planned interview with each principal. I specifically asked him to develop a set of questions which would be circulated to the principals prior to the interview. These interviews, held during the summer, would provide Nat with the background of his position, the principal's point of view of what activities needed to be worked on during the year in the area of Special Services and would provide Nat with an informal opportunity to get to know a group of principals he would be working with very closely during the year. A second interview with the principals to feed back and double-check the data was to be scheduled in the Fall.

7. *How to enter the new school year.* I asked Nat to begin to think about how he would spend his time during the first two months of school.

Index